In Defense of Global Capitalism

In Defense of Global Capitalism

Johan Norberg

CATO
INSTITUTE
Washington, D.C.

Originally published in Sweden as *Till VarldsKapitalismens Forsvar*
(Stockholm: Timbro, 2001). Translated and revised edition
published by the Cato Institute, 2003.
Translation by Roger Tanner with Julian Sanchez.

Library of Congress Cataloging-in-Publication Data

Norberg, Johan, 1973-
  [Till världskapitalismens försvar. English 1]
  In defense of global capitalism / Johan Norberg.
    p. cm.
  Includes bibliographical references and index.
  ISBN 1-930865-46-5 (cloth : alk. paper) --
  ISBN 1-930865-47-3 (paper : alk. paper)
  1. Capitalism. 2. Free enterprise. 3. Free trade--Social
aspects. 4. Globalization--Economic aspects.
5. Globalization--Social aspects. 6. Poverty--Developing
countries. I. Cato Institute. II. Title.

HB501.N6713 2003
330.12'2--dc22   2003055487

Cover design by Elise B. Rivera.

Printed in the United States of America.

CATO INSTITUTE
1000 Massachusetts Ave., N.W.
Washington, D.C. 20001

Contents

Preface   7

I.   **Every day in every way . . .**   19
     The half truth   20
     Poverty reduction   25
     Hunger   31
     Education   36
     Democratization   38
     Oppression of women   43
     China   47
     India   51
     Global inequality   54
     Reservations   60

II. **. . . and it's no coincidence**   63
     That's capitalism for you!   64
     Growth—a blessing   72
     Freedom or equality? Why choose?   84
     Property rights—for the sake of the poor   90
     The East Asian "miracle"   99
     The African morass   104

III. **Free trade is fair trade**   113
     Mutual benefit   114
     Important imports   120
     Free trade brings growth   128

	No end of work	136
	Freedom of movement—for people as well	145
IV.	**The development of the developing countries**	**151**
	An unequal distribution—of capitalism	152
	The white man's shame	156
	The case of Latin America	163
	On the trade route	169
	"Let them keep their tariffs"	173
	The debt trap	177
	The right medicine	186
V.	**Race to the top**	**191**
	I'm all for free trade, but . . .	192
	Child labor	198
	But what about us?	203
	Big is beautiful	210
	"Gold and green forests"	224
VI.	**Irrational, international capital?**	**239**
	The leaderless collective	240
	Regulate more?	249
	Tobin tax	253
	The Asian crisis	259
	Instead of crisis	264
	The "dictatorship of the market"	268
VII.	**Liberalize, don't standardize**	**277**
	The right to choose a culture	278
	The onward march of freedom	286
Notes		**293**
Index		**307**

Preface

Our anarchist party won the school election!

It was the fall semester of 1988 at our school—we were about 16 at the time—in a western suburb of Stockholm. As usual in an election year, we were staging a "school election" of our own. But my best friend Markus and I didn't believe in the system. Majority elections, to our way of looking at things, were like two wolves and a lamb voting on what to have for dinner. The school wanted us to elect someone to rule us, but we wanted to rule our own lives.

Partly, I suppose, we did it because we felt different from the others. I was into listening to electronic music and goth, preferably dressed in black and with my hair combed back. We wanted to play music and read books, while others seemed mostly preoccupied with owning the right accessories and fitting in. The right wing, it seemed to us, was upper class establishment, dead set against anything different. But we didn't feel any more at home with the left, which to us meant drab government bureaucracy and regimentation. Even if we preferred Sisters of Mercy and the Swedish punk singer Thåström, it was John Lennon's "imagine there's no countries" we believed in. Nation states should be abolished and people allowed to move freely, to cooperate of their own free will, everywhere in the world. We wanted a world without compulsion, without rulers. Clearly, then, we were neither right wing nor left wing, neither Conservatives nor Social Democrats. We were anarchists!

7

So we started "Anarchist Front" and put ourselves down as candidates in the school election on a radical, humorous ticket. We put up handwritten posters on the walls at school, asking things like: "Who's going to run your life—you or 349 MPs?" We demanded the abolition of the government . . . and of the ban on bikes in the schoolyard. Most of the teachers took a dim view of this, feeling that we were making a farce of the election, while we thought that we were making our voices heard in true democratic fashion. Being called to the headmaster's office for a chewing-out merely strengthened our rebellious spirit.

We did well in a tough campaign, polling 25 percent of the votes. The Social Democrats came second with 19 percent. We were psyched, convinced that this would be the start of something big. . . .

That was 15 years ago. In the meantime, I have changed my mind about a number of things. I have come to realize that questions concerning individuals, society, and freedom are more complicated than I then believed. There are too many complexities and problems involved for everything to be settled in one drastic Utopian stroke. I have come to realize that we do need some government to protect liberty and prevent the powerful from oppressing individuals, and I now believe that representative democracy is preferable to all other systems for this very purpose of protecting the rights of the individual. I realize now that the modern industrial society of which I was so wary has in fact made possible a fantastic standard of living and widespread freedom. But my fundamental urge for liberty is the same today as in that wonderful election campaign of 1988. I want people to be free, with no one oppressing anyone else, and with governments forbidden to fence people in or to exclude them with tariffs and borders.

That is why I love what is rather barrenly termed "globalization," the process by which people, information, trade, investments, democracy, and the market economy are tending more and more to cross national borders. This internationalization has made us less constricted by mapmakers' boundaries.

Political power has always been a creature of geography, based on physical control of a certain territory. Globalization is enabling us more and more to override these territories, by traveling in person and by trading or investing across national borders. Our options and opportunities have multiplied as transportation costs have fallen, as we have acquired new and more efficient means of communication, and as trade and capital movements have been liberalized.

We don't have to shop with the big local company; we can turn to a foreign competitor. We don't have to work for the village's one and only employer; we can seek out alternative opportunities. We don't have to make do with local cultural amenities; the world's culture is at our disposal. We don't have to spend our whole lives in one place; we can travel and relocate.

Those factors lead to a liberation of our thinking. We no longer settle for following the local routine; we want to choose actively and freely. Companies, politicians, and associations have to exert themselves to elicit interest or support from people who have a whole world of options to choose from. Our ability to control our own lives is growing, and prosperity is growing with it.

That is why I find it pathetic when people who call themselves anarchists engage in the globalization struggle—but against it, not for it! I visited Gothenburg, Sweden, in June 2001 during the big European Union summit. I went there in order to explain why the problem with the EU is that in many ways it is fighting globalization and liberalization, and to present my view that borders should be opened and controls dismantled.

I never got the chance to give my speech. The place where I was to speak was suddenly in the middle of a battle zone, where so-called anti-globalization anarchists were smashing shops and throwing stones at police officers who were trying to defend a democratic meeting. These were "anarchists" demanding prohibitions and controls and throwing stones at people with different values, "anarchists" who insisted that the government retake control of people who no longer found themselves constrained by national boundaries. They made a mockery of the idea of freedom. To our cheerful Anarchist Front, people like that had nothing to do with anarchism. In our simplified teenage vocabulary, they were, if anything, fascists.

But that violence is only part of a broader movement that is critical of increasing globalization. In the past few years, more and more people have been complaining that the new liberty and internationalism have gone too far, giving rise to a "hypercapitalism." The protest movement against this more global capitalism may call itself radical and profess to stand for exciting new ideas, but its arguments actually represent the same old opposition to free markets and free trade that has always been shown by national rulers. Many groups—authoritarian Third World regimes and Eurocrats, agrarian movements and monopoly corporations, conservative intellectuals and new left movements—are afraid of a globalized humanity acquiring more power at the expense of political institutions. All of them are united in viewing globalization as a monster completely out of control, a monster that has to be rounded up and restrained.

Much of the criticism of globalization is based on portraying it as something big and menacing. Often such criticism is not reasoned argument, but flat statements of fact. Critics may say, for example, that 51 of the world's biggest economies are corporations or that something like $1.5 trillion are moved around in financial markets every day, as if size itself were intrinsically dangerous and terrifying. But that is arithmetic, not argument. It remains to be proved that big businesses or high turnover are problems in themselves. Frequently, the detractors forget to prove any such thing. In this book I argue for the opposite view: as long as we are at liberty to pick and choose, there is nothing wrong with certain forms of voluntary cooperation growing large through success.

Such imposing numbers and the abstract term "globalization"—coined in the early 1960s but in common use only since the 1980s—conjure up the image of an anonymous, enigmatic, elusive force. Simply because globalization is governed by people's individual actions across different continents, and not from a central control booth, it seems unchecked, chaotic. Political theorist Benjamin Barber echoed the thoughts of a host of like-minded intellectuals when he bemoaned the apparent absence of "viable powers capable of opposing, subduing, and civilizing the anarchic forces of the global economy."[1]

Many feel powerless in the face of globalization, and that feeling is understandable when we consider how much is determined by the decentralized decisions of millions of people. If others are free to run their own lives, we have no power over them. But in return, we acquire a new power over our own lives. That kind of powerlessness is a good thing. No one is in the driver's seat, because all of us are steering.

The Internet would wither and die if we did not send e-mails, order books, and download music every day through this global computer network. No company would import goods from

11

abroad if we didn't buy them, and no one would invest money over the border if there weren't entrepreneurs there willing to expand existing businesses or launch new ones in response to customer demand. Globalization consists of our everyday actions. We eat bananas from Ecuador, drink wine from France, watch American movies, order books from Britain, work for export companies selling to Germany and Russia, vacation in Thailand, and save money for retirement in funds investing in South America and Asia. Capital may be channeled by finance corporations, and goods may be carried across borders by business enterprises, but they only do these things because we want them to. Globalization takes place from beneath, even though politicians come running after it with all sorts of abbreviations and acronyms (EU, IMF, UN, WTO, UNCTAD, OECD) in a bid to structure the process.

Of course, keeping up with the times doesn't always come easily, especially to intellectuals in the habit of having everything under control. In a book about the 19th century Swedish poet and historian Erik Gustaf Geijer, Anders Ehnmark writes, almost enviously, that Geijer was able to keep himself up to date on all important world events just by sitting in Uppsala reading the *Edinburgh Review* and the *Quarterly Review*.[2] That is how simple and intelligible the world can be when only a tiny elite in the capitals of Europe makes any difference to the course of world events. But how complex and confusing everything is becoming now that the other continents are awakening and developments are also beginning to be affected by ordinary people's everyday decisionmaking. No wonder, then, that influential people, decisionmakers, and politicians claim that "we" (meaning they) lose power because of globalization. *They* have lost some of it to *us*— to ordinary citizens.

Not all of us are going to be global jet-setters, but we don't have to be in order to be a part of the globalization process. In particular, the poor and powerless find their well-being vastly improved when inexpensive goods are no longer excluded by tariff barriers and when foreign investments offer employment and streamline production. Those still living in the place where they were born stand to benefit enormously from information being allowed to flow across borders, and from being free to choose their political representatives. But that requires more in the way of democratic reforms and economic liberalization.

Demanding more liberty to pick and choose may sound trivial, but it isn't. To those of us in the affluent world, the availability of nonlocal options may seem like a luxury, or even an annoyance. Say what you will about Starbucks or trashy American reality shows, but they aren't totally intolerable. Well, not the Starbucks, anyway. The existence from which globalization delivers people in the Third World really is intolerable. For the poor, existence means abject poverty, filth, ignorance, and powerlessness; it means always wondering where the next meal is coming from; it means walking many miles to collect water that may not be fit to drink.

When globalization knocks at the door of Bhagant, an elderly agricultural worker and "untouchable" in the Indian village of Saijani, it leads to houses being built of brick instead of mud, to people getting shoes on their feet and clean clothes—not rags— on their backs. Outdoors, the streets now have drains, and the fragrance of tilled earth has replaced the stench of refuse. Thirty years ago Bhagant didn't know he was living in India. Today he watches world news on television.[3]

The new freedom of choice means that people are no longer consigned to working for the village's only employers, the large and powerful farmers. When the women get work away from

13

home, they also become more powerful within the family. New capital markets mean that Bhagant's children are not compelled to borrow money from usurers who collect payment in future labor. The yoke of usury, by which the whole village was once held in thrall, vanishes when people are able to go to different banks and borrow money from them instead.

Everyone in Bhagant's generation was illiterate. In his children's generation, just a few were able to attend school, and in his grandchildren's generation, *everyone* goes to school. Things have improved, Bhagant finds. Liberty and prosperity have grown. Today the children's behavior is the big problem. When he was young, children were obedient and helped in the home. Now they have grown so terribly independent, making money of their own. Such things can cause tensions, of course, but it isn't quite the same thing as the risk of having to watch your children die, or having to sell them to a loan shark.

The stand that you and I and other people in the privileged world take on the burning issue of globalization can determine whether more people are to share in the development that has taken place in Bhagant's village or whether that development is to be reversed.

***

Critics of globalization often try to paint a picture of neo-liberal* market marauders having secretly plotted for capitalism to attain

---

* I use the term "liberal" in the European sense to refer to people in the 19th-century liberal tradition, who support free trade and open markets—economic as well as civil liberties—rather than in the common American sense meaning politically left of center. In American political parlance, "libertarian" is probably closer to what I have in mind.

world mastery. We find political theorist John Gray, for example, describing the spread of free-market policies as a virtual coup d'etat staged by "radical" ideologues who manage to "infiltrate" government. "The goal of this revolution," according to Gray, "was to insulate neo-liberal policy irreversibly from democratic accountability in political life."[4] Some pundits—among them Robert Kuttner, editor of *The American Prospect*, and economist Joseph Stiglitz—even characterize free-market advocacy as a kind of quasi-religious cult, which they call "market fundamentalism."

Deregulation, privatization, and trade liberalization, however, were not invented by ultra-liberal ideologues. True, there were political leaders—Reagan and Thatcher, for instance—who had been inspired by economic liberalism. But the biggest reformers were communists in China and the Soviet Union, protectionists in Latin America, and nationalists in Asia. In many other European countries, the progress has been spurred by Social Democrats. In short, the notion of conspiratorial ultra-liberals making a revolution by shock therapy is completely off the mark. Instead, it is pragmatic, often anti-liberal politicians, realizing that their governments have gone too far in the direction of control-freakery, who have for this very reason begun liberalizing their economies. The allegation of liberal-capitalist world dominion has to be further tempered by the observation that today we probably have the biggest public sectors and the highest taxes the world has ever known. The liberalization measures that have been introduced may have abolished some of the past's centralist excesses, but they have hardly ushered in a system of laissez faire. And because the rulers have retreated on their own terms and at their own speed, there is reason to ask whether things really have gone too far, or whether they have not gone far enough.

When I say that I mean to defend capitalism, what I have in mind is the capitalistic freedom to proceed by trial and error, without having to ask rulers and border officials for permission first. That is the liberty that I once thought anarchy would bring, but under the control of laws ensuring that one person's freedom will not encroach on other people's. I want everyone to have that liberty in abundance. If the critics of capitalism feel that we already have a superabundance of that liberty today, I would like to have more still—a superduper abundance if possible—especially for the poor of the world's population, who as things now stand have little say regarding their work and consumption. That is why I do not hesitate to call this book *In Defense of Global Capitalism,* even though the "capitalism" I celebrate is really more a possible future than a currently existing system.

By capitalism I do not specifically mean an economic system of capital ownership and investment opportunities. Those things can also exist in a command economy. What I mean is the liberal market economy, with free competition based on the right to use one's property and the freedom to negotiate, to conclude agreements, and to start up business activities. What I am defending, then, is individual liberty in the economy. Capitalists are dangerous when, instead of seeking profit through competition, they join forces with the government. If the state is a dictatorship, corporations can easily be parties to human rights violations, as a number of Western oil companies have been in African states.[5] By the same token, capitalists who stalk the corridors of political power in search of benefits and privileges are not *true* capitalists. On the contrary, they are a threat to the free market and as such must be criticized and counteracted. Often, businessmen want to play politics, and politicians want to play at being businessmen. That is not a market

16

economy; it is a mixed economy in which entrepreneurs and politicians have confused their roles. Free capitalism exists when politicians pursue liberal policies and entrepreneurs do business.

What I really believe in, first and foremost, isn't capitalism or globalization. It isn't the systems or regulatory codes that achieve all we see around us in the way of prosperity, innovation, community, and culture. Those things are created by people. What I believe in is man's capacity for achieving great things, and the combined force that results from our interactions and exchanges. I plead for greater liberty and a more open world, not because I believe one system happens to be more efficient than another, but because those things provide a setting that unleashes individual creativity as no other system can. They spur the dynamism that has led to human, economic, scientific, and technical advances. Believing in capitalism does not mean believing in growth, the economy, or efficiency. Desirable as they may be, those are only the results. At its core, belief in capitalism is belief in mankind.

Like most other liberals, I can endorse the opinion of French socialist prime minister Lionel Jospin that we must have a "market economy, not a market society." My aim is not for economic transactions to supplant all other human relations. My aim is freedom and voluntary relations in all fields. In the cultural arena, that means freedom of expression and of the press. In politics, it means democracy and the rule of law. In social life, it means the right to live according to one's own values and to choose one's own company. And in the economy, it means capitalism and free markets.

It is not my intention that we should put price tags on everything. The important things in life—love, family, friendship, one's own way of life—cannot be assigned a dollar value. Those who believe

17

that, to the liberal mind, people always act with the aim of maximizing their income know nothing about liberals, and any liberal who does think that way knows nothing of human nature. It is not a desire for better payment that moves me to write a book about the value of globalization instead of becoming an accountant or a fisherman. I am writing about something I believe in, something that matters. And I wish to live in a liberal society because such a society gives people the right to choose what matters to them.

Last of all, I offer my heartfelt thanks to the friends who helped me to marshal my thoughts on these matters, for the simple reason that this subject also matters to them, especially in the case of Fredrik Erixon, Sofia Nerbrand, and Mauricio Rojas. A big thank you also to Barbro Bengtson, Charlotte Häggblad, and Kristina von Unge for their efficiency in making my manuscript presentable.

Johan Norberg
Stockholm, January 2003

I

Every day in every way...

The half truth

At least since 1014, when Archbishop Wulfstan, preaching in York, declared that "The world is in a rush and is getting close to its end," people have believed that everything is growing worse, that things were better in the old days. Much of the discussion surrounding globalization presupposes that the world is rapidly going to hell in a handbasket. A few years ago, Pope John Paul II echoed his colleague of a thousand years ago by summing up world development in the following terms:

> *Various places are witnessing the resurgence of a certain capitalist neoliberalism which subordinates the human person to blind market forces and conditions the development of peoples on those forces. . . . In the international community, we thus see a small number of countries growing exceedingly rich at the cost of the increasing impoverishment of a great number of other countries; as a result the wealthy grow ever wealthier, while the poor grow ever poorer.*[1]

The world is said to have become increasingly unfair. The chorus of the debate on the market economy runs: "The rich are getting richer, and the poor are getting poorer." This statement is offered as a dictate of natural law, not as a thesis to be argued. But if we look beyond the catchy slogans and study what has actually happened in the world, we find this thesis to be a half-truth. The first half is true: the rich have indeed grown richer—not all of them everywhere, but generally speaking. Those of us who are privileged to live in affluent countries have grown appreciably richer in the past few decades. So too have the Third World rich. But the second half is, quite simply, wrong. The poor have not, generally speaking, come to be worse off in recent decades. On the contrary, absolute poverty has diminished, and where it was quantitatively greatest—in Asia—many hundreds of millions of people who barely twenty years ago were struggling to make ends meet have begun to achieve a secure existence and even a modest degree of affluence. Global misery has diminished and the great injustices have started to unravel. This opening chapter will contain a long succession of figures and trend descriptions that are necessary to correct the very widespread misunderstanding that exists concerning the state of the world.[2]

One of the most interesting books published in recent years is *On Asian Time: India, China, Japan 1966–1999*, a travelogue in which Swedish author Lasse Berg and photographer Stig Karlsson describe new visits to Asian countries where they traveled during the 1960s.[3] Then, they saw poverty, abject misery, and imminent disaster. Like many other travelers to those countries, they could not bring themselves to hold out much hope for the future, and they thought that socialist revolution might be the only way out. Returning to India and China in the 1990s, they could not help seeing how wrong they were. More and more people have extricated themselves from poverty; the problem of hunger is steadily diminishing; the streets are cleaner. Mud huts have given way to brick buildings, wired up for electricity and sporting television aerials on their roofs.

When Berg and Karlsson first visited Calcutta, a tenth of its inhabitants were homeless, and every morning trucks sent by the public authorities or missionary societies would go around

21

collecting the bodies of those who had died in the night. Thirty years later, setting out to photograph people living on the streets, they had difficulty in finding any such people. The rickshaw, a passenger cart pulled by a barefoot man, is disappearing from the urban scene, and people are traveling by car, motorcycle, and subway instead.

When Berg and Karlsson showed young Indians photographs of what things looked like on that last visit, they refused to believe that it was even the same place. Could things really have been so dreadful? One striking illustration of the change is provided by a pair of photographs on page 42 of their book. In the old one, taken in 1976, a 12-year-old Indian girl named Satto holds up her hands. They are already furrowed and worn, prematurely aged by many years' hard work. The recent picture shows Satto's 13-year-old daughter Seema, also holding up her hands. They are young and soft, the hands of a child whose childhood has not been taken away from her.

The biggest change of all is in people's thoughts and dreams. Television and newspapers bring ideas and images from the other side of the globe, widening people's notions of what is possible. Why should one have to spend all one's life in one place? Why must a woman be forced to have children early and sacrifice her career? Why must marriages be arranged—and the untouchables excluded from them—when family relations in other countries are so much freer? Why make do with this kind of government when there are alternative political systems available?

Lasse Berg writes, self-critically:

Reading what we observers, foreigners as well as Indians, wrote in the 60s and 70s, nowhere in these analyses do I see anything of present-day India. Often nightmare scenarios—overpopulation, tumult, upheaval or stagnation—but not this calm and steady forward-jogging, and least of all this modernization of thoughts and dreams. Who foresaw that consumerism would penetrate so deeply in and among the villages? Who foresaw that both the economy and general standard of living would do so well? Looking back, what the descriptions have in common is an overstatement of the extraordinary, frightening, uncertain (most writers had their personal hobby-horses and favorites) and an understatement of the force of normality.[4]

The development described by Lasse Berg has resulted, not from socialist revolution, but rather from a move in the past few decades toward greater individual liberty. Freedom of choice and international exchange have grown, and investments and development assistance have transmitted ideas and resources, allowing the developing world to benefit from the knowledge, wealth, and inventions of other countries. Imports of medicines and new health care systems have improved living conditions. Modern technology and new methods of production have stepped up output and improved the food supply. Individual citizens have become more and more free to choose their own occupations and to sell their products. We can tell from the statistics how this enhances national prosperity and reduces poverty among the population. But the most important thing of all is liberty itself, the independence and dignity that autonomy confers on people who have been living under oppression.

With the spread of humanist ideas, slavery, which a few centuries ago was a worldwide phenomenon, has been beaten down in one continent after another. It lives on today illegally but, since the liberation of the last slaves in the Arabian Peninsula in 1970, has been forbidden practically everywhere on earth. The forced

23

labor of precapitalist economies is being rapidly superseded by freedom of contract and freedom of movement where the market breaks through.

Poverty reduction

Between 1965 and 1998, the average world citizen's income practically doubled, from $2,497 to $4,839, adjusted for purchasing power and inflation. That increase has not come about through the industrialized nations multiplying their incomes. During this period the richest fifth of the world's population increased their average income from $8,315 to $14,623, or by roughly 75 percent. For the poorest fifth of the world's population, the increase has been faster still, with average income more than doubling during the same period from $551 to $1,137.[5] World consumption today is more than twice what it was in 1960.

Thanks to material developments in the past half century, the world has over three billion more people living above the poverty line. This is historically unique. The United Nations Development Program (UNDP) has observed that, all in all, world poverty has fallen more during the past 50 years than during the preceding 500. In its *Human Development Report 1997,* the UNDP writes that humanity is in the midst of "the second great ascent." The first began in the 19th century, with the industrialization of the United States and Europe and the rapid spread of prosperity. The second began during the post-war era and is now in full swing, with first Asia and then the other developing countries scoring ever-greater victories in the war against poverty, hunger, disease, and illiteracy.

The great success in reducing poverty in the 20th century shows that eradicating severe poverty in the first decades of the 21st century is feasible.[6]

Poverty is still rapidly diminishing. "Absolute poverty" is usually defined as the condition of having an income less than one dollar a day. In 1820 something like 85 percent of the world's population were living on the equivalent of less than a dollar a day. By 1950 that figure had fallen to about 50 percent and by 1980 to 31 percent. According to World Bank figures, absolute poverty has fallen since 1980 from 31 to 20 percent (a figure of 24 percent is often mentioned, meaning 24 percent of the population of the developing countries). The radical reduction of the past 20 years is unique in that not only the proportion but also the total number of people living in absolute poverty has declined—for the first time in world history. During these two decades the world's population has grown by a billion and a half, and yet the number of absolute poor has fallen by about 200 million. That decrease is connected with economic growth. In places where prosperity has grown fastest, poverty has been most effectively combated. In East Asia (China excluded), absolute poverty has fallen from 15 to just over 9 percent, in China from 32 to 17 percent. Six Asians in 10 were absolutely poor in 1975. Today's figure, according to the World Bank, is fewer than 2 out of 10.

Even those encouraging findings, however, almost certainly overestimate world poverty significantly because the World Bank uses notoriously unreliable survey data as the basis for its own assessments. Former World Bank economist Surjit S. Bhalla recently published his own calculations, supplementing survey results with national accounts data. This method, he argues convincingly, is far more likely to provide an accurate measurement.

Bhalla found that poverty had fallen precipitously, from a level of 44 percent in 1980 to 13 percent at the end of 2002. If those figures are correct, then the last 20 years have seen an extraordinary, unprecedented reduction of poverty—twice that achieved in any other 20-year period on record. The UN's goal of lowering world poverty to below 15 percent by 2015 has already been achieved and surpassed.[7]

"But," the skeptic asks, "what do people in the developing countries want consumption and growth for? Why must we force our way of life upon them?" The answer is that we must not force a particular way of life on anyone. Whatever their values, the great majority of people the world over desire better material conditions, for the simple reason that they will then have more options, regardless of how they then decide to use that increased wealth. As Indian economist and Nobel laureate Amartya Sen has emphasized, poverty is not just a material problem. Poverty is something wider: it is about powerlessness, about being deprived of basic opportunities and freedom of choice. Small incomes are often symptomatic of the absence of these things, of people's marginalization or subjection to coercion. Human development means enjoying a reasonably healthy and secure existence, with a good standard of living and freedom to shape one's own life. It is important to investigate material development because it suggests how wealth can be produced and because it contributes to development in this broader sense. Material resources, individual and societal, enable people to feed and educate themselves, to obtain health care, and to be spared the pain of watching their children die. Those are pretty universal human desires, one finds, when people are allowed to choose for themselves.

Average life expectancy is increasing

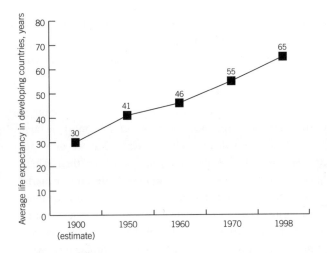

Source: UNDP, *Human Development Report 1997* (New York: Oxford University Press for the United Nations Development Program, 1997).

The worldwide improvement in the human condition is reflected in a very rapid growth of average life expectancy. At the beginning of the 20th century, average life expectancy in the developing countries was under 30 years; by 1960 it had risen to 46, and in 1998 it was 65. Longevity in the developing countries today is nearly 15 years higher than it was a century ago in the world's *leading* economy at the time, Britain. Development has been slowest in sub-Saharan Africa, but even there life expectancy has risen, from 41 to 51 years since the 1960s. Average life expectancy remains highest in the most affluent countries—in the Organization for Economic Cooperation and Development (OECD) countries it is 78—but the *fastest improvement* has been in the poor

28

countries. In 1960, their average life expectancy was 60 percent of that of the affluent countries. Today it is more than 80 percent. Nine out of every 10 people in the world today can expect to live beyond 60, which is more than twice the average only a hundred years ago.

In *On Asian Time*, Berg describes returning to Malaysia 30 years after his first visit and suddenly realizing that in the meantime the average life expectancy of the population has risen by 15 years. That means that the people he meets there have been able to celebrate every birthday since his last visit having come only half a year closer to death.[8]

The improvement in health has been partly because of better eating habits and living conditions, but also because of improved health care. Twenty years ago there was one doctor for every thousand people; today there are 1.5. In the very poorest countries, there was 0.6 of a doctor per thousand inhabitants in 1980; this statistic has almost doubled to 1.0. Perhaps the most dependable indicator of the living conditions of the poor is infant mortality, which in the developing countries has fallen drastically. Whereas 18 percent of newborns—almost one in five!—died in 1950, by 1976 this figure had fallen to 11 percent and in 1995 was only 6 percent. In the past 30 years alone, mortality has been almost halved, from 107 deaths per thousand births in 1970 to 59 per thousand in 1998. More and more people, then, have been able to survive despite poverty. And even as more people in poor countries survive, a progressively smaller proportion of the world's population is poor, which in turn suggests that the reduction of poverty has been still greater than is apparent from a superficial study of the statistics.

Infant mortality is declining

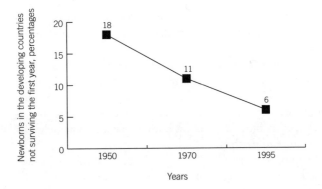

Source: UNDP, *Human Development Report 1997* (New York: Oxford University Press for the United Nations Development Program, 1997).

Hunger

Longer lives and better health are connected with the reduction of one of the cruelest manifestations of underdevelopment—hunger. Calorie intake in the Third World has risen by 30 percent per capita since the 1960s. According to the UN Food and Agriculture Organization, 960 million people in the developing countries were undernourished in 1970. In 1991 the figure was 830 million, falling by 1996 to 790 million. In proportion to population, this is an immensely rapid improvement. Thirty years ago nearly 37 percent of the population of the developing countries were afflicted with hunger. Today's figure is less than 18 percent. Many? Yes. Too many? Of course. But the number is rapidly declining. It took the first two decades of the 20th century for Sweden to be declared free from chronic malnutrition. In only 30 years the proportion of hungry in the world has been reduced by half, and it is expected to decline further, to 12 percent by 2010. There have never been so many of us on earth, and we have never had such a good supply of food. During the 1990s, the ranks of the hungry diminished by an average of 6 million every year, at the same time as the world's population grew by about 800 million.

Things have moved fastest in East and Southeast Asia, where the proportion of hungry has fallen from 43 to 13 percent since 1970. In Latin America, it has fallen from 19 to 11 percent, in North Africa and the Middle East from 25 to 9 percent, in South Asia from 38 to 23 percent. The worst development has occurred in Africa south of the Sahara, where the number of hungry has actually increased, from 89 to 180 million people. But even there the proportion of the population living in hunger has declined, albeit marginally, from 34 to 33 percent.

World hunger is declining

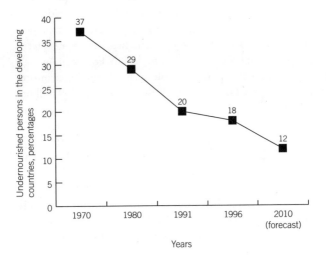

Source: Food and Agriculture Organization of the United Nations, "The State of Food and Agriculture," Document C99/2 to FAO conference, 30th Session, Rome, Nov. 12-13, 1998.

Global food production has doubled during the past half century, and in the developing countries it has tripled. Global food supply increased by 24 percent, from 2,257 to 2,808 calories per person daily, between 1961 and 1999. The fastest increase occurred in the developing countries, where consumption rose by 39 percent, from 1,932 to 2,684 calories daily.[9] Very little of this development

32

is due to new land having been converted to agricultural use. Instead, the old land is being farmed more efficiently. The yield per acre of arable land has virtually doubled. Wheat, maize, and rice prices have fallen by more than 60 percent. Since the beginning of the 1980s alone, food prices have halved and production from a given area of land has risen by 25 percent—a process that has been swifter in poor countries than in affluent ones.

Such is the triumph of the "green revolution." Higher-yield, more-resistant crops have been developed, at the same time as sowing, irrigation, manuring, and harvesting methods have improved dramatically. New, efficient strains of wheat account for more than 75 percent of wheat production in the developing countries, and farmers there are estimated to have earned nearly $5 billion as a result of the change. In southern India, the green revolution is estimated to have boosted farmers' real earnings by 90 percent and those of landless peasants by 125 percent over 20 years. Its impact has been least in Africa, but even there the green revolution has raised maize production per acre by between 10 and 40 percent. Without this revolution, it is estimated that world prices of wheat and rice would be nearly 40 percent higher than they are today and that roughly another 2 percent of the world's children—children who are now getting enough to eat—would have suffered from chronic malnourishment. Today's food problem has nothing to do with overpopulation. Hunger today is a problem of access to the available knowledge and technology, to wealth, and to the secure background conditions that make food production possible. Many researchers believe that if modern farming techniques were applied in all the world's agriculture, we would already be able, here and now, to feed another billion or so people.[10]

The incidence of major famine disasters has also declined dramatically, largely as a result of the spread of democracy. Starvation has occurred in states of practically every kind—communist regimes, colonial empires, technocratic dictatorships, and ancient tribal societies. In all cases they have been centralized, authoritarian states that suppressed free debate and the workings of the market. As Amartya Sen observes, there has never been a famine disaster in a democracy. Even poor democracies like India and Botswana have avoided starvation, despite having a poorer food supply than many countries where famine *has* struck. By contrast, communist states like China, the Soviet Union, Cambodia, Ethiopia, and North Korea, as well as colonies like India under the British Raj, have experienced starvation. This shows that famine is caused by dictatorship, not by food shortage. Famine is induced by leaders destroying production and trade, making war, and ignoring the plight of the starving population.

Sen maintains that democracies are spared starvation for the simple reason that it is easily prevented if the rulers of a society wish to prevent it. Rulers can refrain from impeding the distribution of food, and they can create jobs for people who would not be able to afford food purchases in times of crisis. But dictators are under no pressure: they can eat their fill however badly off their people are, whereas democratic leaders will be unseated if they fail to address food distribution problems. Additionally, a free press makes the general public aware of the problems, so that they can be tackled in time. In a dictatorship, even the leaders may be deceived by censorship. Much evidence suggests that China's leaders were reassured by their own propaganda and their subordinates' laundered statistics while 30 million people died of starvation during "the Great Leap Forward" between 1958 and 1961.[11]

At the same time as more people are getting the food they need, the supply of potable drinking water has doubled, which is hugely important for the reduction of disease and infection in

34

developing countries. Worldwide, 8 people in 10 now have access to pure water. A generation ago, 90 percent of the world's rural population were without pure water. Today that applies to only 25 percent. At the beginning of the 1980s, little more than half of India's population had access to pure water, while 10 years later the figure was more than 80 percent. In Indonesia that percentage rose from 39 to 62. Countries like Kuwait and Saudi Arabia today derive large parts of their water supply from desalination of seawater, which is available in practically unlimited quantities. Desalination is a costly process, but it shows that growing prosperity can solve problems of scarce resources.

Education

Education is one of the most reliable methods of increasing people's development and earning prospects, yet many people are denied access to it. Access to education is very much a gender issue: roughly 65 percent of those who are not allowed to attend school, and who therefore remain illiterate, are girls. It is also a poverty problem. In many countries the poorest people have no education at all. Poor families cannot send their children to school, either because school is too expensive to afford at all or because the return on education is insufficient. In India, children from the wealthiest 15 percent of families receive 10 years more schooling than those from the poorest 15 percent. And so it is no surprise that education is quickly extended when the economy gathers speed. Rising levels of education in turn act as a spur to economic growth.

Participation in elementary education has come close to 100 percent the world over. The big exception, once again, is Africa south of the Sahara, and even there it has reached three-quarters of the population. Participation in high school education rose from 27 percent in 1960 to 67 percent in 1995. During that time, the proportion of children allowed to attend school rose by 80 percent. Today there are nearly 900 million illiterate adults. That sounds like a lot, and indeed it is, but it reflects a significant decrease, from 70 percent of the population of the developing world in the 1950s to 25–30 percent today. The very rapid spread of literacy in the world today is readily apparent from an examination of literacy rates across generations. Where the youngest people are concerned, illiteracy is rapidly disappearing.

Illiteracy is diminishing

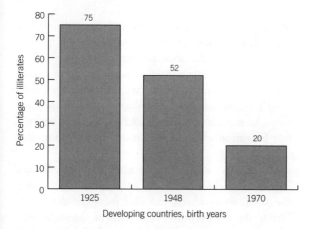

Developing countries, birth years

Source: United Nations Educational, Scientific and Cultural Organization, *The World Education Report 2000* (Paris: UNESCO Publishing, 2000).

Democratization

The accelerating spread of information and ideas throughout the world, coupled with rising education standards and growing prosperity, is prompting demands for genuine political rights. Critics of globalization maintain that a dynamic market and international capital are a threat to democracy, but what they really see threatened is the use that *they* would like to make of democracy. Never before in human history have democracy, universal suffrage, and the free formation of opinion been as widespread as they are today.

A hundred years ago, no country on earth had universal and equal suffrage. The world was ruled by empires and monarchies. Even in the West, women were excluded from the democratic process. During the 20th century, large parts of the world were subjugated by communism, fascism, or National Socialism, ideologies that led to major wars and the political murder of more than a hundred million people. With just a few exceptions, those systems have fallen. The totalitarian states have collapsed, the dictatorships have been democratized, and the absolute monarchies have been deposed. A hundred years ago, one-third of the world's population was governed by remote colonial powers. Today the colonial empires have been dismantled. In the past few decades alone, dictatorships have fallen like bowling pins, especially following the tearing down of the communist Iron Curtain. The end of the Cold War also put an end to the unpleasant American strategy of supporting Third World dictatorships as long as they opposed the Soviet bloc.

According to the think tank Freedom House, there were 121 democracies with multiparty systems and with universal, equal suffrage in 2002. Living in those democracies are some 3.5 billion people, or roughly 60 percent of the world's population. Freedom House regards 85 countries, with a total of 2.5 billion inhabitants, as "free" (i.e., democratic countries with civil rights). That is more than 40 percent of the world's inhabitants, the biggest proportion ever. That many, in other words, are living in states that guarantee the rule of law and permit free debate and an active opposition.

The world is being democratized

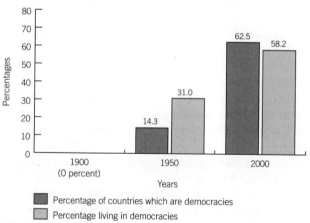

■ Percentage of countries which are democracies

▫ Percentage living in democracies

Source: Freedom House, "Democracy's Century: A Survey of Global Political Change in the 20th Century" (New York: Freedom House, 2000), *http://www.freedomhouse.org/reports/century/pdf.*

In 2002, there were 47 states that violated basic human rights. Worst among them were Burma, Cuba, Iraq, Libya, North Korea, Saudi Arabia, Sudan, Syria, and Turkmenistan—that is, the countries least affected by globalization and least oriented in favor of the market economy and liberalism. While deploring and combating their oppression, suppression of opinion, government-controlled media, and wiretapping, we should still remember that such was the normal state of affairs for most of the world's population only a few decades ago. In 1973, only 20 countries with populations of more than a million were democratically governed.[12]

During the 1990s the number of "free" states in the world increased by 21, at the same time as the number of unfree ones declined by 3. This expansion of freedom has proceeded parallel to the formation of many new states, following the disintegration of old ones like the Soviet Union. The democratic trend continues. And there is no reason to expect it to end now. Now and then it is alleged that democracy is hard to reconcile with Islam, and so it may seem in the world today. But we should remember that many researchers were saying the same about Catholicism as recently as the 1970s, when Catholic countries included, for example, the military regimes of Latin America, the communist states of eastern Europe, and dictatorships like the Philippines under Ferdinand Marcos.

The number of wars has diminished by half during the past decade, and today less than 1 percent of the world's population are directly affected by military conflicts. One reason is that democracies simply do not make war on each other; another is that international exchange makes conflict less interesting. With freedom of movement and free trade, citizens are not all that interested in the size of their country. People create prosperity,

40

not by annexing land from another country, but by carrying on trade with that land and its resources. If, on the other hand, the world consists of self-contained nation states, the land of other countries has no value until one is able to seize it.

"The ox made peace" is a 16th-century saying from the border country between Denmark and Sweden. Farmers near the border made peace with each other against the wishes of their rulers because they wanted to trade meat and butter for herring and spices. In the trenchant words of the 19th-century French liberal Frédéric Bastiat, "If goods do not cross borders, soldiers will." Mutual dependence means fewer potential causes of conflict between states. Cross-ownership, multinational corporations, investment, and privately owned natural resources make it hard to tell where one country really ends and another begins. Several centuries ago, when the Swedes pillaged Europe, it was other people's resources they wrecked and stole. If they were to do the same thing today, the victims would include many Swedish companies, not to mention Swedish capital and Swedish export markets.

It has been asserted that the globalist challenge to nation-states leads to separatism and to local and ethnic conflicts. There is indeed a risk of separatist activity when national power is called into question, and the tragedy of the former Yugoslavia is evidence of the bloody conflicts that can follow. But the number of major internecine conflicts—those costing more than a thousand lives— fell from 20 to 13 between 1991 and 1998. Nine of those conflicts occurred in Africa, the world's least democratized, least globalized, and least capitalist continent. The conflicts that follow the collapse of totalitarian states are primarily power struggles in temporary power vacuums. In several countries, centralization has prevented the evolution of stable, democratic institutions and civil societies, and when centralization disappears, chaos ensues pending the establishment of new institutions. There is no reason for believing this to be a new trend in a more internationalized and democratic world.

Oppression of women

One of the world's cruelest injustices is the oppression of women. There are parts of the world where women are regarded as the property of men. A father is entitled to marry off his daughters, and it is the husband who decides what work his wife is to do. In many countries, a husband owns his wife's passport or ID card, with the result that she cannot even travel freely in her own country. Laws disqualify women from divorce, from ownership of property, and from work outside the home. Daughters are denied the rights of inheritance enjoyed by sons. Girls receive nothing like the same education as boys, and very often no education at all. Women are abused and subjected to genital mutilation and rape without any intervention by the authorities.

It is true, as many complain, that globalization upsets old traditions and habits. How, for example, do you maintain patriarchal family traditions when children are suddenly earning more than the head of the family? One of the traditions challenged by globalization is the long-standing subjugation of women. Through cultural contacts and the interchange of ideas, new hopes and ideals are disseminated. Indian women who can see on television that women are not necessarily housewives begin to contemplate careers in law or medicine. Some Chinese women who had previously been isolated have been inspired to press demands for greater autonomy and to make decisions of their own by the website gaogenxie.com. The site's name, which means "high-heeled shoes," is a symbol of freedom contrasting with the tradition of bound feet. When women begin making their own decisions about their consumer behavior or their employment, they

43

become more insistent in demanding equal liberty and power in other fields.

> "My parents brought me up to be pretty and well-behaved. I was to be obedient and polite, submissive to them and my teachers.... When I eventually have children, I want to go in for equality within the family, between man and woman, between children and parents. It wasn't like that for us. To my parents' generation it went without saying that the married woman's life took place within the four walls of the home, where she did everything, even if she was working. I think that age will soon be gone forever."
> *Shang Ying, a 21-year-old Chinese girl employed as a bank clerk in Shanghai.*[13]

Growing prosperity gives women more opportunity to become independent and provide for themselves. Experience from Africa and elsewhere shows that women are often leading entrepreneurs for various kinds of small-scale production and exchange in the informal sector, which suggests that, absent discrimination and regulation by the government, the market is their oyster. And indeed, the worldwide spread of freer conditions of service and freer markets has made it increasingly difficult for women to be kept out. Women today constitute 42 percent of the world's work force, compared with 36 percent 20 years ago. Capitalism doesn't care whether the best producer is a man or a woman. On the contrary, discrimination is expensive because it involves the rejection of certain people's goods and labor. All studies have shown that respect for women's rights and their ability to exert influence in the home are closely bound up with their ability to find employment outside the home and earn an independent income.

44

Technological progress can expedite social progress. Women in Saudi Arabia are prevented from showing themselves in public unless they cover their whole bodies except the hands, eyes, and feet. They are also disqualified from driving cars and from doing other things. The practical effect of this has been to exclude them from all economic activity. But now the Internet and the telephone have suddenly made it possible for women to carry on business from home, at the computer. Within a short span of time, a profusion of women-owned enterprises has come into being, dealing, for example, in fashion, travel bookings, or conference and party arrangements. That is one reason why something like two-thirds of Internet users in Saudi Arabia are women. When several thousand women suddenly show that they are every bit as competitive as men, discrimination notwithstanding, the prohibitions applying to them are made to look increasingly absurd. Awareness and criticism of gender discrimination is growing.[14]

Democratization gives women a voice in politics, and in more and more countries the laws have been reformed to establish greater equality between the sexes. Divorce laws and rights of inheritance are becoming less and less biased. Equality before the law spreads with democracy and capitalism. The idea of equal human dignity spreads, knocking out discrimination.

Gender equity also grows with prosperity. A World Bank study of education in India found that, although boys are more likely than girls to receive schooling at all income levels, the *extent* of the disparity is highly wealth-dependent. In the wealthiest households, the study found only a 2.5 percentage point difference in the enrollment of male and female children. The difference was a whopping 34 percentage points for children from the poorest households.[15] In the most unequal parts of the world—South Asia, Africa, and the Middle East—the proportion of girls attending school has doubled in the past 25 years. The global difference between the proportion of women and men respectively enabled to attend school has diminished by more than half in two decades. On average in basic education worldwide, 46 percent of the pupils are girls.

That statistic is important, not only for women but also for their children. Better education and extra earnings for a mother quickly result in better nourishment and education for her children, whereas the connection between paternal income and child welfare is less strong. In South Asia, where an inhuman attitude concerning the value of women resulted—and still does—in high mortality rates among girls during the first years of life, girls now have a greater life expectancy at birth than boys. The average life expectancy of women in the developing countries has increased by 20 years during the past half century. Development is also giving women more power over their own bodies. Increased power for women in poor countries, and improved availability of contraception, go hand in hand with reduced birthrates.

Helen Rahman of Shoishab, an Oxfam-funded organization working in Dhaka, Bangladesh, with disadvantaged and homeless children and with working women, maintains that the emergence of the country's textile industry during the past 20 years has given women better status: "The garment industry has stimulated a silent revolution of social change. It used not to be acceptable for a woman to work outside her neighborhood. Before, anyone who left the countryside to go to the city was in disgrace; they were assumed to be involved in prostitution. Now it is acceptable for five girls to rent a house together." Helen has noticed changes in social behavior too: "The income the women earn gives them social status and bargaining power. One very positive thing is that the average marriage age has increased."[16]

China

About half of the world's poor live in the two most populous countries, India and China, hence the great importance of what happens in those countries. Both their economies have been extensively liberalized in the past 20 years. China's communist dictatorship realized at the end of the 1970s that collectivization was impeding development. Stifling centralized control—such as the requirement that farmers deliver their own produce—impeded land renewal and lowered crop yields. Deng Xiaoping, China's ruler, wanted to keep faith with the distributive ideas of socialism. Yet he realized that he would have to distribute either poverty or prosperity, and that the latter could only be achieved by giving people more freedom. And so in December 1978, two years after the death of Chairman Mao, Deng embarked on a program of liberalization. Rural families that had previously been forced into collective farming were now entitled to set aside part of their produce for sale at market prices, a system that became increasingly liberal as time went on. The Chinese were thereby impelled to invest in agriculture and improve its efficiency. The option to drop out of the collective and formally lease land from the government was taken advantage of to such a huge extent that nearly all farmland passed into private hands in what may have been the biggest privatization in history. It paid off, with crop yields rising between 1978 and 1984 by an incredible 7.7 percent annually. The same country that 20 years earlier had been hit by the worst famine in human history now had a food surplus.

Before long, similar market incentives began to be introduced in the rest of the economy. First, economic free zones were set up. Exempted from socialist controls, these zones allowed Chinese entrepreneurs to engage in foreign trade, and the great success of this arrangement inspired liberalization measures across the board. Trade was permitted in the countryside, and also between town and country. The formerly self-sufficient villages were integrated with regional and even national markets. Increased productivity and purchasing power induced many farmers to invest their capital in starting up private and cooperative industrial production. Since then, more and more previously inconceivable phenomena—freer labor markets, foreign trade, direct foreign investments—have become commonplace.

Information about those developments is partly contradictory, owing to the difficulty of obtaining hard facts in an immense dictatorship. But all observers agree that the economic growth and the rise in incomes observed in China are unique. There has been talk of almost 10 percent growth annually in the 20 years following the early reforms, and China's gross domestic product (GDP) has more than quadrupled. In 20 years, China's economy has moved from equaling Germany's to exceeding the German, French, Italian, and Nordic economies combined. The 1978 liberalization enabled 800 million Chinese farmers to double their incomes in only six years. Economist Shujie Yao contends that absolute poverty was long concealed by China's official statistics, but in terms of actual development half a billion Chinese have left absolute poverty behind them. The World Bank has characterized this phenomenon as "the biggest and fastest poverty reduction in history."[17]

Dramatic economic reversals may still take place in China. Under the protection of capital regulations, colossal loans have

48

been channeled into the inefficient national government sector and companies favored by state officials, while small and medium enterprises (SMEs) are undercapitalized. The authorities have protected banks and corporations from outside scrutiny, which could precipitate a crisis of huge proportions. But the economy has undergone too much of a fundamental transformation for a reversion to the pre-1978 situation, in terms of either policy or prosperity, to be possible.

The Tiananmen Square massacre, the ban in many regions on having more than one child, oppression in Tibet and Sinkiang, the persecution of the Falun Gong movement, labor camps for political prisoners—these things show that, sadly, not everything has changed in China. Communist party oppression lives on, but fewer and fewer people expect it to survive economic liberalization in the long term. Simply through economic liberalization, citizens have come to enjoy important liberties. Whereas formerly they had to work wherever they were ordered to, today the Chinese can choose their own employment. Travel and relocation used to be almost impossible, and moving from countryside to town or city was out of the question. Now the Chinese can travel almost freely, wear whatever clothing they like, and spend their money almost as they please.

The ability of villages to choose their local representatives has grown. The elections are typically still controlled by the Communist Party, but where they are not, the people have shown that a change is what they want. In nearly one-third of the villages, party control has broken down, and in some, villagers are even insisting on the right to elect national party officials. Combining increased local democracy with central dictatorship will be difficult in the long term. Although people can still be arrested for dissent, a wide range of opinions can now be heard—in large part because of international influence and the Internet. Independent organizations are emerging and information is no longer controllable. Even the newspapers are showing greater independence, and corrupt officials can be criticized.

India

Unlike China, India has been a democracy ever since Independence in 1947, but at the same time it has opted for a strictly regulated economy. The government invested in large-scale industries that had been protected by fierce import and export barriers in an effort to make them self-sufficient. That investment turned out to be a very expensive fiasco. All economic activity was ensnared in regulations and impeded by required permits, which were all but unobtainable without pulling strings and paying bribes. The British Raj was succeeded by a "permit raj." Power passed to the bureaucracy. Indians wishing to engage in business had to devote a great deal of their time to buttering up officials, and if successful they were rewarded with protection against competition from others. Economic growth barely kept pace with population growth, and the proportion falling below the Indian poverty line grew from 50 percent at Independence to 62 percent in 1966.

In the mid-1970s India began a slow reordering of its economy. Exclusion and self-sufficiency were replaced with reliance on the country's advantage in labor-intensive industry. Growth started to accelerate in the 1980s, and poverty began to decline. But this expansion was fueled with borrowed money, resulting in a profound crisis at the beginning of the 1990s. In 1991, the government embarked on a series of reforms aimed at putting its finances in order, welcoming trade and foreign investments, and encouraging competition and enterprise. Tariff levels, which had averaged a crippling 87 percent, were lowered to 27 percent. The economy was freed from numerous restrictions by three consecutive governments, even though the governments represented different party constellations.

Although a massive process of reform still remains to be accomplished before India becomes a genuine market economy, great results have already been achieved through more productive use of the country's resources. Since the reforms began, India has received a steady stream of investment from abroad, and growth has been running at 5 to 7 percent annually. The proportion of inhabitants below the Indian poverty line has now fallen to about 32 percent. Things have moved fastest following the change of system. During the reform years of 1993–99 alone, poverty fell by 10 percentage points. Without this reduction, something like 300 million more Indians would have been poor today. Population growth has fallen by 30 percent since the end of the 1960s and average life expectancy has doubled from about 30 years after Independence to about 60 today.[18] Half the poor households of India today own a clock, one-third have a radio, and 40 percent have access to television.

Developments have varied, however, depending on the extent of reform in the various states of India. Large parts of the countryside, which is where the poor live, have not had the benefit of any major liberalization measures, and poverty rates there have remained stable. At the same time, the southern states in particular—Andhra Pradesh, Karnataka, and Tamil Nadu—have made very swift progress with liberalization. Growth in these states has been above the national average, sometimes approaching an incredible 15 percent annually, and it is these states that have attracted most investments, both from abroad and from the rest of India. The economy has experienced an information technology miracle, with the software sector growing by 50 percent annually. In Andhra Pradesh, Microsoft opened its first full-fledged development center away from its headquarters in Redmond. Economic growth has also left its mark on social development. On average, the reforming states have succeeded best with medical care and education, and have achieved the fastest reductions of infant mortality and illiteracy. Girls, who hardly ever received any education at all, are now catching up with boys in terms of school attendance. In several of the states (Andhra Pradesh, Maharashtra) poverty has declined by about 40 percent since the end of the 1970s, while in nonliberalized states like Bihar and Uttar Pradesh it has hardly diminished at all.[19]

The Indian caste system—a form of apartheid that divides, assesses, and treats people according to the family they come from—has been officially abolished but has proved very persistent. At the local level, people of lower caste are still treated as inferior human beings with fewer rights than others. But now the system is slowly breaking up, with an unprejudiced market hiring the best workers instead of people from the right families. In more and more places, "untouchables" are, for the first time, taking part in village council meetings. Instead of strengthening the caste system, the government is launching anti-discrimination campaigns. One sure sign of progress came when an untouchable, K. R. Narayanan, served as president from 1997 to 2002.

Global inequality

This progress is all very well, many critics of globalization will argue, but even if the majority are better off, gaps have widened and wealthy people and countries have improved their lot more rapidly than others. So inequality has grown. The critics point to the fact that the combined per capita GDP of the 20 richest countries was 15 times greater than that of the 20 poorest countries 40 years ago and is now about 30 times greater.

There are two reasons why this objection to globalization does not hold up. First, even if this were true it would not matter very much. If everyone is coming to be better off, what does it matter that the improvement comes faster for some than for others? Surely the important thing is for everyone to be as well off as possible, not whether one group is better off than another. Only those who consider wealth a greater problem than poverty can find a problem in some becoming millionaires while others grow wealthier from their own starting points. It is better to be poor in the inegalitarian United States, where the poverty line for individuals in 2001 was about $9,039 per year, than to be equal in countries like Rwanda, where in 2001 GDP per capita (adjusted for purchasing power) was $1,000, or Bangladesh ($1,750), or Uzbekistan ($2,500).[20] Often the reason why gaps have widened in certain reforming countries, such as China, is that the towns and cities have grown faster than the countryside. But given the unprecedented poverty reduction this has entailed in both town and country, can anyone wish that this development had never happened?

The poor do not always experience poverty. Many concepts of poverty are relative, which is to say that, instead of measuring how poor someone is, they say how poor that person is in relation to others. One poverty concept frequently used, for example, by the UNDP, rates people as poor if they have less than half the median wage in the country where they live. That means that a person regarded as "loaded" when living in a poor country like Nepal is considered as poor as a church mouse when living in the affluent United States. These relative figures, consequently, cannot be compared internationally. Those who are rated poor in the United States are not always living in circumstances that we would term poverty. Thus, 72 percent of poor American families have one or more cars, 50 percent have air conditioning, 72 percent have a washing machine, 20 percent have a dishwasher, 60 percent have a microwave, 93 percent have a color television, 60 percent have a video player, and 41 percent own their homes (the poverty reference is to regular income only; real estate is not included in the income level).[21]

Second, the allegation of increased inequality is just wrong. The notion that global inequality has increased is largely based on figures from the UN Development Program, in particular its *Human Development Report* from 1999. But the problem with these figures is that they are not adjusted for purchasing power. That is, the UNDP numbers don't take into account what people can actually buy for their money. Without that adjustment the figures mainly show the level of a country's official exchange rate and what its currency is worth on the international market, which is a poor yardstick of poverty. Poor people's actual living standard, needless to say, hinges far more on the cost of their food, clothing, and housing than on what they would get for their money when vacationing in Europe. The odd thing is that the UNDP itself uses purchasing power–adjusted figures in its Human Development Index (HDI), which is its universal yardstick of living standards. It only resorts to the unadjusted figures in order to prove a thesis of inequality.

A report from the Norwegian Institute for Foreign Affairs investigated global inequality by means of figures adjusted for purchasing power. Their data show that, contrary to the conventional wisdom, inequality between countries has been continuously *declining* ever since the end of the 1970s. This decline was especially rapid between 1993 and 1998, when globalization really gathered speed.[22] More recently, similar research by Columbia University development economist Xavier Sala-i-Martin has confirmed those findings. When the UNDP's own numbers are adjusted for purchasing power, Sala-i-Martin found that world inequality declined sharply by any of the common ways of measuring it.[23] Bhalla and Sala-i-Martin also independently found that if we focus on inequality between *persons*, rather than inequality between *countries*, global inequality at the end of 2000 was at its lowest point since the end of World War II. Estimates that compare countries rather than individuals, as both authors note, grossly overestimate real inequality because they allow gains for huge numbers of people to be outweighed by comparable losses for far fewer. Country aggregates treat China and Grenada as data points of equal weight, even though China's population is 12,000 times Grenada's. Once we shift our focus to people rather than nations, the evidence is overwhelming that the past 30 years have witnessed a global equalization.[24] Comparing just the richest and poorest tenths, inequality has increased, suggesting that a small group has lagged behind (we shall be returning to see which countries and why), but a study of all countries clearly points to a general growth of equality. If, for example, we compare the richest and poorest fifth or the richest and poorest third, we find the differences diminishing.

Economists usually measure the degree of inequality by means of the "Gini coefficient." If that number is zero, complete equality prevails, and everyone owns the same amount. If it is one, there is total inequality, with one person owning everything. The Gini coefficient for the whole world declined from 0.6 in 1968 to 0.52 in 1997, a reduction of more than 10 percent.

Because equality between the rich and poor *within* these countries appears to have been roughly constant during this time (having increased in half and diminished in half), global equality, quite contrary to popular supposition, is increasing. The 1998/99 World Bank report reviews among other things the difference in incomes going to the richest and poorest 20 percent in the developing countries. The review shows, of course, that the difference is very great, but it also shows that the difference is diminishing on all continents! The real exception is post-communist Eastern Europe, where inequality has grown fastest in the countries where reform has been slowest.[25]

The 1999 UNDP report appears to contradict this finding, but its conclusions are doubtful, not least because the UNDP omitted its own statistics for the years when inequality declined fastest, 1995–97. Furthermore, their own welfare statistics, as aggregated in the HDI, point to an even faster reduction of inequality in the world than is indicated by the Norwegian report. HDI adds together various aspects of welfare—the income, education standard, and life expectancy of the population. This index ranges from 0, representing the profoundest misery, to 1, representing complete welfare. The HDI has increased in all groups of countries over the past 40 years, but fastest of all in the poorest countries. In the OECD countries, HDI rose from 0.8 to 0.91 between 1960 and 1993, and in the developing countries it rose faster still, from 0.26 to 0.56.

One sometimes hears it said, on the basis of that same UNDP report, that the richest fifth of the world's population is 74 times wealthier than the poorest fifth. But if we measure wealth in terms of what these groups get for their money—that is, if we use figures adjusted for purchasing power—then the richest fifth is only 16 times richer than the poorest.[26]

World income distribution, 1960, 1980, and 2000

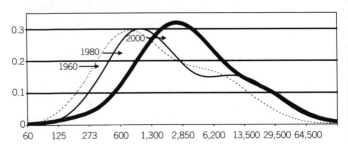

Annual Per Capita Income at 2000 Prices

Source: Surjit Bhalla, *Imagine There's No Country* (Washington: Institute for International Economics, 2002), p. 176.

Standard of living is rising everywhere

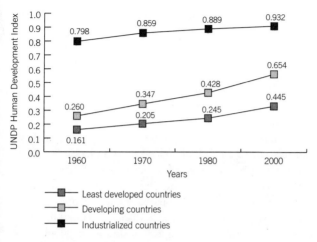

Source: UNDP, *Human Development Report 1997* (New York: Oxford University Press for the United Nations Development Program, 1997).

Reservations

This is not by any means to say that all is well with the world, or even that everything is getting better and better. AIDS deaths in 2000 totaled 3 million, the highest figure ever. One of the cruel consequences of the epidemic is that it leaves children without parents: more than 13 million have been orphaned by AIDS, the vast majority in sub-Saharan Africa.[27] In several African countries, more than 15 percent of the adult population are suffering from HIV or AIDS. Something like 20 million people are now living as fugitives from oppression, conflicts, or natural disasters. Even though forecasts concerning the world's water supply have grown more optimistic, we still risk a huge shortage of pure water, possibly resulting in disease and conflicts. About 20 countries, most of them in southern Africa, have grown poorer since 1965. Illiteracy, hunger, and poverty may be diminishing, but many hundreds of millions of people are still afflicted by them. Armed conflicts are growing fewer, but this is cold comfort to the hundreds of thousands of people who are still being beaten, raped, and murdered.

The remaining problems are made all the more intolerable by our knowledge that something can actually be done about them. When underdevelopment appears to be a natural and inevitable part of the human condition, it is considered a tragic fate. But when we realize that it is not at all necessary, it becomes a problem that can and should be solved. This phenomenon is not unfamiliar: the same thing happened when the Industrial Revolution started to improve living standards in the West more than 200 years ago. When misery is everywhere, we can easily become oblivious to it. When it is contrasted with something else, with abundance and prosperity, our eyes are opened to it—a good thing, because our new awareness spurs our efforts to do something about the problems that remain. But this must not deceive us into thinking that the world has actually grown worse, for it has not.

No one can doubt that the world has more than its share of serious problems. The fantastic thing is that the spread of democracy and capitalism has reduced them so dramatically. Where liberal policies have been allowed to operate longest, they have made poverty and deprivation the exception instead of the rule—and they had previously been the rule everywhere in the world, at all times in history. Colossal changes await all of us, but at the same time our eyes have been opened to the political and technical solutions now available to us. And so, all things considered, there is no reason why we should not be optimistic.

II

... and it's no coincidence!

That's capitalism for you!

The growth of world prosperity is not a "miracle" or any of the other mystifying terms we customarily apply to countries that have succeeded economically and socially. Schools are not built, nor are incomes generated, by sheer luck, like a bolt from the blue. These things happen when people begin to think along new lines and work hard to bring their ideas to fruition. But people do that everywhere, and there is no reason why certain people in certain places during certain periods in history should be intrinsically smarter or more capable than others. What makes the difference is whether the environment permits and encourages ideas and work, or instead puts obstacles in their way. That depends on whether people are free to explore their way ahead, to own property, to invest for the long term, to conclude private agreements, and to trade with others. In short, it depends on whether or not the countries have capitalism. In the affluent world we have had capitalism in one form or another for a couple of centuries. That is how the countries of the West *became* "the affluent world." Capitalism has given people both the liberty and the incentive to create, produce, and trade, thereby generating prosperity.

During the past two decades, this system has spread throughout the world via the process termed globalization. The communist dictatorships in the East and the military dictatorships of the Third World collapsed, and the walls they had raised against ideas, people, and goods collapsed with them. Instead, we have seen the dissemination and widespread acceptance of the idea that creativity cannot be centralized, that it can only be encouraged by entitling citizens to decide for themselves, to create, to think, to work.

Capitalism means that no one is subject to arbitrary coercion by others. Because we have the option of simply refraining from signing a contract or doing a business deal if we prefer some other solution, the only way of getting rich in a free market is by giving people something they want, something they will pay for of their own free will. Both parties to a free exchange have to feel that they benefit from it; otherwise there won't be any deal. Economics, then, is not a zero-sum game. The bigger a person's income in a market economy, the more that person has done to offer people what they want. Bill Gates and Madonna earn millions, but they don't steal that money; they earn it by offering software and music that a lot of people think are worth paying for. In this sense, they are essentially our servants. Firms and individuals struggle to develop better goods and more efficient ways of providing for our needs. The alternative is for the government to take our resources and then decide which types of behavior to encourage. The only question is why the government knows what we want and what we consider important in our lives better than we ourselves do.

Prices and profits in a market economy serve as a signaling system by which the worker, the entrepreneur, and the investor can navigate. Those who want to earn good wages or make a good profit have to seek out those parts of the economy where they can best cater to other people's demands. Excessive taxes and handouts pervert these signals and incentives completely. Price controls are destructive because they directly distort the necessary price signals. If the government puts a ceiling on prices—if it imposes a lower price than the market would have, as it does for apartment rentals in New York—a shortage will result. People will hang onto the apartments they have, even if they don't need them for the moment and even if someone else would be willing to pay more for the use of that same apartment. Denied the ability to charge higher rents, landlords find it less worthwhile to invest in the purchase of new buildings, and housing companies stop new construction. Result: housing shortage. If instead the government sets a price floor—that is, deliberately bids up the price of a good higher than the market would have, as many governments do for agricultural products—a surplus will result. When the EU pays more for foodstuffs than the market, more people than necessary will go into farming, resulting in surplus production and wasted resources.

Capitalism also requires people to be allowed to retain the resources they earn and create. If you exert yourself and invest for the long term, but someone else appropriates most of the profit, the odds are that you'll give up. Protection of ownership lies at the very heart of a capitalist economy. Ownership means not only that people are entitled to the fruits of their labors, but also that they are free to use their resources without having to ask the authorities first. Capitalism allows people to explore the economic frontier for themselves.

That is not to say that any given person in the market will necessarily be *smarter* than a bureaucrat. But market participants are in direct touch with their own particular corner of the market, and by responding to price fluctuations, they have direct feedback on supply and demand. Central planners can never collect all this information from all fields, nor are they nearly as motivated to be guided by it. Even if any one person in the market is no smarter than a bureaucrat, a million people together certainly are!

Their million different attempts at determining the best uses of resources are generally wiser than a single, centralized solution. If the government decides that all resources are to be committed to a certain kind of collective farming and this fails, the whole of society will be economically affected and, in the worst case scenario, will starve. If, instead, one group of people attempts the same type of farming, they alone will suffer the adverse effects if the enterprise fails, and surpluses elsewhere in the market mean that those effects won't be as dire as starvation. A society needs this kind of experimentation and innovation to develop, but at the same time the risks of experimentation have to be limited so that the whole society will not be jeopardized by a few people's mistakes. Therein lies the virtue of individual decisionmaking and individual responsibility.

Personal responsibility, no less than personal freedom, is essential to capitalism. A politician or bureaucrat handling huge sums of money for infrastructure investment or a campaign to host the next Olympics is not under the same pressure to make rational decisions as entrepreneurs and investors are. If things go wrong and expenditure exceeds income, it isn't the politician who foots the bill.

People who own their property act on a long-term basis because they know that they will reap the rewards (and bear the costs) of their actions. This is the core of a capitalist economy—people saving part of what they already have in order to create more value for the future. We do the same thing, create "human capital," when we devote some of our time and energy today to getting a good education that will increase our earning potential in the long run. In the economy, this means that instead of living from hand to mouth we set aside part of what we have and are rewarded with interest or profits by whoever can use the money more efficiently than we can ourselves. Saving and investment elevate the economy to progressively higher levels as they finance new machinery and organizational structures to make the workforce more productive.

Organization is important because people can produce far more through voluntary cooperation than they could by doing everything single-handed. It may take a single craftsman a week to produce a chair, but if he is especially skilled at constructing the wooden frame, and if he joins forces with someone who can paint and someone else who's good at sewing chair cushions, together they may be able to turn out one chair a day. With modern machinery, another product of specialization and cooperation, they can make a hundred chairs a day, which augments the value of their labor.

Technical progress enabled new machines to manufacture old types of goods less expensively, placing new inventions and goods at people's disposal. As a result of this continuous improvement of productivity through the division of labor and technical advancement, one hour's labor today is worth about 25 times more than it was in the mid-19th century. Employees, consequently, now receive about 25 times as much as they did then, in the form of better pay, better working conditions, and shorter working hours. When a person's labor grows more valuable, more firms want to buy it. In order to get it, they then have to raise wages and improve the work environment. If, instead, wages increase more rapidly than productivity, through legislation or union contracts, then jobs will have to be eliminated, because the workers' input is not worth what the employer is forced to pay for it. In this case, the "surplus" created by the price floor in wages comes in the form of unemployment.

Politicians can create the appearance of rising wages by accelerating inflation, which is precisely what Swedish politicians did for a long time. Because each dollar is then worth less, however, those increases are entirely chimerical. Growth and productivity alone are capable of raising real wages in the long run.

All political and economic systems need rules, and this includes even the most liberal capitalism, which presupposes rules about legitimate ownership, the writing of contracts, the resolution of disputes, and many other matters. Those rules are a necessary framework required for markets to operate smoothly. But there are also rules that prevent the market economy from working—detailed regulations specifying the uses people can make of their property and making it difficult to start up a certain kind of activity, owing to the need for licenses and permits or to restrictive rules on pricing and business transactions. Those regulations mainly serve to give more power over the economy to public authorities who are not themselves a part of it and who have not risked their own money. They add up to a heavy burden on the creators of our prosperity. Just at the federal level, American entrepreneurs have to keep track of more than 134,000 pages of regulations, with 4,167 new rules issued by the various regulatory agencies in 2002 alone. Little wonder, then, that more people do not translate their good ideas into entrepreneurial activity.[1]

Such rules are also harmful in another way. When regulation raises barriers to necessary activity, a large portion of a firm's time—time that could otherwise be devoted to production—ends up being spent either complying with or circumventing the rules. If this proves too burdensome, people join the informal economy instead, thereby depriving themselves of legal protection for their business dealings. Many firms will use their resources—resources that could otherwise have been used for investment—to coax politicians into adapting the rules to their needs. Many will be tempted to take shortcuts, and bureaucrats will oblige in

69

return for generous bribes, especially in poor countries where salaries are low and regulatory systems more or less chaotic. The easiest way of corrupting a nation through and through is to demand that citizens get bureaucratic permission for production, for imports, for exports, for investments. As the Chinese philosopher Lao Tzu declared more than two and a half millennia ago, "The more laws are promulgated, the more numerous thieves and bandits become."

Economic freedom reduces corruption

(Freedom from corruption, by Transparency International,s rating).

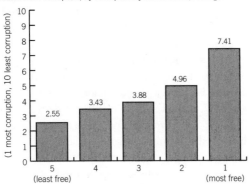

The countries of the world, divided into fifths by degrees of economic freedom

Source: James Gwartney and Robert Lawson, eds., *Economic Freedom of the World 2001* (Vancouver: Fraser Institute, 2001).

If the goal is to have impartial rules and incorruptible officials, there is no better means than substantial deregulation. Amartya Sen argues that the struggle against corruption would be a perfectly good reason for developing countries to deregulate their economies even if no other economic benefits would accrue from doing so.[2]

Growth—a blessing

All experience indicates that it is in liberal regimes that wealth is created and development is sustained. Politics and economics are not exact sciences: we cannot perform laboratory experiments in order to ascertain which systems work and which do not. But the conflict between capitalism and central planning gives us something close. History provides us with several instances of similar populations, with similar preconditions and sharing the same language and norms, subjected to two different systems, one a market economy and the other a centrally controlled command economy. With Germany divided into capitalist West and communist East, people talked of an "economic miracle" in the Western part, while the East fell further and further behind. The same thing happened with capitalist South Korea and communist North Korea. The former was numbered among the Asian tigers, convincing the world that "developing" countries can actually develop. Whereas in the 1960s it was poorer than Angola, today, with the world's thirteenth largest economy, South Korea is almost as affluent as a Western European country. The North Korean economy, by contrast, underwent a total collapse, and the country is now afflicted with mass starvation. One can also see the difference between Taiwan, a market economy that experienced one of the swiftest economic developments in history, and communist mainland China, which suffered starvation and misery until it saw fit to start opening up its markets.[3]

The same comparison can be made all over the world. The greater the degree of economic liberalism in a country, the better that country's chances of attaining higher prosperity, faster growth, a higher standard of living, and higher average life expectancy. People in the economically freest countries are nearly 10 times as rich as those in the least free, and they are living more than 20 years longer!

The economic development of the past two centuries has no counterpart in the period prior to the breakthrough of the market economy in the 19th century. Historically, the human condition has been one of destitution, with people surviving from one day to the next. Most medieval Europeans were chronically undernourished,

Economic freedom brings prosperity

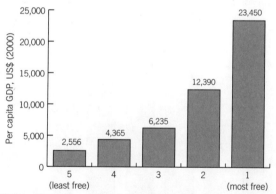

The countries of the world, divided into fifths by degrees of economic freedom

Source: James Gwartney and Robert Lawson, eds., *Economic Freedom of the World 2001* (Vancouver: Fraser Institute, 2001).[4]

73

Economic freedom brings growth

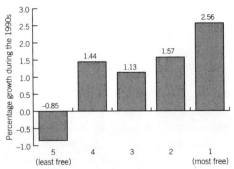

The countries of the world, divided into fifths by degrees of economic freedom

Source: James Gwartney and Robert Lawson, eds., *Economic Freedom of the World 2001* (Vancouver: Fraser Institute, 2001).

Economic freedom raises living standards

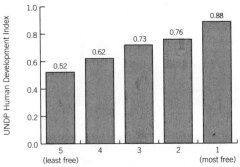

The countries of the world, divided into fifths by degrees of economic freedom

Source: James Gwartney and Robert Lawson, eds., *Economic Freedom of the World 2001* (Vancouver: Fraser Institute, 2001).

Economic freedom increases average life expectancy

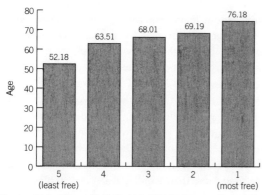

The countries of the world, divided into fifths by degrees of economic freedom

Source: James Gwartney and Robert Lawson, eds., *Economic Freedom of the World 2001* (Vancouver: Fraser Institute, 2001).

owned only one article of clothing, and worked in houses which were so filthy and vermin-ridden that, in the words of one historian, "From a health point of view the only thing to be said in their favour was that they burnt down very easily!"[5] After the 16th century, when different parts of the world very slowly and tentatively began trading with each other, we do find examples of growth, but that growth was extremely marginal.

Poverty in the 18th century was much the same on every continent. According to the best estimates, which are still highly uncertain, Europe was only 20 percent wealthier than the rest of the world. Then, in about 1820, Europe began moving further ahead as a result of the Industrial Revolution. But poverty remained appalling. Per capita income in the very richest European countries was the equivalent of $1,000–$1,500 annually—

less than in present-day Bolivia or Kazakhstan. Even if all incomes had been perfectly equally distributed, that amount would still have been insufficient for more than a state of abject misery, with neither clean water nor daily bread and with little more than one garment per person. Almost the entire world population lived at a level of poverty scarcely to be seen anywhere today: only the very poorest countries—Mali, Zambia, and Nigeria, for example—come anywhere near it. During the 200 years since then, per capita incomes have multiplied several times over, worldwide. Global growth during the 320 years between 1500 and 1820 has been estimated at a mere 30th of what the world has experienced since then.[6] Over the course of the last two centuries, incomes in Europe have risen more than tenfold. Asia has also picked up speed during the past half-century and, with the path to prosperity already known, has grown still faster. Living standards today are eight times higher in Japan and six times higher in China than they were in 1950.

Increased investment and the urge to devise better, more efficient solutions to old problems enable us to produce more, and growth accelerates. This acceleration generates new ideas and machinery, enabling the workforce to produce more. GDP, or gross domestic product, is a measure of the value of all goods and services produced in a country. Dividing that by the number of inhabitants in a country gives us GDP per capita ("per head"), which serves as a rough measure of that country's wealth. Growth—the production of more goods and services—may not strike everyone as the most exciting thing on earth, and certain radical circles have even come to disdain it, branding those who do care about it as "economistic" or "growth fanatics." That may be partly a healthy reaction to an excessive focus on high GDP as an end in itself, but growth, quite simply, means that production grows, and prosperity and opportunities grow with it. In the affluent world, growth may allow societies to save, to consume more, to invest in welfare, or to enjoy more leisure time. In the developing countries, it can mean the difference between life and death, development and stagnation, for it is growth that makes wider access to healthy foods and pure drinking water possible.[7]

For everyday life in India, growth since the 1980s has meant mud huts being replaced by brick buildings and muddy paths being paved. Electricity has become available to everyone, and the dark alleys now have streetlights. The alleys no longer reek of garbage, and hotbeds of infection are removed by proper drainage. The poor can afford clothing and footwear. As the clearest example of what growth implies, Indian women no longer wash their saris one half at a time. This was once necessary because

Incomes and living standards go hand in hand

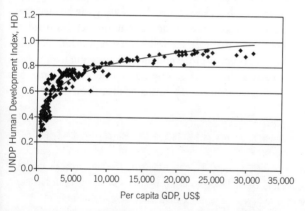

Source: Arne Melchior, Kjetil Telle, and Henrik Wiig, *Globalisering och ulikhet: Verdens inntektsfordeling og levestandard 1960–1998.* (Oslo: Royal Norwegian Ministry of Foreign Affairs, 2000).

77

most women possessed only one sari and thus had to wash it while still wearing it.

Growth also means opportunities and power for people. It means that, instead of resorting to the local usurer and getting into debt for a lifetime, the ordinary Indian can turn to a bank. People can look for jobs in different places, with different entrepreneurs, which emancipates the poor from the power of life and death that the village landlord once had over them. Although India has democratic elections, they do not make all that much difference so long as the poor are completely at the mercy of the local elite because they still have to vote as they are told. Parents in poor parts of the world do not send their children out to work because they like doing it, but because they need the money to feed the family. Growth gives them better incomes and improves the return on education, which means they can send their children to school instead. That also gives the individual greater opportunity within the family. A law against wife beating can be ineffective if the woman is economically dependent on her husband for survival, because in that case she will neither report him nor leave him. When the economy grows and more production materializes, the woman has a chance of getting a job away from home. She becomes less dependent on the husband's caprices.

"In my mother's day women had to grin and bear it. I wouldn't have any of it. I can speak my mind. Life isn't just meant to be sacrifice; you also have to be able to enjoy it. That, I think, is the great change that is happening in Japan. People no longer want to work and work. Today they also want to have time for a good life and a little enjoyment."
29-year-old Eriko, who instead of following in her parents' footsteps and working on the land became an advertising artist.[8]

78

It is sometimes argued that growth only benefits the rich, while the poor lag behind. This is a curious notion. Why should poor people benefit less than others from society growing richer? Two World Bank economists, David Dollar and Aart Kraay, studied 40 years of income statistics from 80 countries to see whether this was really true. Their studies show that growth benefits the poor just as much as the rich. With 1 percent growth, the incomes of the poor rise by 1 percent on average; with 10 percent growth, they rise, on average, by 10 percent. Not always and not every-

Growth benefits the poor

(Correlation between prosperity and incomes of the poor in 80 studied countries).

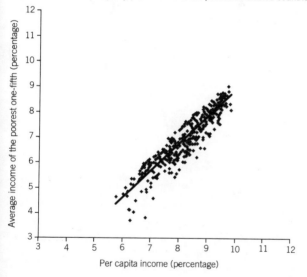

Source: David Dollar and Aart Kraay, *Growth Is Good for the Poor* (Washington: World Bank, April 2001).

where—there are exceptions and variations—but on average. This finding tallies with a long line of other surveys, whereas studies suggesting the contrary are very hard to find.[9]

Thus, growth is the best cure for poverty. Some economists have spoken of a "trickle-down" effect, meaning that some get rich first, after which parts of this wealth trickle down to the poor as the rich spend and invest. This description may evoke the image of the poor man getting the crumbs that fall from the rich man's table, but this is a completely mistaken picture of the

Growth benefits the poor

(Correlation between economic growth and incomes of the poor in 80 studied countries).

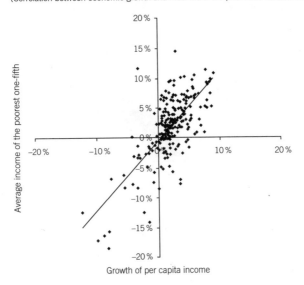

Growth of per capita income

Source: David Dollar and Aart Kraay, *Growth Is Good for the Poor* (Washington: World Bank, April 2001).

true effect of growth. On the contrary, what happens is that the poor benefit from growth to roughly the same extent and at the same speed as the rich. They benefit immediately from an increase in the value of their labor and from greater purchasing power.

No country has ever succeeded in reducing poverty without having long-term growth. Nor is there any case of the opposite, that is, of a country having had long-term, sustainable growth that didn't benefit the poor population. Still more interestingly, there is no instance of a country having had steady levels of growth in the long term without opening up its markets. The World Bank's *World Development Report 2000/2001* contained a good deal of rhetoric about growth not being everything and not being sufficient for development—rhetoric influenced, no doubt, by the growth of the anti-globalization movement. But that report's own tables show that the higher a country's growth has been in the past 20 years, the faster it has reduced poverty, infant mortality, and illiteracy. In the countries at the bottom of the growth league, illiteracy had actually increased. It may be that growth in itself is not sufficient to bring good development for everyone, but growth is manifestly necessary.

If we have 3 percent growth annually, this means that the economy, our capital, and our incomes double every 23 years. If growth is twice as fast, they double about every 12 years. This growth represents an unparalleled increase in prosperity. By comparison, the effects of even vigorous government income redistribution policies are insignificant—not just insignificant, but downright dangerous, because high taxes to finance these measures can jeopardize growth. If so, great long-term benefits for everyone are sacrificed in favor of small immediate gains for a few.

A society's economy is above all improved by people saving, investing, and working. High taxes on work, savings, and capital, in the words of John Stuart Mill, "impose a penalty on people for having worked harder and saved more than their neighbors."[10] That means punishing what is most beneficial to society. Or, as a bumper sticker slogan has it, "A fine is a tax for doing something wrong; a tax is a fine for doing something right." We have alcohol taxes to reduce consumption of alcohol, tobacco taxes to reduce smoking, and environmental taxes to reduce pollution. So where do we expect the taxation of endeavor, work, and saving to get us? It results in many people not exerting themselves to work, invest, and hatch new ideas, because most of the proceeds will go to the government. It leads to firms devoting more and more time to tax avoidance—time that could have been devoted to constructive work. It leads to people spending more time on things they are not good at. The surgeon stays at home to paint the living room instead of doing what he is best at—saving lives— because that way he avoids having to pay taxes on both his own work and on the painter's wages.[11]

In a dynamic market economy there is also social mobility. Someone who is poor today will not necessarily be poor tomorrow. In the absence of legal privileges and high taxes, there are great possibilities of raising one's standard of living through one's own exertions, education, and thrift. Four-fifths of American millionaires have made their money themselves, as opposed to merely inheriting it.

It is true that the poorest one-fifth in a capitalist economy like that of the United States earn only 3.6 percent of the country's GDP. But viewing income gaps in these static terms makes it easy to forget that there is always mobility between the various groups—mostly upward mobility, because wages rise with higher education and longer working experience. Only 5.1 percent of the Americans belonging to that poorest quintile in 1975 were still there in 1991. In the meantime nearly 30 percent of them had moved up into the wealthiest one-fifth, and 60 percent of them had arrived in the wealthiest two-fifths.

The best remedy for poverty is a chance to do something about it. On average, those who fall below the poverty line in the United States only stay there for 4.2 months. Only 4 percent of America's population are long-term poor, that is, remain poor for more than two years. Meanwhile the poorest fifth is replenished with new people—students and poor immigrants—who then have the opportunity of quickly climbing the ladder of wealth.[12]

Freedom or equality? Why choose?

Many believe that liberalization and economic growth entail a growth of inequality in a society. Once again, I would like to point out that this is not the most important thing. If a better standard of living is worth pursuing, then what matters is how well situated you are, period, not how well situated you are in relation to others. The important thing is for as many people as possible to be better off, and across-the-board improvement doesn't become deterioration just because some people improve their lot faster than others. But there are several reasons why equality is worth aiming for. For one thing, most of us probably believe that people should not get off to tremendously unequal starts in life. It is important that everyone have similar opportunities—not so important that it is worth reducing everyone's chances in order to make them as equal as possible, but still important enough for great social inequality to be a problem. This, then, is a crucial objection to scrutinize.

Another reason is that equality actually stimulates growth, quite contrary to what is often claimed. True, in a very poor society some degree of inequality may be necessary in order for anyone at all to be able to start saving and investing, but many studies have shown that societies with a high degree of equality achieve, on average, greater economic growth than unequal societies, especially if the inequality takes the form of very uneven land ownership. One reason for this connection is that societies with greater equality can be expected to have greater stability and less political turbulence. Inequality can lead to conflicts, or demands for higher taxes and more redistribution, which are threats to growth.

But a more important reason is that people must have some basic assets—things like land in an undeveloped economy and education in a modern one—to be able to work effectively. What matters, then, is a degree of equality in terms of those assets and not in what is usually meant in the political debate, equality of incomes and profits. The crucial reform in a developing country that has ancient, unfair feudal structures and a small, land-owning elite is land reform, so that more people will have a share of the land and thus will be able to participate in the economy. The important thing is for the whole population to obtain an education and have the opportunity to borrow money when they have ideas for business projects. No one must be discriminated against or marginalized, or prevented by licensing requirements, prohibitions, and legal privileges from competing for positions and incomes. This kind of equality spurs the economy, whereas a reallocation of incomes, if anything, reduces it because education, work, and the introduction of new ideas become less profitable.

To simplify matters somewhat, it is equality of opportunity that matters, not equality of results. The goal is for all people to have certain basic opportunities and then be at liberty to explore their way forward and achieve different results. These are two sides of the same coin: people have the opportunity of working and trying new things and the right to make a profit out of the enterprise if it does well. This results in a society that encourages social mobility and rewards initiative and effort—and consequently also achieves greater prosperity. It is not income differences in themselves that are dangerous for development, but the discrimination and privileges that cause the difference in incomes in undemocratic states. This is corroborated by the fact that the connection between inequality and growth is quite clear in non-democratic states, but not apparent in modern, liberal ones.[13]

But can the opposite effect also hold? Is it true that increased growth leads to greater inequality, as is widely maintained? Economists sometimes refer to "Kuznets's inverted U-curve," which is based on a 1955 article by the economist Simon Kuznets, who argued that economic growth in a society initially leads to greater inequality and only after some time to a reduction of inequality. Many have accepted this thesis as truth, and it is sometimes used to discredit the idea of growth, or at least to demand redistributive policies. Kuznets himself did not draw any such drastic conclusions. On the contrary, he declared that his article was based on "perhaps 5 percent empirical information and 95 percent speculation," adding that "so long as it is recognized as a collection of hunches calling for further investigation rather than a set of fully tested conclusions, little harm and much good may result."[14]

If we follow Kuznets's recommendation and investigate what has happened since the 1950s, we can see that his preliminary conclusion is not universally valid. True, it can happen that growth initially leads to inequality, but this is not a general connection. There are countries that have had high growth followed by a reduction in income differences, such as Indonesia, Malaysia, Taiwan, South Korea, and Mauritius, and there are countries like China, Thailand, Pakistan, and Brazil where growth has led to greater income differences. Similarly, things have moved in different directions in countries with low or negative growth. Equality has increased in Cuba, Colombia, and Morocco, while diminishing in Kenya, Ethiopia, and Mexico during the 1980s, and Russia during the 1990s. Distribution hinges on other factors, such as a country's initial position and domestic policy. The World Bank sums up the state of affairs by saying,

"The available data show no stable relationship between growth and inequality. On average, income inequality within countries has neither decreased nor increased over the last 30 years." [15]

Economic growth does not increase inequality

(Correlation between economic growth and inequality in 80 studied countries).

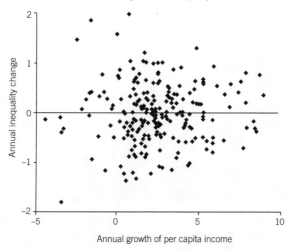

Source: David Dollar and Aart Kraay, *Growth Is Good for the Poor* (Washington: World Bank, April 2001).

Studying equality in 70 countries, the economist G. W. Scully found that incomes were *more evenly distributed* in countries with a liberal economy, open markets, and property rights. This was, above all, because the middle class had more and the upper class less in free than in unfree economies. The share of national income going to the richest fifth of the population was 25 percent lower in the "freest" economies than in the "least free" economies. The proportion going to the poorest fifth in a society was unaffected by how free the economy was, but their actual incomes were far greater in liberal economies.[16]

Economic freedom increases equality

(Incomes of the one-fifth richest are this many times higher than of the poorest one-fifth, in various countries).

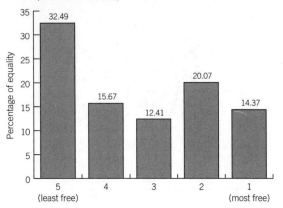

The countries of the world, divided into fifths by degrees of economic freedom

Source: James Gwartney, Robert Lawson, and Dexter Samida, eds., *Economic Freedom of the World 2000* (Vancouver: Fraser Institute, 2000).

Contrary to popular suppositions, then, a higher degree of economic liberalism appears to mean more economic equality. But what about the effects of the *transition* to a liberal economy? Does rapid liberalization have a negative impact on equality? Here, too, the answer would appear to be that it does not. The Swedish economist Niclas Berggren has investigated how the growth of economic freedom affects economic equality. In countries that have liberalized their economies since 1985, equality has *increased*, while stagnating or diminishing in countries that have refrained from liberalization. Equality is growing fastest in poor developing countries that are quickly reforming their economies. Berggren's findings indicate that there are two main determinants of equality in a society: freedom of international trade and freedom of international movements of capital—the two most "globalizing" reforms.[17]

This pattern is corroborated by a different classification of countries, one measuring how "globalized" they are. *Foreign Policy* magazine and the consulting firm A. T. Kearny have tried to devise a "globalization index," an estimate of how much a country's inhabitants shop, invest, communicate, and travel across its borders. The globalized countries, they discovered, are not at all more unequal. On the contrary,

> *The general pattern of higher globalization and greater income equality holds for most countries, both in mature economies and emerging markets.*[18]

People on the left often say that individual liberty and economic equality are in conflict, which explains why they think they must oppose one of these widely appreciated values. They may be right in the sense that legislators must decide which to focus on more in their deliberations, but it is not correct to say that the two values are mutually exclusive. On the contrary, there is much to suggest that equality of liberty also leads to economic equality. Rights of ownership, freedom of enterprise, free trade, and reduced inflation confer both growth and equality.

Property rights—for the sake of the poor

That economic freedom is not an enemy of equality comes as a surprise to everyone who has been told that capitalism is the ideology of the rich and the privileged. In fact, this is precisely backward. The free market is the antithesis of societies of privilege. In a market economy, the only way of holding on to a good economic position is by improving your production and offering people good products or services. It is in the regulated economies, with their distribution of privileges and monopolies to favored groups, that privilege can become entrenched. Those who have the right contacts can afford to pay bribes. Those who have the time and knowledge to plow through bulky volumes of regulations can start up business enterprises and engage in trade. The poor never have a chance, not even of starting small businesses like bakeries or corner shops. In a capitalistic society, all people with ideas and willpower are at liberty to try their luck, even if they are not the favorites of the rulers.

Globalization contributes to this tendency because it disturbs power relations and emancipates people from the local potentates. Free trade enables consumers to buy goods and services from a global range of competitors instead of the local monopolists. Free movements of capital enable poor people with good ideas to finance their projects. Freedom of migration means that the village's one and only employer has to offer higher wages and better working conditions in order to attract labor, because otherwise the workers can go elsewhere.

The left often portrays economic liberalism as the ideology of the rich, because it stands up for rights of ownership. But defending private property is not the same as cementing the prevailing property conditions. Empirical facts tell us that it is not mainly the rich who benefit from the protection of property rights. On the contrary, it may be the most vulnerable citizens who have most to lose in a society without stable rights of ownership, since the people with political power and contacts are most able to seize control of resources. Where there is private property, resources and incomes are channeled mainly to those who are productive and who offer services in the market and the workplace, and underprivileged groups then have a much better chance of asserting themselves than in a system governed by power and graft. Besides, it is the poor who have most to gain from goods becoming progressively cheaper in relation to incomes, and competition in the context of private ownership helps to achieve just that result. Property rights provide an incentive for foresight and personal initiative, spurring growth and distributing the fruits of it equally, on average, between rich and poor. Thus the introduction of safeguards for private property in a society has a distributive effect as favorable to the poor as a commitment to universal education. Studies indicate that protecting private ownership is the economic reform most conducive to growth.[19]

The Peruvian economist Hernando de Soto has done more than anyone else to show how poor people lose out in the absence of property rights. In his revolutionary book *The Mystery of Capital,* he turns the orthodox view of the world's poor upside down. The problem is not that they are helpless or even that they lack "property," in the sense of the physical assets themselves. The problem, rather, is that they have no formal *rights* of ownership.

The poor are often people with great initiative who save large portions of their income to spend on improvements to their land

and their homes. After many years spent traveling and researching, de Soto roughly estimates that poor people in the Third World and in former communist states have real estate (buildings and the land they stand on) worth about $9.3 trillion more than is officially registered. That is a huge sum, more than the combined value of all companies listed on the stock exchanges of the 20 most affluent countries—the New York Stock Exchange; the NASDAQ; the exchanges of Toronto, Tokyo, London, Frankfurt, Paris, and Milan; and a dozen more besides. The problem is that Third World governments generally do not recognize the rights of ownership without tortuous bureaucratic processes. People in the Third World occupy common lands, build simple houses in shanty towns, which they are constantly improving, and establish small corner shops, just as poor people in the Western world were doing a couple of hundred years ago. The trouble is that in developing countries today it is practically impossible to register this as property. De Soto illustrates these problems through an ambitious experiment. Together with a number of colleagues, he traveled the world attempting to register property. The results of those attempts are horrifying.

Obtaining legal title to a house built on public land in Peru required 207 different administrative steps at 52 different public offices. Anyone wishing to do something as simple as drive a taxi or start a private bus service legally, could expect 26 months of red tape first. In Haiti, people can only settle on a plot of common land by leasing it for five years and then buying it. But just getting a leasehold permit involved 65 steps and took more than 2 years. Buying the freehold then took far longer. In the Philippines, the same process could take more than 13 years. Legally registering a plot of land in the Egyptian desert required permits from 31 authorities, which could take between 5 and 14 years, and doing the same for agricultural land took between 6 and 11 years.

Getting a legal license for a factory with two sewing machines in the shanty towns of Lima took 289 six-hour days of traveling to the authorities, lining up to see the right people, filling in forms and waiting for an answer. In addition to the time required, the process cost a total of $1,231—more than 30 times the minimum monthly wage.

To people without many resources or powerful contacts, these are insuperable barriers. The only option remaining for poor people is to run micro-businesses in the informal sector, outside the law. Consequently, they have no legal protection and do not dare to invest for the long term, even if they have the spare cash to do so. Their property is not included in a uniform system of ownership that records transactions and indicates who owns what. Without clarity on this crucial point, it is not clear how transactions are to proceed, or who is responsible for payments and services to the address. The property remains "dead capital." Properties cannot be mortgaged, depriving the de facto owner of one source of capital for financing an education or investing in and expanding a business. The usual way that small entrepreneurs in affluent countries obtain capital is therefore unavailable in developing countries. Without a registered address and the possibility of having one's creditworthiness investigated, it is often impossible to establish a telephone, water, or electricity connection, and the property cannot even be sold. Nor can entrepreneurs expand their businesses by selling shares in them.

Owners of micro-businesses, being forced to work in the informal sector, always have to beware of bureaucrats and the police or else pay heavy bribes. This means they have to keep their businesses small and hidden, and are thus prevented from taking advantage of economies of scale. Nor do they dare to advertise or to broaden their customer base excessively. They venture to sell to the nearest precincts, but no more. Major deals can only be concluded with members of the family or others one trusts personally.

De Soto maintains that between 50 and 75 percent of citizens in the developing countries work outside the protection of the law, and that roughly 80 percent of homes and land are not registered in the names of their present owners. In one country that de Soto visited, the urban authority had itself established an illegal settlement on common land so that its employees would have somewhere to live. In countries without a functioning property system, then, the great majority of the population has assets that the owners are not allowed to make full use of. In the absence of ownership rights, they cannot use their property as a basis of expansion, which was the Western world's path to prosperity. Only the elite in the developing countries have the contacts that permit them to engage in modern economic activity. Capitalism without property rights becomes capitalism for the elite only. Millions of capable people with initiative, people who could be the entrepreneurs of the future, become entrapped by poverty.[20]

That is one of the reasons why Russia's economy took 10 years to show any growth after the fall of communism. That was how long it took the Russian government to even begin introducing a uniform system of private land ownership. Land in Russia is generally considered government property and is just lent or leased to the farmers, making investment pointless and sale or mortgage unthinkable. By the beginning of the 21st century, fewer than 300,000 out of a total of some 10 million Russian farmers had anything resembling title to their land. The government imposes severe restrictions on what people can do with land that rightfully belongs to them. Land socialism, of course, inhibits any number of investment opportunities, but because land is often the basis of borrowing, it also impedes the development of a modern credit system. Instead, transactions find their way into the informal market. Russia today is sometimes portrayed as a land of manic, unchecked capitalism. By any reasonable definition of capitalism, this is nonsense. Russian land socialism, coupled with a formidable welter of business regulations and trade controls, leads the Heritage Foundation to find it only the 135th freest economy out of 161 investigated. In *Economic Freedom of the World's ranking, it comes 116th out of 123, after countries like Syria and Rwanda.*[21]

Economic freedom reduces poverty

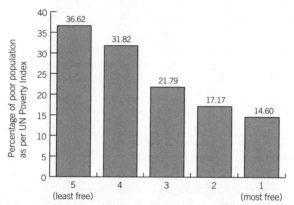

The countries of the world, divided into fifths by degrees of economic freedom

Source: James Gwartney and Robert Lawson, eds., *Economic Freedom of the World 2001* (Vancouver: Fraser Institute, 2001).

Regulation of agriculture is another important cause of inequality. Through price regulations, delivery requirements, and a variety of other means, many developing countries have tried to benefit the urban population at the expense of farmers. This is part of an attempt to force industrialization by taxing and regulating agriculture and transferring the proceeds to industry. The problem is that this has had the effect of shattering agriculture, depriving it of resources that would have been needed in order to streamline food production and actually generate a surplus. In many African and Latin American countries, this has created a vicious circle, with heavy migration from the impoverished countryside to the towns and cities. But there is no great demand for industrial goods because the countryside remains poor, and so unemployment and poverty increase in the towns, and homelessness, crime, and prostitution with them. The property that the poor themselves acquire and save up for is not recognized and is not registered. As a result, demand for agricultural produce does not gather speed, and so urbanization continues. Foreign demand cannot be counted on to fill the domestic gap because the affluent countries have built high tariff barriers to keep out agricultural produce.[22]

Several types of anti-liberal policy hit the poor especially hard. One is inflation, which ruins the value of money. By rapidly increasing the money supply, the government obliterates the small monetary assets of the poor, while the rich who own registered land, properties, and businesses get off more lightly. Reducing inflation—and, above all, avoiding the kind of hyperinflation that has afflicted so many Third World countries—is one of the most important things that can be done to help the less well-to-do, according to Dollar and Kraay's study. One classic example of hyperinflation was Germany's during the 1920s, which ruined the middle class and made people receptive to Hitler's rhetoric. An extreme instance of the opposite occurred at the end of 1989, when Argentina quickly reduced inflation and, in little over a year, reduced the proportion of poor people in greater Buenos Aires from 35 to 23 percent.

Another of Dollar and Kraay's findings is that public spending seems to harm not only growth but also a country's poorest inhabitants. This does not ring true to those who believe that public spending involves taking from the rich and giving to the poor. In fact, the opposite is frequently what happens. In poor, undemocratic countries especially, it is the elite—the leader, his relatives and friends, and powerful corporations—who are allowed to help themselves to public funds, while the bill is paid by those without influence in the palaces of the capital. Bloated military establishments co-opt the lion's share of resources. The rulers prefer to invest in prestigious international airports, universities, and city hospitals rather than in the roads, schools, and local hospitals that would really help people. In undemocratic countries, moreover, public medical care and education are often directed to staunch supporters of the regime. This shows how wrong many left-wing intellectuals were in the 1960s and 1970s when they declared that democratic rights and liberties did not matter all that much in the developing countries, because what they first needed to invest in was welfare policy. Without democracy, whatever welfare policy is implemented cannot be expected to benefit the great mass of the population.

Inefficient systems of government will not make the best possible use of money—or, for that matter, the second best. "I heard rumors about assistance for the poor," said one poor Indonesian of his country's welfare policy, "but no one seems to know where it is." Presumably the money went into a local bigwig's pockets. The same problem exists in India, where bureaucracy and corruption have turned poor relief into black holes for tax money. The government there spends $4.30 to effect a transfer to the poor of just $1.00 through a program of food subsidization. It is, of course, a straight loss to the poor, whose supplies are taxed heavily so that the government can "generously" give them back a far smaller amount in the form of aid.[23]

Capitalism is not a perfect system, and it is not good for everyone all the time. Critics of globalization are good at pointing out individual harms—a factory that has closed down, a wage that has been reduced. Such things do happen, but by concentrating solely on individual instances, one may miss the larger reality of how a political or economic system generally works and what fantastic values it confers on the great majority compared with other alternatives. Problems are found in every political and economic system, but rejecting all systems is not an option. Hunting down negative examples of what can happen in a market economy is easy enough. By that method water or fire can be proved to be bad things, because some people drown and some get burned to death, but this isn't the full picture.

A myopic focus on capitalism's imperfections ignores the freedom and independence that it confers on people who have never experienced anything but oppression. It also disregards the calm and steady progress that is the basic rule of a society with a market economy. There is nothing wrong with identifying problems and mishaps in a predominantly successful system if one does so with the constructive intent of rectifying or alleviating them. But someone who condemns the system as such is obligated to answer this question: What political and economic system could manage things better? Never before in human history has prosperity grown so rapidly and poverty declined so heavily. Is there any evidence, either in history or in the world around us, to suggest that another system could do as well?

The East Asian "miracle"

To gauge the impact of politics on development, it may be enlightening to compare the continents presenting the big contrast in postwar history, namely the growth "miracle" of East Asia and the disastrous track record of Africa. Zambia in 1960 was almost as wealthy as South Korea. Today South Korea has a standard of living comparable to Portugal's and is roughly 20 times wealthier than Zambia. The Taiwanese used to be poorer than the population of the Congo. Today they are as rich as the Spaniards, while the Congo has stood still. How could things go so well for Asia and so badly for Africa?

The end of the Second World War found Japan's economy in ruins and the countries it had recently occupied destitute, starving, and wretched. The rest of the world expected these countries to be torn apart by corruption, crime, and guerrilla warfare. But since the 1960s these East Asian "miracle economies" have had annual growth rates between 5 and 7 percent, and their incomes have doubled every decade. Savings, investments, and exports have all been impressive, and the countries have quickly industrialized. Former colonies like Singapore and Hong Kong are now as prosperous as their former colonizers.

In nearly all these countries, sometimes called the "Asian tigers," this process of development has preserved or even increased economic equality—without any significant redistribution. Poverty has rapidly declined. In Indonesia, the proportion living in absolute poverty has fallen from 58 to 15 percent, and in Malaysia from 37 to 5 percent. Between 1960 and 1990, average life expectancy in the East Asian countries rose from 56 to 71 years. With growth came the eventual democratization of countries like Taiwan, South Korea, Thailand, and now Indonesia as well.

These states have proved that it is perfectly possible for developing countries to industrialize and develop. They also showed that this could happen only in an open, capitalistic economy, not in a secluded command economy. Recently, many economists have pointed out that the miracle economies also had a great deal of government control, implying that they actually provide counter-examples to the claim that liberalism alone creates development. The first point is correct. The first states in the region to develop—Japan, South Korea, and Taiwan—had a great deal of government intervention, though the subsequent miracles—Indonesia, Malaysia, and Thailand—got their economies moving with less intervention. In the former countries, the state governed investments, regulated the banks, invested in and protected chosen industries, and kept a whole battery of interventions in its arsenal. But there was nothing unique about this: developing countries in all continents have done the same. The World Bank, in its broad evaluation of the miracles, observes:

> *Other economies attempted similar interventions without success, and on average they used them more pervasively.*[24]

What distinguished the Asian tigers from other developing countries was that they committed themselves to establishing and protecting rights of ownership, creating a legal code that would protect enterprise and competition, and having a stable monetary policy and low inflation. They implemented universal education, producing skilled populations capable of developing their countries. Because the governments concentrated on elementary education, leaving higher education to the privately funded market, higher education establishments were attuned to the needs of the economy.

The East Asian states introduced reforms that deprived old elites of the land and privileges they had seized in the past. Those reforms enabled the entire population to participate in the economy. Farmers could now dispose relatively freely of their surplus, saving and investing as they saw fit, which gave them an interest in making agriculture more efficient. The increased yield kept these countries supplied with food while releasing manpower for industry, which in turn encountered rising demand as rural earnings improved. The tigers were more interested in creating job opportunities than in setting minimum wages and regulating the labor market. This provided work for most people, and wages then rose with productivity. Because wages could also be lowered in a recession (as the goods those wages bought also became cheaper), many of these countries coped with crises more smoothly and with lower unemployment than others.

In other developing countries, enterprise is hamstrung by regulations, and licenses and permits are needed in order to start up business. East Asian states, by contrast, have had a notable freedom of enterprise. Individual citizens with ideas have been able to start up firms with a minimum of red tape and to work untrammeled by elaborate controls and price regulations. Hong Kong went furthest in this direction. There, one could just start a business and then inform the authorities afterwards in order to obtain a permit. This has been hugely important, not only opening the field to initiative but also providing an effective antidote to the corruption that often flourishes in the shade of permit procedures.

Although many of the East Asian countries have steered tax credits and subsidies into the private sector, they have been less swayed than other developing countries by cronyism and nepotism, vested interests, or the temptation to pursue ostentatious but unproductive showcase projects. Instead, they have focused their attention on genuine productive achievement and the exigencies of the market. Prices have been far more market driven than in other developing countries. These countries have not had price controls and have not distorted world market prices, so investments have occurred where they have been most likely to succeed. Absent those distortions, investment has flowed to the sectors where those countries are most efficient and have advantages relative to other countries.

Many of those in the debate demand that the government intervene and govern investments in order to slow the pace of growth and protect existing businesses. This is precisely what was *not* done by the Asian governments, which regarded ability to withstand international competition as crucial for businesses. The Japanese government let large corporations go bankrupt because they did not have sufficient profit potential, and South Korea was quite unsentimental about shutting down firms that were unable to produce for an open market. This absence of sentimentality has also been applied to the government itself. Whenever subsidies and expenditure have threatened economic stability, the government has quickly scaled down its commitments, thereby avoiding budget crises and inflation.

Above all, these countries have been fiercely committed to integration with the international economy. They are among the world's most export-oriented economies, and most of them have welcomed investments by foreign companies. The larger the share of these countries' GDP accounted for by trade, the faster their economic growth has been. Most of them have had tariff barriers against imports, but the same goes for the rest of Asia, Africa, and South America. The East Asian countries are different in that they applied this policy to a lesser extent than other developing countries and dropped it much earlier. While the others were busily pursuing self-sufficiency and avoiding trade, the East Asian countries committed themselves to internationalization. In the 1960s they began encouraging exports, partly by abolishing permit requirements and exempting exporters and their suppliers from import duties. Tariffs on capital goods have been low. According to the index of openness constructed by Harvard economists Jeffrey Sachs and Andrew Warner, East Asian countries were among the first developing countries to open up their economies by reducing tariffs, abolishing quotas, freeing exports, and deregulating foreign exchange. The economies of Taiwan, Thailand, and Malaysia were "open" since 1963 at the latest, Japan since 1964, South Korea since 1968, and Indonesia since 1970. Hong Kong has pursued a more liberal trade policy than any other country in the world.[25] The same revolution did not occur in Latin America until the beginning of the 1990s and has yet to come in most parts of Africa.

It is highly enlightening to compare these miracle economies with those of neighboring countries that are culturally and demographically similar but committed to quite the opposite kind of policy. North Korea and Burma had no time for the market, opting instead for an ultra-protectionist policy and a rigorously controlled economy. They were completely left out of the regional upturn and ensnared by abject poverty, and today they are governed by inhuman dictatorships. Far from demonstrating the viability of regulation and state control, the East Asian miracle shows an open, free-enterprise economy to be the sine qua non of development.

The African morass

Africa, especially sub-Saharan Africa, presents a painful contrast to the East Asian miracles. In southern Africa, we find most of the countries whose per capita GDP has actually decreased since the mid-1960s, as well as the world's heaviest concentration of poverty, disease, malnourishment, illiteracy, and child labor. Instead of the growth and prosperity that have prevailed in most of the rest of the world, over the past 30 years this continent has grown accustomed to a declining standard of living and growing distress. Certain natural factors help to account for this. The tropical climate causes parasitic diseases to flourish; the soil is less fertile and natural disasters more common than in Europe. One-third of the population live in completely landlocked countries, which makes it far more difficult for them to connect with international markets and trade movements. The curious border definitions and discriminatory policies of the old colonial powers have contributed to a severe ethnic and linguistic fragmentation within African states. A large part of the continent is being torn apart by wars and conflicts.

But other regions with both nature and culture against them have managed far better than Africa. Even factors like war and famine have political causes—no democracy has ever been afflicted by famine, and as a rule, democracies do not make war on each other, which shows that to a great extent it is a country's institutions and politics that determine its prospects for development. Africa, unfortunately, is notable for a far higher degree of political oppression, corruption, economic dirigisme, and protectionism than the other continents. The African countries inherited a hierarchical, repressive political structure from the colonial powers, and have used it to oppress other ethnic groups and the countryside, limit enterprise, and violate fundamental rights.

African leaders have, by and large, been intent on avoiding both the policies of the old colonial powers and the risk of becoming commercially dependent on their European ex-rulers. So they have tried to build self-sufficient economies via draconian tariffs, nationalization, and detailed control of industry. African economies have been governed by price and exchange controls, and public expenditure has at times run riot. The urban elites have systematically exploited the countryside. Instead of creating markets, countries established purchasing monopolies that paid wretched prices and introduced government distribution of food. The government thereby confiscated the entire agricultural surplus, impoverishing the farmers and effectively abolishing trade. Production fell and farmers were driven into the informal market. That impeded plans for industrialization and posed a threat to society when the economic downturn set in during the 1970s. After trying to borrow their way out of the crisis, many African states were in free fall by the mid-1980s. Structures collapsed, people starved, there were no medicines, and machinery simply stopped when spare parts were missing and batteries went flat and could not be replaced. The fall has stopped since then, but has not yet been followed by an upturn. Between 1990 and 1998, southern Africa's combined GDP declined by 0.6 percent.

The cause of Africa's hunger and suffering is not the desert and drought but political oppressors who have systematically shattered the countries' potential. Instead of becoming "dependent" on trade, these states have become dependent on development aid. Sub-Saharan Africa has received more development assistance per capita than any other region in the world. Some states have received development assistance equal to twice their own incomes. But instead of going to people in distress, the money has often been used to sustain rogue regimes that exploited their people. Many Western donors declared that these countries were not ripe for democracy and individual rights, that they should rely on planning the economy and reducing their dependence on trade. The consequences of following that prescription were not long in coming. Potential entrepreneurship has been snuffed out, and whereas in the 1960s Africa had 5 percent of the world's trade, today it has only 1 percent.

Africa has been afflicted with long-lived leaders like Mugabe in Zimbabwe, Moi in Kenya, and Mobutu in Zaire who have clung to power with the support of development aid from the Western world. African economist George Ayittey has characterized many of those governments as "vampire states," marked by public sectors that are not interested in stimulating creativity and growth, only in feathering their own nests with the productive resources of society—much like an army of occupation. Often the leaders, and the clique surrounding them, have seized property by means of direct expropriation and massive peculation of government funds. Mobutu is understood to have amassed a fortune of about $4 billion while his country was bleeding to death.

Anyone who believes that hierarchy is synonymous with efficiency should study some of these countries. Chaos prevails throughout the public sector. The bureaucracy often ignores routine matters; officials disregard orders from superiors and, not infrequently, do the opposite of what they are told to. The courts, which are seldom impartial, do not protect contracts or property rights. Corruption is amazingly widespread, paralyzing whole states. Officials demand bribes simply to allow people to work and trade, which makes it hard for businesses—and impossible for the poor—to do so. Political decisions are often based on ties of friendship and kinship, not merit. Arbitrary rule and corruption have deterred entrepreneurship, and many of these countries are receiving no foreign investments at all. Africa has been marginalized—on that point the anti-globalization movement is perfectly right—but the reason is that the African countries have retreated from globalization and have instead been subjected to socialism, gangster rule, and protectionism. To the peoples of Africa, globalization has meant little more than their leaders flying off to conferences in other countries.[26]

Some African countries have in recent years succeeded in balancing their national budgets, but such change is only marginal. Challenging strong vested interests, taking vigorous action against corruption, reducing the apparatus of government, and opening the economy to competition have proved more difficult. A bare majority of the countries south of the Sahara have relatively democratic regimes, and those countries have the world's least liberal economic systems. Estimating the amount of economic freedom in the region, the Canadian Fraser Institute found that, ignoring those countries too war torn to make measurement possible, 14 of the world's 20 least free economies are in Africa. All but four of the African countries for which data were available fell into the least free half of the 123 countries ranked.[27]

Zimbabwe, a long-standing recipient of Western development assistance, has undertaken the world's fastest and most consistent retreat from the alleged evils of globalization and liberalization. Under dictator Robert Mugabe, the country's trade with the outside world has been drastically limited, government spending has skyrocketed, and price controls have been introduced. Recently, oppression has escalated, with large-scale expropriation of property, suppression of freedom of expression, and acts of terror against the opposition. In just five years, the country has lost more than a third of all its wealth, and absolute poverty has grown by more than 10 percentage points. Zimbabwe was once a major exporter of foodstuffs, but over the course of only a few years, cereal production has collapsed to one-third its former level, and more than 6 million people are now facing starvation.[28]

Nigeria is another example. This huge country, despite abundant natural resources and agricultural land, has remained abysmally poor because of a very strictly regulated and corrupt economy. On the advice of the IMF, among others, certain structural reforms were inaugurated at the end of the 1980s, but their unpopularity led the Nigerian government to drop them at the beginning of the 1990s. Regulations were reintroduced, the credit and exchange market was abolished, and interest rates were controlled. Inflation and unemployment resulted. Between 1992 and 1996, the proportion of the absolutely poor rose from 43 to an incredible 66 percent of the national population. Nigeria today accounts for a quarter of all absolute poverty in sub-Saharan Africa, and despite the advent of a new, democratic government, reforms have progressed very slowly. Per capita income today is lower than it was thirty years ago, and health and education standards have fallen.

The economists Jeffrey Sachs and Andrew Warner have studied the growth that different political reforms have brought in various African countries. They have attempted, on the basis of various country studies, to calculate what growth the continent would have had if it had adopted the East Asian policy of open markets, freedom of enterprise, protection of property rights, and a high level of saving. Sachs and Warner maintain that, despite its poor natural conditions, Africa would then have been capable of achieving an average per capita growth of about 4.3 percent annually between 1965 and 1990. That would almost have tripled the population's incomes. Of course, any such estimate has to be taken with a grain of salt, but even with a generous margin of error, the figure remains shockingly high compared with Africa's actual growth during the years in question—a mere 0.8 percent per year.[29]

If we examine the track record of the African countries that *have* opted for free trade and more open economies, it seems entirely plausible that a liberal policy could have been so successful. The cattle farmers of Botswana were quick to realize that it was in their interest to campaign for more open markets, and that meant that large parts of the economy were already exposed to competition by the end of the 1970s. Botswana has protected rights of ownership and has never nationalized businesses. Through its association with the EU, the country's exports to Europe are exempt from duties and quotas. Since independence in 1966, Botswana has been the exception in a continent dominated by dictatorships, which has helped to make it one of the least corrupt nations in Africa, on par with European countries. Botswana's economic growth has actually surpassed that of the East Asian countries, with annual growth levels of more than 10 percent between 1970 and 1990. Another state that committed itself to free trade early on is the island nation of Mauritius. Through reduced military expenditure, protection of property rights, reduced taxes, a free capital market and increased competition, the country has achieved growth rates on the order of 5 percent annually. Today nearly everyone there has access to clean water, and education and health care are expanding. If countries like Mauritius and Botswana can achieve this degree of growth, why shouldn't the rest of Africa be able to? The populations of the other African countries are no less inventive and enterprising than the people of Mauritius or Botswana, but they are forced to use their creative powers to evade corruption and regulations and to cope with working in the informal sector.

Another interesting African country is Ghana, which began liberalizing its economy in 1983 and gradually became more prosperous while its neighbors grew slowly poorer. In particular, Ghana deregulated agriculture and abolished tariffs, price controls, and subsidies. Production has risen fast, which above all has benefited cocoa farmers—but because the farmers have now been able to invest and to afford more goods and services, many others have also benefited from the farming boom. Absolute poverty in Ghana fell during the 1990s from 36 to slightly more than 29 percent of the population, and in 2000 the leadership of the country was, for the first time, transferred peacefully and democratically.

Uganda has developed along similar lines and is one of the countries that liberalized fastest over the course of the 1990s. Trade there has been quickly liberated, price controls abolished, taxes lowered, inflation reduced, and the first steps taken toward protecting property rights and deregulating financial markets. Those factors, coupled with extensive development assistance, have produced annual growth of more than 5 percent, while inequality has diminished. During the 1990s, absolute poverty in Uganda fell from 56 to 35 percent. A relatively high degree of openness and the educational work of independent organizations have made Uganda the first country in Africa where the incidence of HIV/AIDS in the towns and cities has begun to diminish.

These examples of African "lion economies" (the counterpart of Asian "tigers" and "dragons") have shown, despite their setbacks, that poverty is not imposed by some law of nature. Slowly, very slowly, certain sub-Saharan states are beginning to use their resources more efficiently and to give their citizens greater economic liberties. The democracies are growing in number and urbanization is breaking up old tribal loyalties that have hitherto stood in the way of equality before the law. Competition is reducing corruption because rulers no longer have the same power to confer and withhold permits and privileges. Interest in foreign investments is another motive force, because companies shun investment in corrupt economies. The controlled economies are becoming a little frayed at the edges. The proportion of national budgets devoted to health and medical care increased, albeit marginally, during the 1990s.

Africa has an incredibly long way to go, but contrary to what some maintain, improvement is possible. From being in free fall, many African countries have been stabilized, albeit at an extremely low level. It will take determined democratic and liberal reforms to move things forward, and the implementation of those reforms will require leaders with the courage to put the people's interests before those of their friends, or of the bureaucracies. Given the grim starting point, it is unlikely but not impossible for the 21st century to be Africa's century.

III

Free trade is fair trade

Mutual benefit

Following demonstrations against the Seattle meeting of the World Trade Organization by tens of thousands of people at the end of 1999, the benefits of free trade have once again begun to be questioned in public debate. Voices have been raised calling for countries to be self-sufficient, or saying that the developing countries should "protect" themselves with tariffs until their industries have become mature, or that we need "new rules" for international trade. Often, the criticisms are summed up in the slogan that we ought to have "fair trade, not free trade." But in my view, free trade is by nature fair trade, because it is based on voluntary cooperation and exchange. Free trade means you, not the government, decide where you will buy your goods, without extra costs being imposed on them merely because they happen to cross a border. Tariffs, which impose a tax on products whenever they cross a border, and quotas, which limit the number of goods of a particular kind that may enter a country, are direct restrictions of citizens' freedom to make decisions about their own consumption for themselves. Freedom from those things—free trade—gives us freedom of choice and gives all people the opportunity of raising their living standard.

It may seem odd that the world's prosperity can be augmented just by people swapping things with each other. But every time you go shopping, you realize (if only subconsciously) how exchange augments wealth. You pay a dollar for a carton of milk because you would rather have the milk than your dollar. The shopkeeper sells it at that price because he would rather have your dollar than keep the milk. Both parties are satisfied with the deal, otherwise it would never have taken place. Both of you emerge from the transaction feeling that you have made a good exchange, that your needs have been better provided for.

Trade results in the person who has a knack for making bicycles doing just that, the person who is best at cutting hair working as a hairdresser, and the person who is best at manufacturing television sets taking a job in the TV factory. Then those workers exchange, so as to get what they each want. Through free trade, we can consume goods and services that we could never have produced ourselves. The possibility of free choice means that we can choose the best and cheapest goods possible. Free choice gives us access to goods that we cannot procure by ourselves. In a Minnesota grocery, we can buy bananas and pineapples, even though neither is likely to be found on a Minnesota farm. Even in northern latitudes, fresh green vegetables are on sale all winter, and people in landlocked countries can buy salmon from Norway. Free trade results in goods and services being produced by whoever is best at producing them and then being sold to whoever wants to buy them. That's really all there is to it.

But in fact the argument for free trade is even stronger. Perhaps most people are aware that you can make money out of trade so long as you produce something better than everyone else, but much of the criticism of free trade is based on the fear that some countries may be better at everything. Certain countries and enterprises are more advanced than others, and can perhaps do everything more efficiently than their weaker trading partners. But the fact is that you gain by trade even if you manufacture things less well than others could. The important thing is to do what you are relatively best at, not to be better than everyone else at doing it.

115

Imagine a simple case of trade between two people. Julia is highly trained, an outstanding surgeon, and also a pretty good cook. The other is John, who has not trained for any particular occupation and, moreover, is not quite as good at baking as Julia. John would like to do something simple that he can learn easily, in the home, and then use it in exchange for things that are more difficult to produce, such as surgery and medical care. But why should Julia agree to any such exchange when she is also the better cook? For the simple reason that she profits by concentrating on what she does best of all. Even if she is twice as good a chef as John is, she is a thousand times better at surgery than he is. So she produces the greatest value by devoting her limited time to surgery and then using part of her earnings from that source to buy dinner from somebody else. By concentrating on what she is best at, she has still more resources left over, and can thus afford to buy other goods and services that she wants.

Those who do not want free trade because it takes place "on unequal terms" and is based on "unequal circumstances" would urge John to shut himself off and not do business with Julia. But the fact is that he would profit handsomely by free trade. Through trade, he can concentrate on what he does best, in relative terms, and exchange it for what he needs, things that he would be far worse at producing, such as bicycles or medical care. This example illustrates what economists call "comparative advantage." John does not need to be *absolutely* best at his kind of production. It is enough for him to be best at it in relative terms—producing it better than other things he needs. It will still be worth his while to concentrate on that particular thing instead of trying to produce everything he needs by himself. He concentrates on the area in which he has a comparative advantage.

There need not even be any difference of training or education—different degrees of industry or good luck will suffice.

Imagine the two people in our example are stranded on a desert island, where each needs to eat a fish and a loaf of bread every day in order to survive. To achieve this, Julia has to spend two hours baking and one hour fishing. John needs two and one-half hours to bake and five hours to fish. So again Julia is best at both jobs. But she still gains by swapping with John, because then she can devote her time to what she is absolutely best at—fishing. She can then catch three fish in that same three hours, while John in the course of his same seven and one-half hours can bake three loaves. They then exchange the surplus, getting one and a half of each. Thus, without working an iota harder or a minute longer, John and Julia have increased their daily output from two fish and two loaves to three fish and three loaves. They can opt for this higher output level and have a better meal, or they can each work a bit less and make do with the old quantities. Or they can spend the additional time they've freed up on building a hut or a boat. If they were able to trade with other islands in the vicinity, they would be able to trade off their surplus for clothing or tools that represented someone else's comparative advantage.

Of course, this is a greatly simplified example, but it illustrates how specialization works in more complicated cases as well. Comparative advantage is just as important between countries as between individuals. In the above examples, John and Julia can be replaced with the United States and Canada, and the fish and bread with computers, clothing, tractors, or medicine. The principle that it is a good idea to concentrate on what one is relatively best at still applies. One's comparative advantage need not be a result of naturally given factors, such as the United States having plenty of farmland and Venezuela and the Middle East having oil. A country can acquire comparative advantages by chance. Computer corporations pop up in Silicon Valley and fashion tycoons set up shop in Milan, not because nature smiles on them, but because they can make use of the specialized contacts, knowledge, and manpower that, for one reason or another, have begun to accumulate in each place.

Free trade brings prosperity

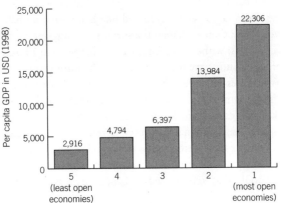

The countries of the world, divided into fifths by degrees of economic freedom

Source: James Gwartney and Robert Lawson, eds., *Economic Freedom of the World 2001* (Vancouver: Fraser Institute, 2001).

The simple examples given above expose the hollowness of the argument that countries should be self-sufficient and produce for their own populations. Under free trade, producing for others *is* producing for yourself. It is by producing and exporting what we are best at that we are able to import what we need. After World War II, many developing countries in South America, Africa, and elsewhere believed that self-sufficiency was the right policy.

Cheered on by the Western world, they were going to produce "for use and not for profit." In practice, this meant trying to do everything themselves, at huge expense. The East Asian countries

Free trade brings growth

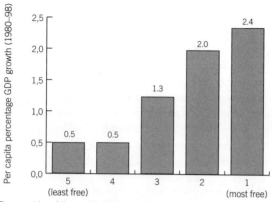

The countries of the world, divided into fifths by degrees of economic freedom

Source: James Gwartney and Robert Lawson, eds., *Economic Freedom of the World 2001* (Vancouver: Fraser Institute, 2001).

did the opposite. They made what they were best at and exported it, and in return were able to purchase, at lower cost, what they themselves needed. South Korea's first export commodities included wigs and particleboard; Hong Kong prospered with plastic flowers and cheap toys. Those aren't the first things a central planning committee would decide that people needed, but by exporting those things they acquired economic scope for catering to their own needs.[1]

Important imports

The logic above exposes the vacuity of another myth about trade, the notion that exports to other countries are a good thing but that importing from other countries is somehow a bad thing. Many still believe, like the "mercantilist" economists of the 18th century, that a country grows powerful by selling much but buying little. All experience indicates that this is not a stable situation. Import quotas designed to keep out products from abroad would just drive up prices in the United States by shielding domestic producers from competitive pressures. Those producers would then find it more profitable to focus on the high-priced American market than to export and sell their goods at lower world prices. Import barriers, then, actually reduce exports as well.

The truth is that we get richest by exporting what we make best, so as to be able to import things we make (relatively) less well. Otherwise we have to do everything ourselves and forsake the advantages of specialization. We can make a pile of money by just selling, but our standard of living will not rise until we use that money to buy things that we would not have had otherwise. One of the first trade theorists, James Mill, quite rightly argued, in 1821, "The benefit which is derived from exchanging one commodity for another, arises, in all cases, from the commodity *received*, not the commodity given."[2] The only point of exports, in other words, is to enable us to get imports in return.

The absurdity of the idea that we must avoid cheap imports becomes clear if we imagine it applied to non-national boundaries—for example, if Los Angeles were to try to prevent the importation of goods from San Francisco, on the grounds that it had to protect its markets. If imports really were economically harmful, it would make sense for one city or state to prevent its inhabitants from buying from another. According to this logic, Californians would lose out if they bought goods from Texas, Brooklyn would gain by refusing to buy from Manhattan, and it would be better for a family to make everything themselves instead of trading with their neighbors. It's obvious that such thinking would lead to a tremendous loss of welfare: the self-sufficient family would be hard pressed just to keep food on the table. When you go to the store, you "import" food—being able to do so cheaply is a benefit, not a loss. You "export" when you go to work and create goods or services. Most of us would prefer to "import" so cheaply that we could afford to "export" a little less.

Trade is not a zero-sum game, in which one party loses what the other party gains. On the contrary, there would be no exchange if both parties did not feel that they benefited. The really interesting yardstick is not the "balance of trade" (where a "surplus" means that we are exporting more than we are importing) but the quantity of trade, since both exports and imports are gains. Imports are often feared as a potential cause of unemployment: if we import cheap toys and clothing from China, then toy and garment manufacturers here will have to scale down. If we take a more internationalist perspective, we might ask why jobs and investments are more important in the United States than in poorer countries. Don't those countries need the jobs more than we do, unable as they are to compensate the unemployed? But this is also a mistaken way of looking at things. By obtaining cheaper goods from abroad, we save resources in the United States and can therefore invest in new industries and occupations, which

"Nothing, however, can be more absurd than this whole doctrine of the balance of trade, upon which, not only these restraints, but almost all the other regulations of commerce are founded. When two places trade with one another, this doctrine supposes that, if the balance be even, neither of them either loses or gains; but if it leans in any degree to one side, that one of them loses and the other gains in proportion to its declension from the exact equilibrium. Both suppositions are false. A trade which is forced by means of bounties and monopolies may be, and commonly is, disadvantageous to the country in whose favor it is meant to be established, as I shall endeavour to show hereafter. But that trade which, without force or constraint, is naturally and regularly carried on between any two places is always advantageous, though not always equally so, to both."

Adam Smith, 1776[3]

results in the Chinese having more money to spare and being able to buy software or Britney Spears albums from us. Besides, most businesses and producers are dependent on raw materials from suppliers and subcontractors in other countries. For the production of mobile phones, for example, the Swedish company Ericsson needs electronic components produced in Asia. So when the EU raises tariff barriers against Asia, allegedly for the protection of European jobs, European companies like Ericsson sustain added costs and therefore sell less, which means they are not able to create as many new jobs as they otherwise could have.

Thus, the world's politicians are in one sense acting foolishly when they gather in Seattle or Qatar to negotiate the reduction of tariffs within the framework of the World Trade Organization (WTO). The politicians say that they will consent to reduce a tariff only on the condition that other countries do the same. But that is fundamentally irrational, because each country benefits by reducing its own tariffs and being able to import cheaply, whether or not other countries follow suit. The best policy is unilateral free trade, that is, the United States dismantling its own tariffs and quotas even if other countries retain or even increase theirs. Why should we subject our population to more tariffs and prohibitions merely because other countries do so to their populations? To borrow an analogy from the British economist Joan Robinson, there is nothing very clever about tipping boulders into your own harbors just because your neighbors have rocky and inaccessible coastlines that make it hard for your own ships to dock. Saying "I'm not going to allow myself to choose from a wider range of good, cheap products unless you do the same" is a sacrifice, not a cunning reprisal.

Even so, there are good arguments in favor of multilateral trade negotiations between lots of countries under WTO auspices. For one thing, such negotiations can make it easier for vested interests to accept free trade reforms. If the United States unilaterally reduces its tariffs, the reduction may meet with fierce resistance from American companies and trade unions that would rather not have the competition. That competition would benefit consumers, of course, but consumers as a class are dispersed and unorganized, unlikely to make too much noise about any single tariff. The industries for whom those trade barriers represent a kind of monopoly protection, however, will fight tooth and nail to retain the captive market tariffs give them. Multilateral agreements can shift the balance of political interests. When many countries reduce their tariffs at the same time, businesses and unions in export industry will support the reform in hopes of opening up new markets. Negotiations can make it easier to introduce tariff reductions and to get other countries to do the same, but they can also make it more difficult. If politicians behave as though tariffs are something beneficial, something to remove only if we get something in return, voters will end up believing this is true. Voters will get the impression that tariffs are a good thing that the politicians are selling out, whereas in fact tariffs are harmful. If trade talks are not combined with a strong mobilization of opinion against tariffs and quotas and in favor of imports, there may come a protectionist backlash, as the collapse of negotiations following the December 1999 WTO meeting in Seattle suggests.[4]

The WTO offers the promise of a second, broader benefit as well: the establishment of an impartial code of rules to ensure that all countries honor their agreements. The norm throughout history has been that powerful countries could behave as they liked toward the weaker ones. Many of the world's countries wanted a trade organization with uniform rules to prevent, above all, unilateral actions by the United States against its trading partners. The United States, on the other hand, had wanted only a weaker agreement to begin with, not an organization to resolve disputes. Through the WTO, member states have pledged not to discriminate against foreign enterprises and not to introduce arbitrary trade barriers—over and above the ones they have already, anyway. It was in order to benefit from these protections that the poorer countries of the world quickly ratified the 1995 WTO agreement, whereas the EU, the United States, and Japan— accustomed to doing as they liked—held back. Powerful countries like the United States have since been defeated in WTO disputes, something that could never happen at the United Nations, where they have a veto.

Another advantage of the WTO is that all member states have pledged to give the others "most favored nation" treatment, which entails automatic access to all tariff reductions granted to any other country. The United States and the EU used to reduce tariffs in relation to each other without a thought of increasing freedom of trade with the rest of the world. Now tariff reductions also have to apply to the poor countries, with the unfortunate exception of those contained in regional trade agreements of the sort existing between EU countries or the signatories of the North American Free Trade Agreement (NAFTA).

But the obstacles to unfair tariffs are not all that great. The WTO has no specific rights to forbid anyone to impose tariffs; it can only entitle the injured party to introduce compensatory trade barriers. This is not an ideal situation, because countries should phase out their tariffs regardless of what others do. It would be better if the losing party had to pay monetary compensation or lower other tariffs to compensate. But these relatively stable procedures are at least an improvement on the old days, when a petty dispute could develop into a full-scale trade war. Now states are at least prevented by their honor from reneging on their agreements. In several widely noted instances, however, the EU has tried to retain trade barriers condemned by the WTO. One example is the attempt made for many years to discriminate against Latin American bananas and hormone-treated meat. The EU governments act as though one yardstick should apply to the industrialized nations and another to the developing countries, which in the long term will severely damage the WTO's credibility.

Once the benefits of imports are perceived, it also follows that antidumping measures are harmful. Politicians often say that they must protect the people from "price dumping" by other countries, meaning, for example, that if Malaysia sells us extremely cheap shoes, priced below production cost or cheaper than they are sold in the Malaysian market, this is "unfair competition." The

Malaysian producers are then "dumping," and this is something we have to protect ourselves against. But, as economist Murray Rothbard has quipped, you should keep a sharp eye on your wallet when somebody says that they want "fair competition," because it means that your pocket is about to be picked. That certainly is true where antidumping tariffs are concerned. What they really "protect" us from is cheap shoes, TV sets, and food-stuffs. The question is why we should need protection from these things. There need not be anything unfair at all about foreign producers engaging in "dumping." For example, they may be forced to do so in order to penetrate a new market, surely a legitimate goal. New domestic firms are allowed to do this, so why not foreign ones? Surely, having different rules for domestic and foreign businesses amounts to a greater injustice than dump-ing. It may also be that the Malaysian shoe manufacturers sell their products more expensively in the home market because they have advantages there that they do not enjoy here—advantages like protective tariff walls!

The United States, which claims to support free trade, is in fact the biggest transgressor when it comes to introducing anti-dumping tariffs. Not only do these tariffs harm the enterprise sectors of other countries, but the American economy loses billions of dollars every year to higher prices and lower efficiency. The use of such tariffs has grown in the past decade. When the WTO and international agreements make protectionism harder to intro-duce through the front gate, the United States and the EU let it in the back door with antidumping tariffs.[5]

WTO rules notwithstanding, countries can and do still erect de facto trade barriers in the form of domestic subsidies. The American steel industry, for example, has been the beneficiary of a welter of government pension guarantees, loan guarantees, special tax and environmental exemptions, and research and development grants. Conservative estimates place the value of those subsidies at some $23 billion since 1975, and other studies found that they totaled more than $30 billion just in the 1980s. American taxpayers have ample reason to resent this massive outlay of corporate welfare, which, in addition to wasting tax money, props up noncompetitive firms and thereby ties up resources inefficiently. But consumers abroad, far from demanding "protection" against this "unfair" practice, should be grateful (if a bit perplexed) that the United States has chosen to underwrite cheaper steel for *them*. American taxpayers are in fact subsidizing Swedish consumption of steel and other products. By the same token, we should regard a decision by a foreign government to subsidize export industry, not as a threat, but as a somewhat misguided gift.[6]

Free trade brings growth

Free trade is primarily a good thing because it brings freedom: freedom for people to buy what they want from whoever they please, but also to sell to whoever wants to buy. As an added economic benefit, this freedom leads to the efficient use of resources and capital. A company, a region, or a country specializes where it has comparative advantages and can therefore generate the greatest value. Capital and labor from older, less competitive sectors are transferred to newer, more dynamic ones. That means that a country switching to a more free-trade-friendly policy rises to a higher level of production and prosperity, and can therefore anticipate a substantial acceleration of growth for at least the first few years. But economic openness also leads to an enduring effort to improve production, because foreign competition forces firms to be as good and cheap as possible, and this leaves consumers free to choose goods and services from the seller making the best offer. As production in established industries becomes ever more efficient, resources are freed up for investment in new methods, inventions, and products. This same argument supports competition generally; it simply extends competition to even bigger fields, thus making it more intensive.

One of the most important benefits of free trade, but one that is particularly hard to measure, is that a country trading a great deal with the rest of the world imports new ideas and new techniques in the bargain. If the United States pursues free trade, our companies are exposed to the world's best ideas in their particular fields.

That compels them to be more dynamic themselves, and they can borrow other companies' ideas, buy their technology, and hire foreign manpower. Openness to other people and other ways of doing business has always been a path to development, while isolation means stagnation. It is no coincidence that the most dynamic regions in history have often been in coastal locations, close to towns and cities, while those that lag behind are inaccessible, often in mountain regions.

The world's output today is 6 times what it was 50 years ago, and world trade is 16 times greater. There is cause to believe that production has been led and driven by trade. Exactly what difference open markets make is hard to tell, but virtually no economist denies that the effect is positive. There are huge quantities of empirical fact to show that free trade creates economic development.

One comprehensive and frequently cited study of the effects of trade was conducted by Harvard economists Jeffrey Sachs and Andrew Warner.[7] They examined the trade policies of 117 countries between 1970 and 1989. After controlling for other factors, the study reveals a statistically significant connection between free trade and growth that the authors were unable to find, for example, between education and growth. Growth was between three and six times higher in free trade countries than in protectionist ones. Open developing countries had on average an annual growth rate of 4.49 percent those two decades, while closed developing countries had only 0.69 percent. Open industrialized countries had an annual growth of 2.29 percent, while closed ones experienced only 0.74 percent growth.

It must be emphasized that this is not a matter of how much countries earn because others are open to their exports, but of how much they earn by keeping their own markets open. The results show that the open economies had a faster growth rate than the closed ones every year between 1970 and 1989. No free trade country in the study had an average growth rate of less than 1.2 percent annually, and no open developing country had a growth rate of less than 2.3 percent!

Free trade and growth during the 1970s and 1980s

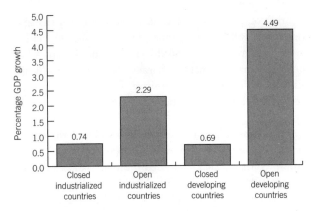

Source: Jeffrey Sachs and Andrew Warner, "Economic Reform and the Process of Global Integration," *Brookings Papers on Economic Activity 1, 1995.*

In all regions, free trade policies led to an acceleration of growth after a short time, even in Africa. The positive results of free trade were even apparent when liberalization was only temporary. Countries that opened up their economies briefly and then closed them again showed faster growth during the open period than before or after.

Slower growth and reduced investments did not afford the protectionist economies greater stability, either. Sachs and Warner showed that closed economies were far more liable than free trade economies to be affected by financial crises and hyperinflation. Barely 8 percent of the developing countries judged open from the 1970s onward suffered from crises of this kind during the 1980s, whereas more than 80 percent of the closed economies did so.

Criticism has been leveled at this type of regression analysis, which is based on statistics from many economies and tries to control for other factors that can affect economic outcomes, because of the many problems of measurement that such analysis involves. Coping with enormous masses of data is always a problem. Where exactly is the line between open and closed economies? How does one distinguish between correlation and causation? How can the direction of causation be established? Consider, after all, that it is common for countries implementing free trade to also introduce other liberal reforms, such as protection for property rights, reduced inflation, and balanced budgets. That makes it hard to separate the effects of one policy from the effects of another.[8] The problems of measurement are real ones, and results of this kind always have to be taken with a grain of salt, but it remains interesting that, with so very few exceptions, those studies point to great advantages with free trade. All the same, they have to be supplemented with theoretical analysis and case studies of individual countries before and after trade liberalization measures. Such studies also quite clearly bring out the advantages of free trade.

The economist Sebastian Edwards maintains that the important thing is not to devise exact, objective measurements but to test many different variables, so as to see whether a pattern emerges. Using 8 different yardsticks of openness, he has made 18 calculations based on several data sets and using a variety of calculation methods. All but one of the calculations indicated a positive connection between free trade and growth. Edwards estimates that growth rates have been twice as high in free-trading developing countries as in protectionist ones. In a report to the Swedish parliamentary committee Globkom, the economist Håkan Nordström reviews 20 different studies of free trade, all of which clearly show that open markets give rise to better economic development.[9]

Another attempt to quantify the benefits of trade has been made by the economists Jeffrey Frankel and David Romer. On the basis of their research, they maintain that if a country increases its trade in relation to GDP by 1 percent, its per capita income can be expected to rise by between 0.5 and 2 percent. That means that if a country boosts its trade volume by 10 percentage points, the incomes of the poor rise by 5–20 percent. These are, of course, averages, not universal truths. But if we work out what this actually means to the poor of the world, we find that a 10 percent increase in trade relative to GDP in a country like Nigeria would enable 25 million people to escape from poverty. In a country like India, it could mean ten times that number being lifted out of absolute poverty. This is a hypothesis, not an ironclad guarantee, but it conveys something of the explosive potential inherent in free commercial exchange.[10]

A clear connection exists between greater free trade and growth on the one hand and poverty reduction on the other. We can see the differences between similarly situated countries that have introduced, or refrained from introducing, liberalization measures and open markets. We see this difference between liberalizing Vietnam and nonliberalizing Burma, between Bangladesh and Pakistan, between Costa Rica and Honduras, between Uganda and Kenya, between Chile and its neighbors in Latin America, and so on.

What about trade and inequality? There does not seem to be any strong and unambiguous connection between increased trade and changes in equality—except, possibly, a slightly positive connection. Certain groups lose out by free trade, but they are as likely to be the protected rich as the poor. Changes in equality depend primarily on overall policy. Results in trade-liberalizing countries varied during the 1990s: in China, inequality increased, in Costa Rica and Vietnam it remained constant, and in countries like Ghana and Thailand it diminished. After many years of a communist-planned economy and deepest poverty, Vietnam since the end of the 1980s has introduced free trade reforms and measures of domestic liberalization. Those changes have made possible a substantial growth in exports of such labor-intensive products as shoes, and of rice, which is produced by poor farmers. This has resulted in rapid growth and a uniquely swift reduction of poverty. Whereas 75 percent of the population in 1988 were living in absolute poverty, by 1993 this figure had fallen to 58 percent, and 10 years later had been reduced by half, to 37 percent; 98 percent of the poorest Vietnamese households increased their incomes during the 1990s.[11]

One seldom observed aspect of Sachs and Warner's findings is that they show open poor economies to have grown faster than open affluent ones. It may seem natural for poor countries to have higher growth than affluent ones. They have more latent resources to harness, and they can benefit from the existence of wealthier nations to which they export goods and from which they import capital and more advanced technology, whereas affluent countries will have already captured many of those gains. But economists had not found any such general connection previously. The reason is simple: the economies of protectionist developing countries cannot make use of these international opportunities, and so grow less rapidly than those of the affluent countries. But when Sachs and Warner studied the developing countries that had been open to trade and investments, those in a position to benefit from the opportunities provided by the industrialized nations, those countries were found to grow more rapidly than the open affluent countries. The poorer they were at the outset, the faster their economies grew once they were opened up. No such connection exists for closed countries, which suggests that free trade is not only the best way to promote growth, but also the best way for developing countries to catch up with the industrialized nations. In short, poor countries grow faster than rich ones as long as the two are united by flows of trade and capital.

The same pattern was even clearer in the 1990s. During that decade, per capita GDP fell by an average of 1.1 percent in closed developing countries. In the industrialized countries it rose by 1.9 percent, but the fastest growth of all—5 percent annually on average—occurred in developing countries that had opened their markets and frontiers. It is free-trading developing countries that are developing their economies fastest, more so than the affluent countries. One pair of economists sum up their findings as follows:

Thus, the globalizers are catching up with rich countries while the non-globalizers fall further and further behind.[12]

History shows that economies can grow faster by riding on the prosperity and technology of other countries. From 1780, it took England 58 years to double its wealth. A hundred years later, Japan did it in only 34 years, and another century later it took South Korea only 11 years.[13] The convergence, in terms of wealth, of countries associated with one another is confirmed by many other epochs and groups of countries. During the globalization of the late 19th century, poorer economies like Ireland and Scandinavia moved closer to the wealthier countries. During the post-war era, poor OECD countries have moved closer to the more affluent ones. Differences between countries have diminished within the European Free Trade Association (EFTA) and EU free trade zones. The same result has also been discovered in different parts of such large economies as the United States and Japan. Free trade and mobility, then, make the poor richer and the rich also richer, but the rich do not get richer as fast as the poor do.[14]

Globalization and growth during the 1990s

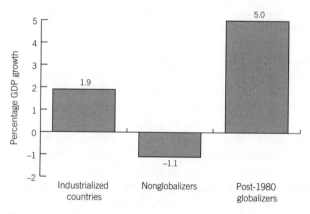

Source: David Dollar and Aart Kraay, *Trade, Growth and Poverty* (Washington: World Bank, 2001).

No end of work

If free trade is constantly making production more efficient, won't that result in the disappearance of job opportunities? When Asians begin manufacturing our cars and South Americans producing our meat, auto workers and farmers in the United States lose their jobs and unemployment rises—so the argument goes, anyway. Foreigners, developing countries, and machines will compete to produce the things we need, until in the end we will not have any jobs left. If everything we consume today could be produced by half the U.S. labor force in twenty years' time, doesn't that mean that the other half will be put out of work? Such is the horror scenario depicted in many of the anti-globalization writings of our time. In the book *The Global Trap*, two German journalists maintain that, in the future, 80 percent of the population will not be needed for production. American readers may be more familiar with *One World, Ready or Not: The Manic Logic of Global Capitalism*, a breathless tome in which William Greider, then a reporter for *Rolling Stone*, frets that global supply is outstripping demand, leaving the world poised on the verge of mass unemployment. Those fears are based on an unpleasant view of human nature, according to which few people will have the qualities that cause society to "need" them. I'm happy to report that this view is completely misguided.

The notion that a colossal unemployment crisis is looming just around the corner began to grow popular in the mid-1970s, and since then production has been streamlined and internationalized more than ever. All over the world, however, far more jobs have been created than have disappeared. In the past few decades, the number of gainfully employed people in the world has risen by about 800 million. We have more efficient production than ever before, but also more people at work. Between 1975 and 1998, employment in countries like the United States, Canada, and Australia rose by 50 percent and in Japan by 25 percent. Within the EU, where unemployment has gained a stronger hold than in many other places, more people found jobs during this period in almost every country. Sweden, Finland, and Spain were the only exceptions, but in these countries the employment participation rate has risen since 1998.

It is also interesting to note that it is in the most internationalized economies, those making the most use of modern technology, that employment has grown fastest. The United States is the clearest instance. Between 1983 and 1995 in the United States, 24 million more job opportunities were created than disappeared. And those were not low-paid, unskilled jobs, as is often alleged in the course of debate. On the contrary, 70 percent of the new jobs carried a wage above the American median level. Nearly half the new jobs belonged to the most highly skilled, a figure which has risen even more rapidly since 1995.[15]

So allegations of progressively fewer people being needed in production have no empirical foundation. And no wonder, for they are wrong in theory too. It is not the case that only a certain number of jobs exist and that when these can be done by fewer people, more become unemployed. Imagine a pre-industrial economy where most of what people earn is spent on food. Then food production is improved by new technologies; machines begin doing the work of many farmers, and foreign competition makes farming more efficient. That results in a lot of people having to

137

leave the agricultural sector. Does this mean there is nothing for them to do, that consumption is constant? No, because it also means more scope for consumption. The money that used to go to labor costs in agriculture can now be used to buy other commodities, such as better clothing, books, and industrial goods. The people who are no longer needed in agriculture can then switch to those lines of business instead.

This is not merely conjecture; it describes precisely what happened in Sweden with the improvement of agricultural efficiency from the beginning of the 19th century onward. Before then, about 80 percent of Sweden's population had been employed on the land. Today the figure is less than 3 percent. But does this mean that 77 percent of the Swedish population are now unemployed? No, because instead people started demanding other goods and better services, and manpower went into industry and services in response to that demand. By doing a job efficiently, we get a larger total of resources with which to satisfy our needs. The manpower which used to be necessary in order to feed us could then clothe us and provide us with better housing, entertainment, travel, newspapers, telephones, and computers, thus raising our standard of living.

The notion that the quantity of work to be done is constant, that a job gained by one person is always a job taken from someone else, has provoked a variety of responses. It has led some to advocate that jobs be shared, others to smash machinery, and many to advocate raising tariffs and excluding immigrants. But the whole notion is wrong. Greider's turgid and rigorous-seeming book has been enormously influential among anti-globalization activists. Yet all of its dire predictions are based on this one simple error, which Princeton economist Paul Krugman, in his scathing review of the book, described as a "transparent fallacy."[16] But

Greider is not alone in making this mistake. Susan George, vice chairman of the French anti-globalization organization ATTAC, declares that globalization and international investments rarely provide any new jobs at all:

> *Not everything called investment leads to new job opportunities. Eight out of ten investments the world over in the past five years have been concerned with mergers and take-overs, and things like that mostly result in job losses.*[17]

But it is this very process—a task being done more efficiently, thus enabling jobs to be shed—that enables new industries to grow, providing people with new and better jobs.

Here, somebody might reasonably ask: "Will it never end? What happens when *all* our needs are being satisfied by a small portion of the workforce?" And when, I wonder, is that supposed to happen? I believe that people will always, for example, be in need of more security, convenience, and entertainment. I don't believe we will ever come to think that we are giving our children enough education, that we know enough, that we are doing just the right amount of research or that we are getting enough remedies for our aches and pains. It is hard to see a limit to the quality of housing we would like to have, the quality of food we want to eat, the extent we wish to travel, or the quality of entertainment we would like to experience. When our productive abilities increase, we will always choose to satisfy new needs, or to satisfy old ones better than ever. If we think we have all that we need, we can demand more leisure instead. Ask yourself whether you could not conceive of two full-time jobs for people to provide you with services and products. Finding the money to employ them, I suspect, is more difficult than thinking of things for them to do. If you and I and everyone else can think of things that we would like two people to do, we have a permanent manpower deficit, with 6 billion people wanting at least 12 billion employees. This is why we will never have too much manpower, no matter how prosperous we become or how efficient our production gets.

Efficiency does, of course, have a flip side. Economist Joseph Schumpeter famously described a dynamic market as a process of "creative destruction," because it is concerned with "destroying" old solutions and industries, but with a creative end in view, namely the transfer of manpower and capital to more productive occupations. This gives us a higher standard of living, but as the word "destruction" suggests, not everyone benefits from every market transformation in the short term. It is, of course, painful for those who have invested in the old solutions and for those who are laid off in less efficient industries. Drivers of horse-drawn cabs lost out with the spread of automobiles, as did producers of paraffin lamps when electric light was introduced. In more modern times, manufacturers of typewriters were put out of business by the coming of the computer, and LP records were superseded by CDs.

Painful changes of this kind are happening all the time as a result of new inventions and methods of production. Some friends of free trade attempt to explain them away by saying that job losses are primarily due to technical advances, not to competition from other countries. That premise is true as far as it goes, but as a defense it rings hollow because the competition stimulated by free trade helps to accelerate the introduction of those new technologies. Unquestionably, such changes can cause enormous problems and traumas for those affected, especially if a new job is hard to find. The very fear of the risks involved causes certain conservative ideologues to reject the capitalist system entirely. A modern society based on a market economy does indeed present new risks and problems, and of course it is very stressful to be in danger of losing one's job, with the reduction of living standard and blow to self-esteem this implies. But that risk still cannot be compared with the stress in ages past of perhaps not being able to earn one's daily bread or of drought or flood completely obliterating one's livelihood. It cannot be compared with the anxiety of the present-day Ethiopian farmer, whose life may depend on the coming of rain and on the health of his livestock.

The most foolish possible way to counter the problems that such economic adjustments entail is to try to prevent the adjustments. Without "creative destruction," we would *all* be stuck with a lower standard of living. The whole point of trade and development is to direct resources to the point where they can be used most efficiently. A Chinese proverb has it, "When the wind of change begins to blow, some people build windbreaks while others build windmills." The idea that we should halt change now is as misguided as the idea that we should have obstructed agricultural advances two centuries ago to protect the 80 percent of the population employed on the land at that time. Changes are hard to stop anyway, because the most common cause of structural change in different branches of economic activity is the changing tastes of consumers. A far better idea would be to use the economic gains that change brings about to alleviate the consequences for those adversely affected.

There is a lot we can do to make changes proceed as smoothly as possible. We should not try to prop up old industries by means of subsidies or tariff walls. Enterprise and financial markets should be free enough for people to invest in the new industries. Wages should be flexible and taxes low, so that people will be drawn to the new and more productive sectors, and the labor market should be free as well. Schools and other education opportunities must be good enough for people to acquire the skills required by the new jobs. Social safety nets must provide transitional security, without preventing people from entering new jobs.

But these problems are seldom as widespread as a scan of the newspaper headlines might suggest. It is easy to report that 300 people lost their jobs in a car factory due to Japanese competition. It is less easy and less dramatic to report on all the thousands of jobs that have been created because we have been able to use old resources more efficiently. It is less easy to report on how much consumers have gained from the wider selection, better quality, and lower prices spurred by competition. Hardly any of the world's consumers are aware that they have gained between $100 billion and $200 billion annually from liberalization measures implemented following the Uruguay Round of trade negotiations, but the difference is visible in our refrigerators, in home electronics, and in our wallets. Costs affecting a small group on an isolated occasion are easier to see and observe, while benefits that gradually accrue to nearly everyone creep up on us without our giving them a thought.

A review of more than 50 surveys of adjustment following openness reforms in different countries clearly shows these changes to be milder than the debate on them indicates. For every dollar of adjustment costs, roughly $20 is harvested in the form of welfare gains. A study of 13 cases of trade liberalization in different countries showed industrial employment to have already *increased* one year after the liberalization in all countries but one. One reason why changes are less painful in poor countries is that the old jobs mostly offered poor wages and bad working conditions. The people who are usually most vulnerable—those without any specific training—find new work more easily than those with special skills. Poor countries have comparative advantages in labor-intensive sectors, leading, on average, to a rapid rise in wages for the workers concerned. Broadbased liberalization measures also have the effect of cheapening the goods workers need.

Costs are also small compared to benefits in affluent countries that liberalize trade. The sectors badly affected by competition and new breakthroughs of technology go through something resembling an ordinary recession. The number of people in other sectors who retire or leave jobs of their own free will is often so great as to swallow the job loss as the economy adjusts to reforms. If the changes contribute to a high level of growth, they can even subdue painful restructuring problems, which are always at their greatest in downturns. Unemployment usually lasts for only a short time, whereas the positive effects on the economy keep on growing. The process, in other words, turns out to be far more creative than destructive.[18]

The problems ought to be greatest in the United States, with its constant economic transformation, but our job market is a bit like the Hydra in the legend of Hercules. In the myth, every time Hercules cut off one of the beast's heads, two new ones appeared. For every two jobs that disappeared in the United States during the 1990s, three new ones were created. This pattern greatly increases the individual person's chances: there is no better safeguard against unemployment than the prospect of a new job. The danger of having to continue changing between different jobs all one's life is exaggerated, especially as firms are exerting themselves more and more to train employees for new tasks. The average length of time an American stays in a particular job increased between 1983 and 1995 from 3.5 years to 3.8. Nor is it true, as many people believe, that more jobs are being created in the United States because real wages have stagnated or fallen since the 1970s. A growing proportion of wages has been paid in nonmonetary forms, such as health insurance, stock, 401k contributions, day care, and so forth, to avoid taxation. If benefits of this new kind are included in wages, then American wages have gone on rising with productivity. The proportion of consumption among poor Americans that is devoted to food, clothing, and housing has fallen since the 1970s from 52 to 37 percent, which clearly shows that such people have money to spare for more than the bare necessities of life.[19]

One of the most drastic trade liberalizations in modern history has been carried out by the Baltic nation of Estonia. Soon after the country gained its independence from the Soviet Union in 1992, the Estonian government decided to abolish all tariffs in one fell swoop. The average tariff level is now 0 percent. The tariff measure proved an unqualified success. The Estonian economy has been rapidly restructured on a competitive basis. Western Europe, which in 1990 accounted for only 1 percent of Estonia's international trade, today accounts for two-thirds of it. The country is attracting large direct investments and can boast an annual growth rate of around 5 percent. Average life expectancy has grown and infant mortality has fallen, in contrast to those former communist states that have reformed slowly. The change to a liberal system has made Estonia one of the EU's most promising candidate countries. Unfortunately, EU membership will mean that Estonia has to adjust to EU protectionism. Instead of having no tariffs at all, the country will have to introduce 10,794 different tariff levels, which among other things will raise food prices appreciably. In addition, Estonia will have to introduce various quotas, subsidies, and antidumping measures.[20]

Freedom of movement—for people as well

Even if a world in which we are free to buy and sell goods and services across national borders is a long way off, that world is what many people are aiming for. The world's politicians meet regularly in an attempt to extend free trade, albeit far too slowly. But when it comes to the mobility of human beings, the politicians, unfortunately, meet regularly to do everything in their power to reduce it. Reducing mobility has been a very conspicuous aim of the affluent European states ever since the 1970s. At the same time that the Schengen Agreement has given Europeans free mobility within Europe, the EU governments are trying to prevent outsiders from penetrating Europe's borders. The result is very high walls against the outside and stricter controls on the internal movement of persons.

Of course, since the terrorist attacks of September 11, 2001, some new walls and controls have been introduced, with the goal of preventing a recurrence of that horrific event. Some of those controls are doubtless justifiable: citizens everywhere rightfully demand to know that newcomers to their countries have come as workers, tourists, students, and neighbors—not as mass murderers. The fundamental duty of any government is to protect its own citizenry, and one way of doing that is to ensure that terrorists and violent criminals cannot enter the country. The major effort to that end in the United States, the Enhanced Border Security and Visa Entry Reform Act of 2002, is a good example of a reasonable response. The act implemented measures to exclude potential terrorists without rolling back levels of legal immigration or cracking down on undocumented (but harmless) workers.

Sadly, some who have long wanted stricter immigration rules anyway, as a means of closing borders to peaceful workers and immigrants, have seized upon the tragedy of September 11 to advance that agenda by calling for far broader restrictions. Such tactics are not only cynical and exploitative, but also counterproductive. The crucial task of stopping terrorists becomes far more difficult when restrictive immigration laws force law enforcement officers to waste energy and resources combing through the many millions of immigrants who seek only a better life. Surely it would be more efficient to focus on the relatively very few who mean to harm Americans. It is important, then, to distinguish between measures targeted at keeping out the dangerous and measures that would pointlessly sacrifice the very freedom and openness that the terrorists and their allies despise. The latter measures are, sadly, all too common.

Although immigration policy in the United States has, fortunately, grown more enlightened and inclusive since the days when Congress enacted racist legislation, such as the Chinese Exclusion Act of 1882, to keep out "inferior" peoples, tight regulations remain in effect. Strict quotas limit how many people may come to the United States from different regions, and prospective workers must first find a sponsor in the United States who is willing to wade through extensive red tape in order to employ them. Some come to the United States as refugees from war, natural disaster, or persecution, but the number of such immigrants admitted annually has fallen in recent years. Under President George H. W. Bush, the average was 121,000 per year. Under President Clinton, that average dropped to 82,000, and under President George W. Bush it fell below 70,000. Because screening

146

of refugees is extraordinarily thorough, it is difficult to justify this precipitous decline by an appeal to security concerns.[21]

The costs of too-strict immigration policies around the world have manifested themselves in tragic ways. A port official opening a container in England finds 58 Chinese refugees who have died from heat and suffocation after trying to hide from immigration officials. Africans are found dead on the southern coast of Spain, having drowned in the attempt to cross the Mediterranean swimming or in flimsy crafts. The bodies of 11 Mexicans are found sealed in a rail car in Iowa. The big tragedies attract attention, but they have their lesser daily counterparts. The Dutch charity United has estimated that one person dies every day attempting to cross the borders of the EU. There are many women whose only chance of escaping desperate conditions in their home countries is through criminal syndicates that force them into prostitution and, when the women try to break free from this degradation, threaten to report them to the authorities. If, through visa requirements and barriers, people are prevented from entering a country legally, they resort to drastic and dangerous ways of doing so illegally. Often they fall into the clutches of unscrupulous refugee smugglers who demand exorbitant payments but do not think twice about risking the lives of their desperate clients.

When the EU or the United States try to prevent outsiders from moving there, by means of progressively stricter quotas and tougher enforcement, refugees are forced to take even bigger risks. If people are willing to take those risks in order to come to a freer country, politicians should seriously reconsider whether they have correctly assessed the refugees' need for protection. The ultimate goal must be for peaceful people to be able to evaluate their own interests in fleeing or migrating to another country.

The same goes for so-called economic refugees, people who wish to leave economic deprivation behind them and come to a country where they have the chance of creating a better life. No genuine economic globalization can occur so long as people are not allowed to cross national boundaries in search of employment. That is precisely what the ancestors of contemporary Americans did: since 1820, some 66 million immigrants have legally entered the United States. The Western world rightly castigated the communist states for not allowing their citizens to emigrate. But now that they are permitted to do so, we are forbidding them to enter our countries.

There is no concession or generosity involved when rich countries open their borders to refugees and immigrants, any more than there is in opening them up to imports. Greater immigration may be a prerequisite for our still having a viable economy and security of welfare a generation from now, especially in a sparsely populated country like Sweden. The EU countries are greatly troubled by falling birth rates and aging populations. The United Nations Population Fund (UNFPA) has estimated that to keep the EU population at its present level until 2050, 1.6 million immigrants annually will be needed. And to maintain a steady ratio between working and retired populations, the EU would need to take in 13.5 million immigrants *every year*. In the United States, a similar demographic trend threatens to drive the Social Security system into bankruptcy, as fewer and fewer workers finance the benefits of more and more retirees. Immigration alone cannot ultimately solve the system's deeper structural problems, but an influx of immigrant workers could ease the burden of transition to one of the alternative systems that various reformers have advocated. The challenge for the future will consist in attracting new immigrants, not in trying to keep them away.

It is a profound error to regard immigrants as a burden on a country. They represent a manpower and consumption boost that leads to market growth. More immigration means more people to work, spend, and hatch new ideas. Seeing that as a problem makes no more sense than viewing increased domestic birth rates as a problem. So long as wages mirror productivity (the amount workers are able to produce), there is no reason why this should create unemployment. Over the course of a lifetime, even those getting off to a poor start in a new country generally put more back into society—and the national treasury—than they get out of it. Far from being a drain on public resources, extensive research by economist Julian Simon found that the average legal immigrant receives less from government and pays in a greater amount in taxes than the average native-born citizen. Though calculations for illegal immigrants are more difficult, even here Simon found a likely net benefit to the host society. Summing up his findings, Simon even estimates the rough dollar amount of benefit each new immigrant provides his host country:

> *Evaluating the future stream of differences as one would when evaluating a prospective dam or harbor, the present value of a newly arrived immigrant family discounted at 3% (inflation adjusted) was $20,600 in 1975 dollars, almost two years' average earnings of a native family; at 6% the present value was $15,800, and $12,400 at 9%.* [22]

If some immigrants do become permanently dependent on handouts, that merely illustrates one reason to seriously reform our welfare policy and labor market regulations. For people who come to the United States, especially those starting out with few skills and a shaky grasp of the language, not being able to compete by working for lower pay will naturally tend to impair their chances. They will then be made to depend on handouts, perhaps for life, and their self-respect will be correspondingly eroded. Entering the job market at a low pay level, which rises later on with growing experience, is therefore a better option. In a healthy economy, low starting wages need not mean a general reduction of real earnings, because low wages keep down the prices of the goods and services we all consume.

Openness to immigration and emigration is also important for the sake of a living society. A diverse population, comprising people with different starting points and values, provides a greater variety of perspectives on long-standing social problems, and perhaps also a better chance of finding creative solutions to them. Immigrants can take what is most viable in American culture and combine it with traditions of their own, and native-born Americans can do likewise. Cultural innovation almost always flows from the contact or fusion of different cultures. It is no coincidence that the United States, the most dynamic society in history, was built by immigrants. President Franklin Delano Roosevelt once opened a speech by saying, "My fellow immigrants." Even today, in spite of all the restrictions, the United States receives far more immigrants than other countries. In this way the United States is constantly renewing itself and laying the foundations of continued global leadership—economic, cultural, and scientific.

IV

The development of the developing countries

An unequal distribution—of capitalism

Twenty percent of the world's population (we often hear) consumes more than 80 percent of the earth's resources, while the other 80 percent consume less than 20 percent. Critics of globalization never tire of reminding us of this injustice. Far less often do we hear a proper analysis of the reason for this state of affairs. The critics make it sound as though the poor are poor *because* the rich are rich, as if the richest 20 percent had somehow stolen those resources from the other 80 percent. That is wrong. Natural resources were, of course, stolen in the age of imperialism, but those thefts have played a relatively small part in the prosperity of the Western world and the poverty of the poor. Even though colonialism did great harm and was cruelly oppressive in places, this in itself does not account for differences between North and South. The affluent world has grown fastest since losing its colonies. And the regions the imperialist countries subjugated grew faster after becoming colonies than they had previously. Several of the world's richest countries—such as Switzerland and the Scandinavian countries—never had any colonies of importance. Others, such as the United States, Canada, Australia, New Zealand, Hong Kong, and Singapore, were colonies themselves. On the other hand, several of the world's least developed countries—Afghanistan, Liberia, and Nepal, for example—have never been colonies.

Perhaps surprisingly, it is not the countries with abundant raw materials that have grown fastest. In fact, those countries are often held back because abundant natural resources can reduce the incentive to develop good policies and institutions. It is no accident that the major oil producing nations of the Middle East and Africa are all, with the exception of Kuwait, ranked "unfree" by Freedom House. State-owned oil wells provide the region's despotic regimes with funds they could not otherwise obtain without freeing up their economies.

The main reason for that 20 percent consuming 80 percent of resources is that they *produce* 80 percent of resources. The 80 percent consume only 20 percent because they produce only 20 percent of resources. It is this latter problem we ought to tackle— the inadequate productive capacity of the poor countries of the world—instead of waxing indignant over the affluent world producing so much. The problem is that many people are poor, not that certain people are rich.

Critics of capitalism point out that per capita GDP is more than 30 times greater in the world's 20 richest countries than in the 20 poorest. The critics are right to say that this inequality is due to capitalism—but not for the reasons they think. The difference is due to certain countries having taken the path of capitalism, resulting in fantastic prosperity for their inhabitants, while those choosing to impede ownership, trade, and production have lagged behind. Factors such as climate and natural disasters are not unimportant, but most of the gap can still be put down to certain countries having opted for liberalization and others for control. The 20 economically most liberal countries in the world have a per capita GDP about 29 times greater than the 20 economically least liberal. If, then, we are serious about closing the North-South divide, we should hope with all our hearts that the South will also gain access to a free economy and open markets. Developing countries that have had openness in recent decades have not only grown faster than other developing countries—they have grown faster than the affluent countries too.

The world's inequality is due to capitalism. Not to capitalism having made certain groups poor, but to its making its practitioners wealthy. *The uneven distribution of wealth in the world is due to the uneven distribution of capitalism.*

Arguments that capitalism is somehow to blame for world poverty are oddly contradictory. Some argue that capital and corporations make their way only into the affluent countries, leaving the poor ones up the proverbial creek. Others maintain that capital and corporations flock to poor countries with low production costs, to the detriment of workers in the developed world. The truth seems to be that they make their way into both. Trade and investment flows in the past two decades have come to be more and more evenly distributed among the economies that are relatively open to the rest of the world. It is the really closed economies that, for obvious reasons, are not getting investments and trade. Moreover, the differences between these groups of countries are increasing. Clearly, instead of globalization marginalizing certain regions, it is the regions that stand back from globalization that become marginalized.[1]

A quarter of direct international investments between 1988 and 1998 went to developing countries. Since the beginning of the 1980s, investment flows from industrialized to developing countries have risen from $10 billion to $200 billion annually. If we look only at capital flows to the developing world, we find that 85 percent of direct investment there goes to a mere 10 countries, often the most liberalizing. But because those investments have been growing by 12 percent annually in the past three decades, tremendous increases also accrue for countries not included in the top 10.

Between 1990 and 2000, private investors channeled a trillion dollars from the affluent world to the poor countries in direct investments. That is roughly ten times as much as in earlier decades, and it also happens to be rather more than the sum total of assistance given by all affluent countries to all developing countries during the past 50 years. Of course, unlike development assistance, such investments are not primarily intended to alleviate poverty. But in the long term, investment makes a far greater contribution to that goal, because it develops the country's productive forces instead of flowing to governments, which may or may not use that aid wisely.

The affluent OECD countries accounted for 80 percent of world GDP in 1975, a share that has fallen to 70 percent today. As has already been mentioned, poor countries opting for economic liberalization and free trade have had *faster* growth than the affluent countries in recent decades. Free trade and economic liberalism, it seems, are a way for developing countries not only to get richer, but also, possibly, to catch up with the wealthier countries. As UN Secretary-General Kofi Annan said at an UNCTAD Conference held in February of 2000, soon after the demonstrations against the WTO:

> *The main losers in today's very unequal world are not those who are too much exposed to globalization. They are those who have been left out.*

Africa is the most prominent example. Isolation and regulation cause poor countries to remain poor countries.

The white man's shame

Although the Western world has paid lip service to free trade, it has not done very much to aid the process. On the contrary, its highest barriers have been raised against the developing countries, a policy that persists today. In the big rounds of free trade negotiations, tariffs and quotas for the Western world's export products have been steadily reduced. In the areas of greatest importance to the developing countries, such as textiles and agricultural produce, liberalization measures have failed to materialize. The tariff reductions agreed to during the Uruguay Round of WTO negotiations were smallest for the least developed countries. Asia and Latin America gained relatively little. Africa gained nothing at all.

Today, Western duties on export commodities from the developing world are 30 percent above the global average. The iron curtain between East and West has fallen, only to be replaced by a customs curtain between North and South. This is not just an act of omission; it is a deliberate attempt to keep poor states out of the running. We may allow them to sell us a few things that we are unable to produce ourselves, but heaven help them if they threaten to put us out of business by doing something cheaper and better than we can. The Western world maintains higher tariffs on clothing than on cotton, on roasted coffee than on coffee beans, and on marmalades and jams than on the fruits they are made from. Protectionism is a way of penalizing work inputs and development and of ensuring that poor countries sell us only raw materials, which we then process and resell to them as finished products. Duties on processed products from the developing countries are no less than four times higher than duties on corresponding goods from industrialized countries.

It is goods of the very kind that the Third World could produce that are worst hit by protectionism—labor-intensive industrial goods and services such as toys, electronics, transportation services, textiles, and garments. If the duties are between 10 and 30 percent of the value of the goods, a substantial difference in quality and price is necessary for those goods to get into our markets at all. The Western countries have pledged themselves to remove their textile quotas by 2005, but even if that pledge is honored— which is uncertain—textile tariffs will remain, averaging about 12 percent.

The developing countries would be the principal beneficiaries of increased global free trade in manufactures. One study estimated that the world economy would gain about $70 billion a year from a 40 percent tariff reduction, and that some 75 percent of the total gains would be harvested by the developing countries.[2] That would equal the total amount of international development assistance to the developing countries, and it is almost three times the monthly income of all the world's absolutely poor taken together. The absence of a real breakthrough in WTO talks is a tragedy for the people of those countries.

The most startling protectionism on the part of the affluent countries concerns agricultural produce. World trade in agriculture is growing far more slowly than trade in other commodities, and this too is due to the policy of the affluent countries. Most of them are determined at all costs to maintain a large-scale agricultural industry of their own, even if they have no comparative advantages in this sector. They therefore subsidize their own farmers and exclude those of other countries by means of trade barriers.

There is no easier way of squandering money than through an advanced agricultural policy. Affluent countries are drenching farmers with money through protectionism, subsidies, and export grants. The total cost of agricultural policy in the 29 affluent OECD countries burdens taxpayers and consumers with a staggering $360 billion. For that money, you could fly the 56 million cows in these countries once around the world every year—business class—with plenty of change left over. If they're willing to fly coach, the cows could also be given $2,800 each in pocket money to spend in tax-free shops during their stopovers in the United States, the EU, and Asia.[3]

The European Union's Common Agricultural Policy (CAP) involves quotas on foodstuffs, and tariffs of about 100 percent on things like sugar and dairy products. Here again, the EU wishes to exclude processed products that can compete with European ones. Tariffs on basic foodstuffs average only half of those on upgraded foodstuffs. Coffee and cocoa, which European countries don't produce themselves, can slip in without any serious customs markups. Meanwhile EU tariffs on meat are several hundred percent. The hollowness of self-appointed solidarity movements like the French ATTAC is exposed by their defense of such tariffs against the Third World.[4]

Not only is the EU excluding foreign products, but production and transport by European farmers are being subsidized to a fantastic degree, by nearly half the EU budget. The average cow receives $2.50 support daily, at the same time that nearly three billion of the world's human inhabitants have less than $2.00 a day to live on. Because those grants are paid according to acreage and head of livestock, they are mainly a subsidy for the wealthiest large-scale operations—it is rumored that the biggest beneficiary is the British royal family. OECD figures show the wealthiest 20 percent of farmers receiving something like 80 percent of the grants. In other words, nearly 40 percent of the entire EU budget goes to less than one percent of the EU's population.

The grants give rise to a huge surplus of foodstuffs, which has to be disposed of. One way that the EU does this is by paying farmers *not* to grow anything. Worse still, through export subsidies the EU dumps its surplus on the world market, so that poor countries are unable to compete. That means that the CAP not only prevents Third World farms from selling to Europeans, it also knocks them out of business in their own countries.

For consumers in the developed world, as was previously argued, export subsidies in other countries are a gift: the artificially low cost of goods is paid by foreign taxpayers, and the savings can be diverted to other sectors. But for the developing world, the North's agricultural policy is a different story. It is a deliberate and systematic means of undermining the very type of industry in which the developing countries do have comparative advantages. The poor countries don't get a stable supply of specific goods; rather, one year the EU dumps one product that is being overproduced then, but the next year it dumps a totally different product, thus undermining any attempt by producers in the poor country to specialize. It is one thing for imports to spur farmers to produce more competitively, but subsidies guarantee that farmers in the developed world cannot compete, even when they are more efficient. These countries are so poor that there are few other sectors in which to invest: most of them must expand agriculture before other sectors can be developed. The CAP is estimated to cause the developing countries a welfare loss in the region of $20 billion annually, which is twice Kenya's entire GDP.[5]

The EU's trade policy is irrational and shameful. It protects a small circle of lobbyists and farmers who ignore the fact that their walls are condemning people in other continents to poverty and death. That is a moral disaster. The cynicism of the policy is made all the more apparent by the realization that the EU as a whole gains nothing by it either. The Swedish government's calculations suggest that a Swedish household with two children could gain about $250 a year by being spared the EU's duties on garments, and no less than $1,200 a year if all agricultural policies were abolished.[6] European taxpayers pay millions of dollars in taxes every year so that their shops can have a smaller selection of food at higher prices. EU governments subsidize agriculture to the tune of about $90 billion a year and the manufacture of basic industrial products by about the same amount. All cracks through which goods from the developing countries could sneak in are promptly plugged with antidumping tariffs and technical stipulations, concerning, for example, packaging and hygiene—stipulations exclusively tailored to EU enterprises.

On the basis of statistics from the European Commission, the French economist Patrick Messerlin has estimated the cost of all EU trade barriers, including tariffs, quotas, export subsidies, antidumping measures, and the like. His findings indicate a total annual loss of 5–7 percent of the EU's GDP. In other words, completely free trade would mean that the EU could add the equivalent of nearly three Swedens to its prosperity every year. Messerlin maintains that roughly 3 percent of the jobs in the sectors he has investigated have been rescued by protectionism. Each job costs about $200,000 per year, which is roughly 10 times the average wage in these industries. For that money every tariff-protected worker could receive an annual Rolls Royce instead; it would not cost us more, and it would not be done at the expense of the world's poor.[7] "Either a branch of enterprise is profitable, in which case it needs no tariff protection; or else

160

it is unprofitable, in which case it deserves no tariff protection," as economist Eli F. Heckscher once put it.[8] With tariff protection and subsidies, manpower and capital that could have developed the EU's competitive strength linger on in sectors where there is no comparative advantage. Thus the EU ties the developing countries to poverty, not for the benefit of the European people, but for the sake of a narrow, vociferous vested interest.

The United States, which had miraculously bucked the special interests to roll back subsidies in 1996, has recently abandoned many of those gains. A bill passed in 2002 included subsidies projected to total $180 billion over the first 10 years alone. Those subsidies, too, disproportionately benefit the wealthy. The largest 7 percent of farms received 45 percent of subsidy payments in 1999.

Both the United States and the EU have introduced symbolic free trade reforms in relation to the poorest countries in recent years. The only trouble is that those reforms exclude the goods that would provide real competition for domestic producers in the North. The United States Africa Growth and Opportunity Act meant free trade in everything that Africa is not good at producing, and exclusion of goods like tobacco and peanuts. The EU's Everything-but-Arms initiative meant the abolition of tariffs against the world's least developed countries, but with long transitional periods of tariff retention for bananas, sugar, and rice. These measures are often rendered ineffective by strict rules concerning the origin of components of the relevant goods. Haiti is welcome to export coffee to the EU, but not T-shirts if the material is imported from another country, such as China. And other goods can be excluded by arbitrary environmental, security, or safety rules—rules often passed precisely for this protectionist effect, and not for their contribution to safety, security, or environmental quality.

161

It is, of course, hard to quantify the loss that the developing countries sustain as a result of protectionism, but many people try to. The British Labour government's white paper on globalization issues asserts that a 50 percent reduction of import duties in industrialized and developing countries would lead to a growth of prosperity in the developing countries by something like $150 billion, or three times as much as global development assistance. The United Nations Trade and Development Program (UNCTAD) claims that, with greater access to the markets of the affluent countries, exports from the developing world would grow by about $700 billion annually. That is 14 times the development assistance they receive.[9]

The case of Latin America

One traditional fear concerning trade between North and South is that it would make the Third World dependent on selling raw materials to affluent countries in the North. If the developing countries were to practice free trade, on this view, they would never succeed in getting industrialized and selling other products. Many have therefore taken the position that they should go in for "import substitution," with the government building up native industry behind high tariff walls and expanding it by starting to manufacture goods that would otherwise have to be imported. The aim was a kind of self-sufficiency—being able to fend for oneself instead of specializing and making oneself dependent on world trade. This "dependency theory" rapidly gained ground after World War II, and it had plenty of adherents in the West. That is why Western observers in the 1960s expected North Korea, a closed economy, to outdistance export-oriented South Korea, and Mao's China to have far better prospects than pro-trade Taiwan. Import substitution was practiced by India and Africa, but the whole idea was modeled on post-war Latin America.[10]

It was not surprising that politicians in Chile, Brazil, and Argentina, among others, fell for the dependency school. Since the mid-19th century, the region had experienced an economic upturn through the export of a few central raw materials, such as coffee, bananas, sugar, cotton, and copper. But that still did not bring any broad-based national development, because the countries in question were typical societies of privilege. A small, protected landlord class owned enormous tracts of land, which were worked by legions of destitute unskilled workers, who were often paid in kind with goods from the estates. This tiny elite reaped huge profits, but did not invest them. They had no need of labor saving machinery, because there was a superabundance of labor, and they did not need to improve crop yields, because they had vast acreages at their disposal. If new lands were needed, they were simply stolen from the native population. Agriculture did not develop, and no demand was created for manufactured goods, because incomes did not grow. Among the elite, both technology and organizing ability were conspicuously absent. Low education, discrimination, and trade regulations made it impossible for those in the labor force to start up small businesses. The Latin American economies remained dependent on exports of a few raw materials. When, in about 1930, the international economy collapsed and the affluent countries reintroduced protectionism, it came as a deathblow to the states of Latin America. Suddenly everything that had built up their economies had vanished.

What this example shows is that trade alone does not necessarily create dynamic development in an oppressive society. If a country is static and characterized by enormous privileges and discrimination, there is little chance of trade solving all these problems. For that to happen, the population must acquire liberty and the opportunity of economic participation. Land reforms to put an end to centuries of feudalism would have been needed, coupled with a commitment to education and free markets. But those were not the conclusions drawn by the rulers of Latin America and the Marxist academics who developed the theory of dependence. History, they argued, showed that trade was pernicious and that countries should aim for self-sufficiency and internal industrialization. They pointed to the wrong villain. The Latin American

164

countries retained privileges and national intervention, but tried to abolish trade.

The policy the Latin American countries then proceeded to apply was a textbook example of protectionism—and of economic suicide. The government paid heavy grants to a native industry protected by sky-high tariff walls. During the 1950s, strict import prohibitions and quotas were introduced, and tariffs averaged between 100 and 200 percent. Because consumers were unable to buy goods from other countries, native industries were able to raise their output quickly and generate high growth. However, because they were under no pressure from competition, they did not develop technically or organizationally. Instead, an already outmoded and inefficient industry was heavily expanded. Home market prices being higher than those on the world market, the companies became less interested in exporting. The economy became more and more politicized as the government attempted to direct manpower, prices, and production to encourage industrialization. Government power over the economy grew steadily— in Argentina even the circuses were nationalized. Firms therefore began devoting more resources and energy to currying favor with those in power than to streamlining production. Strong interest groups were formed, which campaigned to obtain benefits or to obtain compensation for benefits granted to others. Distribution was governed more and more by the political struggle and less and less by market transactions.

Those who did not occupy a strong position and were not members of powerful coalitions—Indians, rural workers, small entrepreneurs, and the shanty town populations—lagged further and further behind. Tariffs took the bread out of their mouths, and when inflation was accelerated to finance ballooning government spending, they found their small savings obliterated as the value

165

of the currency plummeted. The countries of Latin America remained societies of privilege, and already-large inequalities escalated to appalling levels. Luxury palaces were built even as slums sprawled. Some people were born with silver spoons in their mouths, others as starving street children. Rio de Janeiro has been described as a bit of Paris surrounded by a bit of Ethiopia. The wealthiest 10 percent in Brazil cornered more than half the country's GDP (as compared with roughly a quarter in the United States and a fifth in Sweden). At the same time, the ruling classes diverted discontent by pointing to outside enemies. To protect themselves, they insisted that absolutely nothing was wrong with their own policies—that the fault lay entirely with foreigners and the United States.

Poor consumers were forced to pay exorbitant prices in shops, while big industrialists grew richer and richer behind the tariff walls. A car in the 1960s cost more than three times as much in Chile as it did on the world market, with the result that only the rich could buy one. Price increases also afflicted industry, which needed things like trucks for transporting goods. Because products made on the wrong side of the tariff barriers were not allowed to be sold in the protected market, the governments managed to attract some foreign firms. But Western companies did not bring new methods; instead, they quickly adjusted to the national policy. Instead of specializing and improving efficiency, they became jacks-of-all-trades, manufacturing every conceivable thing that people could not buy from abroad. Whole corporate departments concentrated on bureaucracy in order to obtain start-up permits, cheap credits, special prices, and public contracts. Keeping cozy with the establishment became the path to profit for companies, making them an unsavory political power factor. This internal focus prevented them from achieving economies of scale by

166

expanding their markets, and the lack of competition meant that they never developed their technology and organization.

Latin American industry became more and more antiquated in relation to the rest of the world. Unable to face international competition after long years of protection, Latin America became more and more dependent on privileges and tariffs, which in turn caused it to lag still further behind. Paradoxically, exports of the old raw materials became more and more important as a means of financing the growing imports of machinery and semi-manufactured goods that industry needed. Because the government diverted resources away from agriculture and exports, however, those sectors were hampered more and more. The possibility of developing the only industries capable of withstanding international competition dried up. Millions of people left the land for the city slums. In the end, the exploitative economy could not sustain the antiquated industrial sector. Massive loans during the 1970s merely postponed the inevitable, and the backlash was all the stronger in 1982 when Mexico suspended loan payments and set off a debt crisis of unique proportions. In three years, Latin America's per capita income plunged by 15 percent, and the 1980s brought a long succession of financial crises and hyperinflation. It was only after liberalization and free trade reforms, inaugurated toward the end of the decade, that certain of these countries got back on their feet and were able to raise their growth. The problem is that the huge burden of debt and lack of foreign trade are still making these countries crisis-prone. We saw this in connection with Argentina's 2001 economic crisis. If a country has very few exports with which to pay heavy interest charges and debt installments, even small imbalances in its budget are enough to rock the entire economy. The people of Latin America are still footing the bill for the society of privilege and protectionism.

167

The Chilean example demonstrates the possibility of development, even in this region. When dictator Augusto Pinochet's continuation of the old policy of inflation and central control failed to lift the plunging economy, he began listening to market economists instead. Unlike other authoritarian regimes in the region, Chile replaced its authoritarian economic policy with liberalization and free trade about 1975. Tremendous growth ensued, with real earnings more than doubling by 1995, at the same time as infant mortality fell from 6 percent to just over 1 percent, and average life expectancy rose from 64 to 73 years. Chileans today have almost a southern European standard of living, in stark contrast to their neighbors. Most important of all, the bloodstained dictatorship has been peacefully superseded by a stable democratic regime—just as the liberal advisers advocated and prophesied.[11]

On the trade route

The possibility of breaking free of dependence on raw materials lies in free trade rather than protectionism. Instead of a shield behind which industry could grow strong, the tariff walls became a shield from competition that made them less efficient and innovative. The developing countries that have switched fastest from exporting raw materials to exporting upgraded products are those that have themselves had the most open economies, above all the Asian countries. Sachs and Warner's major survey of the effects of trade shows that protectionist countries have transformed their economic structure very slowly, whereas free trade countries have moved more in the direction of industrial production.[12] This is directly contrary to what the advocates of the dependency theory contended. Some of them have learned from their mistakes. The sociologist Fernando Henrique Cardoso, whose own work had included important contributions to dependency theory, was elected president of Brazil in 1994, and tried to introduce measures to liberalize trade! Now developing countries are demanding in trade negotiations that the affluent markets be opened to their exports.

Free trade has greater possibilities than ever of bringing dynamic growth in developing countries. A hundred years ago, globalization primarily meant the West collecting raw materials from developing countries and bringing them home for processing. This process did little to disseminate new technology and new opportunities. Production and processing could not be established in the developing world, because sending a spare part or important personnel there could take months. Today, a factory almost anywhere on earth can dispatch and receive deliveries to or from any destination within a week and a half, and be reached instantly by phone, fax, or e-mail. That means it is now possible to base activities on what used to be the periphery of the world economy, while still keeping in permanent touch with the rest of the world. Even the very core of production can be relocated to poor countries if they have comparative advantages in the sector concerned, which means fantastic opportunities for those who have not had the good fortune to be born in an affluent country.

The above applies not only to manufacturing but also to the service sector. Thanks to satellite communication and the Internet, many foreign companies can place parts of their administrative routines in countries like India, where local inhabitants can be hired for the remote management of things like payroll, invoicing, ticket reservations, and customer services for European and American corporations. This is especially convenient to American business, with India waking up at roughly the same time as Americans go to bed. Even the surveillance of office blocks can be managed from halfway around the world with the aid of satellite imaging. In these labor-intensive services, developing countries have obvious comparative advantages. They get employment and higher wages, at the same time as the services are made cheaper to their customers in the industrialized countries.

Exports of industrial goods from the developing countries have risen rapidly in the past 30 years, thanks to improved communications and global free trade reforms. The dependency theory has been proved wrong by history. Today, manufactured products account for roughly three-quarters of exports from the developing countries, compared with only a quarter in 1965. The economic centrality of raw material exports is diminishing all the time. Whereas at the beginning of the 1970s the developing countries accounted for only 7 percent of global exports of manufactured goods, today they provide more than a quarter.

The developing countries export more manufactured goods

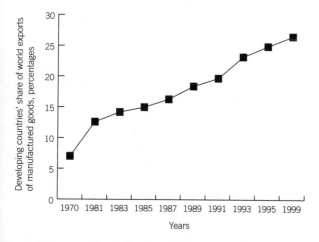

Source: Ajit K. Ghose, *Trade Liberalization and Manufacturing Employment.* Employment Paper 2000/3 (Geneva: International Labour Office, 2000), and Overseas Development Institute, *Developing Countries in the WTO.* Briefing Paper 3 (London: Overseas Development Institute, 1995).

Mexico is a case in point. Long regarded as dependent on rudimentary exports to the United States, Mexico's position has changed rapidly, parallel to its conversion to a policy of free trade. As recently as 1980, only 0.7 percent of its exports were processed. By 1990 this figure had risen to 3.7 percent, and in 1995, after NAFTA had abolished tariffs between Mexico and the United

States, it had risen to 19.3 percent. The country's having advanced, in six short years, from the world's 26th to the 8th largest exporter can be termed a bonus in this connection, and helps to account for the country's growth running at nearly 5 percent annually since 1996.[13]

Critics sometimes complain that labor-intensive industries once emigrated to Japan because wages there were low and, when wages rose, moved on to South Korea and Taiwan. When production costs rose in those countries, the industries moved to Malaysia and Thailand, for example, and today they are beginning to relocate in China and Vietnam. That, the critics believe, is an example of the ruthlessness of capital—leaving countries in the lurch for paying higher wages. As soon as a country's growth and prosperity get started, that country is deserted by companies and investors. But this process is more a case of constantly raising the level of upgrading in production. When a country is poor, it is best at the simplest and least skilled jobs. But when it grows richer, its production more efficient and its population more skilled, it does better out of more qualified, technology-intensive production, and eventually out of knowledge-intensive production. Step by step the economy goes on developing, while poorer countries, relatively speaking, become better performers in more labor-intensive industry. Mexicans are exporting fewer raw materials and more manufactured goods, while Americans are moving more and more from manufactured goods to computer programming and consulting services. In this way the world economy is growing more and more efficient, and at the same time making room for more and more regions and countries. That is why East Asian economies have been likened to a flock of geese. From their different positions in the flock, they have all moved forward to better positions, step by step.

"Let them keep their tariffs"

There are critics of free trade, especially in the churches and in development assistance organizations, whose position stands traditional protectionism on its head. They perceive the absurdity of the affluent world preventing developing countries, by means of tariffs, from exporting to its markets. At the same time, however, they feel that the developing countries should be wary of buying things from us and should therefore protect their markets with tariffs until they have become affluent enough. Often, those critics make it sound as if we do people in developing countries a service by not arguing against their politicians' protectionism. We must "let them keep their tariffs."

This argument may seem reasonable at first blush—if people are poor, they must be allowed to derive earnings from exports, but not made to lose them through imports that might put their own industries out of business. Their industries need "infant industry tariffs" and cannot be exposed to competition until they are competitive. But as we have now seen, it is open countries whose industry develops fastest. Tariffs forced consumers to buy from companies in their own countries, with the result that the companies grew richer. But, not being exposed to competition, they were under no pressure to improve efficiency and realign their production, or to lower the prices of their goods. This policy, accordingly, enabled the elite to enrich themselves while the great mass of the people were forced to pay more for their everyday necessities, being unable to get them anywhere else. To say that the poor gain by just exporting and not importing is to forget that they are consumers as well as producers. "Letting the developing countries keep their tariffs," then, is tantamount to "letting the developing countries forbid their citizens to choose from a wide variety of goods."

The belief that politicians know better than the market and investors which enterprises can become competitive in the long run is sheer superstition. On the contrary, this protective policy is a way of dismantling market mechanisms that separate failed projects from successful ones. There are few good examples of successful governmental industrial initiatives, and any number of examples of expensive flops: India's failed industrial sector, Brazil's attempt to create an information technology industry, the automotive industries of the South American countries, and Suharto's protection of the Indonesian motor industry (headed, coincidentally, by his son). Japan's department of industry, MITI, is sometimes referred to as a planning success, and it did do relatively well, but mainly by responding to signals from the market. By contrast, its efforts to create new industries independently of the market were less successful. MITI invested billions, for example, in fast breeder reactors, a fifth generation computer, and a remote-controlled oil rig, all of which were expensive failures. Happily—for the Japanese—MITI also failed to throttle certain sectors, as it might have in the early 1950s when it attempted to phase out the small car producers and prevent Sony from importing transistor technology.[14] In the West, there are expensive failures like the Anglo-French Concorde and Swedish digital television.

The grim fact is that in many cases political leaders have not even tried to make an objective assessment of what can be profitable, but have based their decisions on lobbying and corruption, or a desire for prestige. Tariff walls, which were supposed to afford temporary protection for viable enterprises, instead gave permanent protection to inefficient corporations. What was intended as a crucible of development became a lush greenhouse for backroom politics and slush money. Even if, in theory, that might occasionally be a successful policy, how do we know that it will be implemented in the right field once the political battle is joined? We ought to ask why poor states should devote their few resources to reckless, mammoth industrial projects when there are other things they could enact that are certain to bring distinct benefits: economic reforms, a liberal regulatory structure, investment in education and health.

The argument for Third World tariffs also rests on ignorance of a very important fact: much developing-country trade is with other developing countries. About 40 percent of exports from the developing countries go to other developing countries. If poor consumers are forced to pay high prices for products from companies in their own countries, they will generally be prevented from buying from companies in neighboring countries, in which case the producers will also lose out. The producers may get a monopoly in their own market, but they are forbidden to sell to other markets. Developing countries' tariffs against other developing countries today are more than two and a half times higher than the industrialized countries' tariffs against developing countries. Tariffs in the industrialized countries average about 8 percent, those of the developing countries 21 percent. Thus, more than 70 percent of the customs dues people in developing countries are forced to pay are levied by other developing countries.[15]

That is the main reason why the developing countries, which constitute only a quarter of the global economy, are forced to bear no less than 40 percent of the global cost of tariffs. One of the greatest benefits the developing countries can derive from free trade is the abolition of the import tariffs, which sometimes multiply commodity prices several times over. Those who believe that supporting tariffs makes them friends of the developing countries fail to realize that they are actually helping a small clique of companies and rulers in the developing countries, to the detriment of the consumers and broader economies of those societies.

If we in the affluent countries truly believe in free trade, we must abolish our tariffs and quotas without demanding concessions from others. Forbidding the poor of the world to develop is immoral. Besides, we ourselves stand to benefit from freer imports, even if others do not want to import from us. But that does not mean that it is wise of the Third World to protect its own industries with trade barriers. On the contrary, the best thing for their populations is for their tariffs also to be abolished. Those who want them to preserve their tariffs may constitute an inverted, mirror image of traditional protectionists, but the face in the mirror is no more attractive than the original.

The debt trap

In the debate on globalization, severe criticism has been leveled at global economic institutions. Most often singled out are the World Bank (WB), which leads multilateral work for long-term development in the Third World, and the International Monetary Fund (IMF), which exists to guide and assist national financial systems, especially in times of crisis. Critics maintain that those institutions serve as collectors of debts from developing countries to the affluent world, and that they force developing countries to implement heavy-handed liberal policies that lead to greater poverty. Left-wing groups and churches the world over say that the WB and the IMF should be democratized and Third World debts should be written off.

"Democratized" means that all countries should have equal voting rights in these institutions, as opposed to power commensurate with the financial contributions they make. That may sound right, but these are basically development aid organizations, and countries choosing to channel their development assistance through them expect to have a say in how the money they give is going to be used. All countries could be given equal power over the funds, but that would only result in countries like the United States withdrawing and sending their money through other channels. That would mean the end of the IMF and the WB, which in its way, of course, would effectively settle the dispute over them, but hardly in the way most of the critics had envisaged.

The IMF and the WB have a great deal on their consciences, mistakes that a liberal should criticize them for. Criticism ought, for example, to be leveled against their many decades of argument in favor of planned economies in the developing countries and against the WB's involvement in sterilization programs—programs that have involved serious abuses against the persons affected by them. The same goes for large-scale projects, such as dam construction projects, which have involved the compulsory relocation of thousands of people. But the opponents of globalization do not often criticize activities of this kind. Instead, they direct their ire at recommendations of low inflation and balanced budgets. But demands of this kind on developing countries are not just orders from above. They are conditions that the institutions place on loans to countries that have acute financial deficits and are on the verge of bankruptcy. Like all credit providers, they would prefer to be paid back, and so they insist on reforms that would allow the country to emerge from its crisis and eventually be capable of repaying what it has borrowed. There is nothing fundamentally wrong with this attitude, and the recommendations (termed structural adjustment programs) have often been healthy: a balanced budget, a lower rate of inflation, greater competition, open markets, less corruption and more rule of law, and a reduction of military spending in favor of things like education and health care. Much work has also been devoted to establishing greater transparency and to cleaning up shady dealings and nepotism between rulers and economic players.

But there are a number of contentious cases where recommendations from these institutions have been destructive—for example, their actions during the Asian crisis. Sharp criticism can be leveled against the demand for contraction in countries that were already entering a profound depression. In September 1997, for instance, tax increases forced on Thailand by the IMF deepened the economic crisis to an alarming degree. In certain cases, the IMF has recommended that governments retain excessively high exchange rates, thereby triggering speculation. Constant crisis packages can also prompt investors and governments to take bigger risks than they otherwise would, because they know that if they get out of their depth, as Russia did in 1998, the IMF will jump in to save them. From a liberal perspective, it is bizarre that taxpayers are forced to pay for the mistakes of speculators. A central canon of the capitalistic system, after all, is that unsuccessful investors must themselves bear the cost of their failure. Other critics say that the IMF has generally been too micromanaging, instead of simply issuing general recommendations. Using promises of multimillion dollar payments, IMF bureaucrats have tried to exercise an almost colonial degree of remote control over other countries' policies. We are perfectly right to insist that Third World rulers extend basic democratic rights and liberties to their peoples, but we must not attempt to control the details of their policymaking.

The foremost lesson to learn from a couple of decades of IMF and WB recommendations is how insignificant is their actual impact on the countries receiving the funds. To many governments in real crisis, IMF and WB loans have provided a last chance to avoid real and drastic economic reforms. Countries have only needed to *promise* reforms in order for huge sums of money to be placed at their disposal. Rulers then play a perilous two-sided game, implementing just enough minor reforms to keep the IMF envoys happy. With the wisdom of hindsight, Russia's finance minister Boris Fyodorov maintains that the IMF's grants to Russia have delayed the liberal reforms that the country would otherwise have been obliged to introduce. Instead of pursuing a good policy, his colleagues decided that it would be more patriotic to raise the biggest possible loans and then start negotiating about the writing off of debts.

It is very dangerous to suppose that reforms can be brought about from outside by means of economic inducements. In the majority of cases, resource transfers of this kind have had the effect of propping up a failed system. Assistance, if it is to have any positive effects, must come after reforms begin. When, in 1994, the WB reviewed 26 different structural adjustment programs, it found that only 6 of them had led to a serious change of policy. Above all, those in power could not, or would not, reduce and streamline bureaucracy and their own control of the economy. Countries have sometimes tried to meet certain important stipulations, such as budgetary balance, by destructive policies such as increasing taxes and tariffs, printing more money, or slashing the most important public spending—on education and health—instead of subsidies, bureaucracy, and the military.

Another problem is that readjustment programs are often too complicated for inefficient governments to implement. When a corrupt government has to take account of perhaps a hundred different stipulations and guidelines at once, things get difficult, especially as it must simultaneously keep track of any number of other aid programs from individual countries. Because these structural adjustment programs are often quite vaguely written, it is easy for governments to delay and undermine them. Breaches of the programs have led to a cancellation of payments, but, bizarrely, the funding tap has been turned full on again as soon as the politicians have verbally promised renewed compliance. That, it seems, can be repeated indefinitely. One analyst maintained that 15 years of structural adjustment programs in Africa had meant only "minimally more openness to the global economy."[17]

The unwillingness of the recipient countries to follow the advice given makes it wrong to point to the IMF's liberalizing recommendations as the cause of those countries' profound crises, as many left-wing movements do. Countries that actually followed the recommendations have apparently done better than countries that have not. Those complying with them—Uganda and Ghana, for example—have on average had higher growth and thus reduced poverty. States that eschewed such liberalization programs—Nigeria, Kenya, and Zambia, for example—remain economically unimpressive, having become bogged down in poverty and inequality of fearful dimensions.[18]

So what about debt cancellation? I believe there are good reasons for it, but also risks involved if we do not go about it in the right way. We should note at the outset, though, that the debate is exaggerated. Critics of the IMF and the WB claim that something like 20,000 people die in the developing countries every day because of debt. That figure is reached by adding up the interest payments that developing countries are forced to make to these institutions and then working out how many human lives could be saved for the same amount of money. Even if we grant the fanciful supposition that all the money would otherwise go to medicines and food instead of munitions, which is not at all credible, the claim overlooks another important fact. These debt-ridden countries receive more credits, grants, and development assistance from the industrialized countries and global institutions every year than they pay in interest. The 41 most highly indebted poor countries (HIPCs) receive about twice as much from the Western world as they pay every year. So to accuse the Western world of causing the deaths of tens of thousands of people in the developing countries every day by collecting interest payments is a grotesque statistical trick.[19]

Even so, debt cancellation is right in principle. Opponents of debt relief say that one should pay one's debts, which of course is true. The only question is why one should be forced to pay other people's debts. Suppose a dictator borrows masses of money to build up his country's military machine and his own fortune, but then, after political upheavals, a democratic regime takes over and finds itself clutching an armful of IOUs. Why should taxpayers be liable for a debt they never chose to take on? Is it not more reasonable for the borrowers to bear the risk of the country not being able to pay the money back? Ordinary market institutions have learned from experience and have long since given up advancing money to deeply indebted countries, while political institutions like the IMF and the WB have gone on sending money at every economic crisis. Through a combination of generosity and irrationality, they lured many developing countries into the debt trap during the 1980s. Most of those countries have absolutely no chance of paying off their debt, and perpetuation of the debt trap will do no one any good. A country like Tanzania has a foreign debt that is twice as large as its annual export revenues, and debt service does displace things like the funding of education for the young. Because challenging privilege, slashing subsidies, and laying off civil servants are politically hazardous, the long-term investments often suffer when cutbacks are needed.

That is not to say that unconditional debt cancellation for all countries, the sort of thing advocated by such popular movements as the Jubilee 2000 campaign, is an entirely good idea. On the contrary, cancellation can mean the Western world financing corrupt regimes that use the money to buy arms and consolidate oppression. In that case we have helped to perpetuate unsavory regimes, which again is not a very moral thing to do. To avoid doing so, certain demands should be made for democracy and reforms, parallel to debts being canceled. One of the problems of debt cancellation is that it distorts the flows of development assistance, in favor, not of the poorest or of democracies, but of those who are most deeply in debt. In 1997, those countries received four times more development assistance per capita than equally poor but nonindebted countries. The Ivory Coast, for example, received 1,276 times more development assistance per capita than India.

Debt cancellation has been going on, to a greater or lesser extent, since 1979, when, following an UNCTAD meeting, the creditors canceled debts of 45 countries totaling $6 billion. The problem is that this policy has encouraged the contracting of further debts. Countries that have gotten rid of their debts have quickly replaced them with new loans. One study has shown that an increase in a country's debt cancellation equaling one percent of GDP between 1979 and 1997 entailed, on average, a 0.34 percent increase in its burden of debt. Moreover, the money has not been spent on good investments, and the respites have not been used to improve policy. On the contrary, one finds that debtor countries pursue worse policies and implement fewer long-term reforms than other poor countries. One grim guess is that these countries often borrow more instead of prioritizing their expenditure because they count on a future cancellation of debts, and that they put off liberal reforms until they can "sell" them to the IMF and WB for the greatest possible cancellation of debts. In September 1996, when the WB and IMF launched their initiative aimed at eventually writing off the debts of 41 countries rated "highly indebted," there had already been two decades of debt cancellation.[20]

These repeated cancellations are a sign of the policy's ineffectiveness. What would actually help is a "once and for all" strategy, whereby the debts of the poor, reform-oriented governments are written off at the same time that it is convincingly indicated that no more debts will be written off in the future. One way of doing this would be to cancel all debts now, then refrain from lending any more money. Instead, any loans would have to be contracted on the international capital market from investors who are willing to take the risk and who personally believe that they will get their money back. That, however, does not appear to have been the strategy when the WB and IMF signaled the exemption of 22 countries from two-thirds of their debts. True, the exemption measure was accompanied by various conditions, such as measures to combat corruption and heavier investment in education and health. But new loans may well be considered after the cancellations, in which case there is a serious risk of debts growing again, making a similar cancellation initiative necessary in 10 years' time.

Since the beginning of the 1960s, Africa has received development assistance equaling six times the aid sent by the United States under the Marshall Plan following World War II. If the money had gone to investments, African countries would have had a Western standard of living by now. Studies of development assistance show discouraging results. In many cases, assistance has been purely destructive and actually reduced national growth. In the words of the great international development economist Peter T. Bauer, development assistance is often tantamount to transferring money "from poor people in rich countries to rich people in poor countries." The problem is that the money sets up the wrong incentives. Trade encourages poor countries to boost their production and develop new ideas. Development assistance has instead given money to leaders who run their countries into poverty instead of developing them, with additional resources going to those who can display the least development. Because aid goes to the state and the politicians, it has become more lucrative in the countries concerned to try to seize government power than to produce and export. This has strengthened the central state, enabling it to exploit the countryside and destroy agriculture and potential industries. Development assistance has in many cases helped corrupt dictators cling to power. (Rulers such as Mobutu, Mugabe, Marcos, and Suharto have amassed fortunes in the billions while their countries' economies deteriorated.) Giving assistance without demanding democracy and reforms is tantamount to subsidizing dictatorships and stagnation. But there is some evidence that development assistance can strengthen economies—if they are already pursuing a successful policy, with property rights, open markets, and a stable budgetary and monetary policy. In those cases, of course, the aid is not really needed. And the likelihood of aid bureaucrats correctly identifying good policies, and then acting wisely, seems slim.[21]

The right medicine

One common objection to the market economy is that it causes people and enterprises to produce for profit, not for needs. This means, for example, pharmaceutical companies devoting huge resources to research and medicines to do with obesity, baldness, and depression, things that westerners can afford to worry about and pay for, whereas only a fraction is devoted to attempting to cure tropical diseases afflicting the poorest of the world's inhabitants, such as malaria and tuberculosis. This criticism is understandable. The unfairness exists, but capitalism is not to blame for it. Without capitalism and the lure of profit, we shouldn't imagine that everyone would have obtained cures for their illnesses. In fact, far fewer would do so than is now the case. If wealthy people in the West demand help for their problems, their resources can be used to research and eventually solve those problems, which are not necessarily trivial to the people afflicted with them. Capitalism gives companies economic incentives to help us by developing medicines and vaccines. That westerners spend money this way does not make things worse for anyone. This is not money that would otherwise have gone to researching tropical diseases—the pharmaceutical companies simply would not have had these resources otherwise. And, as free trade and the market economy promote greater prosperity in poorer countries, their needs and desires will play a larger role in dictating the purposes of research and production.

It is not a problem for the Third World that more and more diseases have been made curable in the Western world. On the contrary, that is something that has proved to be a benefit, and not just because a wealthier world can devote more resources to helping the poor. In many fields, the Third World can inexpensively share in the research financed by wealthy Western customers, sometimes paying nothing for it. The Merck Corporation gave free medicine to a project to combat onchocerciasis (river blindness) in 11 African states. As a result those states have now rid themselves almost completely of a parasite that formerly affected something like a million people, blinding thousands every year.[22] The Monsanto Corporation allows researchers and companies free use of their technique for developing "golden rice," a strain of rice enriched with iron and beta carotene (pro-vitamin A), which could save a million people annually in the Third World who are dying of vitamin A deficiency diseases. A number of pharmaceutical companies are lowering the prices of inhibitors for HIV/AIDS in poor countries by up to 95 percent, on condition that the patents are preserved so that they can maintain full prices in wealthier countries.

Companies can do these things because there are affluent markets with customers who can pay well. Those companies can only do what they have resources for; they cannot simply accept expenditure with no earnings. But that is what many people complaining about efforts by pharmaceutical companies to preserve their patents feel they should do. If patents for HIV/AIDS drugs were abolished altogether, far more poor people in the world would be able to afford them, because they could then be reproduced at very low cost. That might give people greater access to a medicine today, but it would drastically reduce availability in the future, because pharmaceutical companies spend huge amounts developing medicines. For every successful drug, there are on average 20 or 30 unsuccessful ones, and producing a new, marketable medicine can cost hundreds of millions of dollars. The high prices of the few medicines that can be sold are necessary in order to finance all this research. If patents disappeared, hardly any company would be able to afford the research and development of medicines. If we had not had patents before, there would be no controversy over the price of drugs to treat HIV/AIDS, because then those drugs would never have been invented.

It is not the pharmaceutical companies we have to blame for doing too little to cure diseases in developing countries. The industrialized countries could, for example, resolve to pay a certain amount for every child in the world vaccinated for malaria or for everyone receiving inhibitors for HIV/AIDS, as Jeffrey Sachs has proposed. If entrepreneurs and NGOs were to do that, businesses would have an incentive to research cures and vaccines. If curing disease in the Third World is a political goal, then surely it would be more reasonable to divide the costs among us all instead of putting costly demands solely on the pharmaceutical companies.

Unfortunately, the allocation of political resources is subject to—what else?—politics. Nowhere is this more obvious than in the World Health Organization (WHO), which as a specialist UN agency is financed out of tax revenue. Its aim is to assure the world's people the best possible health. There is an easy way of doing this. According to the WHO, six diseases—malaria, tuberculosis, and so on—together account for 90 percent of all deaths from infectious diseases among people under 44. Every year 11 million people die unnecessarily of these diseases. So one might expect the WHO to venture forth and begin vaccinating children and fighting diseases. They could solve one of the world's biggest problems tomorrow if they decided to. But no, the organization has actually moved this idea down on its list of priorities in recent years. Because of lack of resources? Hardly. According to the WHO, it would cost between $4 million and $220 million to prevent these deaths. That is just 0.4–20 percent of the WHO's annual budget! While children die unnecessarily, the WHO is devoting more and more of its annual $1 billion or more to exclusive conferences and to campaigning for the use of seat belts and against smoking. Problems of this kind are considered urgent in the rich countries, so bureaucrats must attend to them in order to preserve their funding.[23]

Personally, I believe we have more to expect from philanthropic capitalists than from politics. Capitalism does not force people to maximize their profit at every turn; it enables them to use their property as they see fit, free of political considerations. Microsoft's Bill Gates, the very personification of modern capitalism, himself devotes more to the campaign against disease in the developing countries than the American government does. Between November 1999 and 2000, through the $23 billion Bill and Melinda Gates Health Fund, $1.44 billion went to vaccinate children in developing countries for common diseases and to fund research into HIV/AIDS, malaria, and TB, for example, in developing countries. That is a quarter of what all industrialized nations combined devote to combating disease in the developing countries. So the fact that Bill Gates is worth more than $50 billion should give the poor and the sick of the world reason to rejoice. Clearly they would stand to gain more from a handful of Gateses than from the whole of Europe and another couple of WHOs.

V

Race to the top

I'm all for free trade, but . . .

The affluent countries take a highly protectionist stance against the developing countries as a result of vigorous lobbying by vested interests. Rarely, though, is this stance defended in public debate. Wanting to get rich at the Third World's expense is not, after all, a very attractive position. There is, however, a closely related type of protectionism that is considered far more presentable, namely the idea of making trade subject to certain conditions. "We're all for free trade," proponents of this approach say, and go on to add something like "but not on any terms whatsoever" or "but it needs a different set of rules." If someone starts off by saying "I'm all for free trade, but . . . ," you should listen very carefully to what follows, because if the "but" is strong enough, it means the person is not for free trade at all.

That is the way the discussion often goes in countries where free trade is a very positive concept.[1] In some countries, though, free trade is a term of abuse. Shout your love of global markets out loud on a Parisian street and you risk being pursued by an angry crowd. Certain globalization skeptics go so far as to assert that the discussion has nothing to do with "being for or against free trade," because everyone is in favor of some form of free trade. But the rules of genuine free trade, complete with rights of ownership and freedom of enterprise, are intended to facilitate free exchange and cannot in any way be equated with rules, prohibitions, and quotas aimed at restricting free exchange. The globalization discussion is necessarily concerned with being for or against free trade, and you are for it if you want more liberal rules of trade; otherwise, you are against it.

A commonly held protectionist view today is that we should not permit trade with countries with unacceptably bad working conditions or those that condone child labor or do not do enough to protect the environment. Otherwise, we permit other countries to put our firms out of business by dint of their inferior social conditions ("social dumping") or disregard for the environment ("eco-dumping"). When drawing up trade agreements with poor countries, some argue, we must always insist on provisions stipulating environmental or labor standards, and require our trading partners to improve their environmental policies or working conditions if they wish to remain trading partners. Not only unions and companies join in this chorus, but social movements as well. But to the developing countries, this approach is little more than the same old protection coupled with a neo-colonialist bid to control their policymaking.

The skeptical attitude of many in the developing world was given voice by Youssef Boutros-Ghali, Egypt's minister for trade: "The question is why all of a sudden, when third world labor has proved to be competitive, why do industrial countries start feeling concerned about our workers? . . . It is suspicious."[2]

It was after President Bill Clinton proposed this kind of boycott of countries not meeting certain requirements that the WTO talks in Seattle deadlocked at the end of 1999. Swedish trade minister Leif Pagrotsky spoke of "Clinton's great blunder," and the developing countries refused to negotiate under such threats.

Whatever well-heeled demonstrators and presidents in economically powerful countries may believe, low wages and poor environmental conditions in developing countries are not due to stinginess. There are, of course, exceptions, but generally the problem

193

is that employers cannot afford to pay higher wages and have better working conditions, because worker productivity is so low at low levels of national development. Wages can be raised as labor becomes more valuable, that is, in step with productivity, and that can be achieved only through increased investment, better infrastructure, more education, new machinery, and better organization. If we force these countries to raise wages before productivity has been improved, firms and consumers will have to pay more for their manpower than it is currently worth, in which case they will be put out of the running by more productive, better-paid workers in the Western world. Unemployment among the world's poor would swiftly rise. Economist Paul Krugman has dubbed this a policy for good jobs in theory and no jobs in practice. Jesus Reyes-Heroles, Mexican ambassador to the United States, has explained:

> *In a poor country like ours the alternative to low-paying jobs isn't high-paying jobs—it's no jobs at all.*[3]

In effect, labor and environmental provisions tell the developing countries: *You are too poor to trade with us, and we are not going to trade with you until you have grown rich.* The problem is that only through trade can they grow richer and thereby, step by step, improve their living standards and their social conditions. This is a catch-22: they cannot trade until their working conditions and environmental protection are of a high standard, but they cannot raise the level of their working conditions and environmental protection if they are not allowed to trade with us. It is reminiscent of that chilling oxymoron from the Vietnam War: "We had to burn the village in order to save it."

194

Suppose this idea had been current at the end of the 19th century. In that case Britain and France would have noted that Swedish wages were only a fraction of theirs, that Sweden had a 12- or 13-hour working day and a six-day week, and that Swedes were chronically undernourished. Child labor was widespread in spinning mills, glassworks, and match and tobacco factories: one factory worker in 20 was under 14 years old. Britain and France, accordingly, would have refused to trade with Sweden and closed their frontiers to Swedish cereals, timber, and iron ore. Would Sweden have gained by this? Hardly. On the contrary, it would have robbed the Swedes of earnings and blocked their industrial development. They would have been left with intolerable living conditions, the children would have stayed in the factories, and perhaps to this day they would be eating tree-bark bread when the harvest failed. But that didn't happen. Sweden's trade was allowed to grow uninterruptedly, industrialization got under way, and the economy was revolutionized. In step with growth, slowly but surely, they were able to tackle the abuses. Wages rose, the working day was shortened, and children began going to school in the mornings, not to the factory.

If today, as a condition for trading with the developing countries, we require their mining industries to be as safe as the West's now are, we are making demands that we ourselves did not have to meet when our own mining industries were developing. It was only after raising our incomes that we were able to develop the technology and afford the safety equipment we use today. If we require the developing countries to adopt those things right away, before they can afford them, then their industry will be knocked out. If we prevent poor countries from exporting to us because their working conditions are not good enough, their export industry will be eliminated and their workers will instead have to look for jobs in native industry, with even lower wages and poorer working conditions. That will not help the world's poor, but it will protect our industry. This, one suspects, is the motive of certain groups in affluent countries for proposing such clauses.

What the adherents of labor and environmental provisions in trade agreements want to do is deny developing countries the chance that the affluent countries were once given. Those who sincerely desire to help the developing countries surely should campaign for the West to help developing countries get rid of their problems by sharing our technology and know-how with them instead of ceasing to trade with them. Instead, some labor organizations, such as the AFL-CIO, are trying to stop the transfer of modern technology to the Third World! There already exist other venues for tackling the specific issues and helping developing countries to improve their labor and environmental standards, such as the United Nations Environmental Program (UNEP) and the International Labor Organization (ILO).

What about the requirement that our trading partners respect patent and intellectual property (IP) rights, which developing countries have to accept in order to be admitted to cooperation within the WTO? Why should we require them to accept patents for a 20-year period, as stipulated in the WTO's TRIPS (Trade-Related Aspects of Intellectual Property Rights) agreement, if we do not require them to maintain even a minimum level of social conditions? There is a simple reason often given: infringements of intellectual property rights act as a trade barrier. Few companies would avoid investing in or selling to a country because it is too poor or its wages are too low, but they might well shun a country where they risked having their product ideas stolen.

Patents are important, both as a recognition of the creator's right to be compensated for a creation and as a means of promoting a climate of innovation and research. Without intellectual property protection, inventors in poor countries would have to sell their ideas abroad in order to protect them.

These are reasonable arguments, but I don't find them strong enough to support the idea that IP rights must be included—as they are today with the TRIPS treaty—in the rules of the WTO. Here again, we should permit trade with everyone, irrespective of the policy they follow. The commercial liberty of Americans should not be infringed just because other countries are pursuing a bad policy, and the citizens of other countries already living under a foolish policy do not need to be punished again by our government. If the policies of these countries turn businesses away and fail to spur innovation at home, then so much the worse for them, but that is no reason why we should forbid citizens of our country to trade freely with them. It is trade that provides the level of economic development that will eventually enable the developing countries to acquire the wealth and technology that make protection of IP rights increasingly vital to the economy. We must not use trade barriers as a weapon for pushing through the policy we want to see. Instead we should keep our frontiers open and at the same time urge the countries in question to start respecting patents and copyrights.

Child labor

But are there really no exceptions? No economic conditions so disgusting that we must prohibit trade because of them? One example often cited in the course of debate is the employment of children. There are today something like 250 million child workers between the ages of 5 and 14. No one can be anything but dismayed at the thought of millions of young people being robbed of their childhood and, in many cases, their health and happiness as well. But are these children helped by the United States or the EU ceasing to trade with the countries in which they live? No, and the absurdity of such a proposition becomes clear as soon as we realize that the great majority of children are employed in sectors having nothing whatsoever to do with trade. About 70 percent of child workers are employed in agriculture. Only 5 percent, about 10 million or 15 million children, are employed in export industries doing things like making footballs and athletic shoes, sewing garments, or knotting carpets. All available sources indicate that children working in export industries are better off than those in other trades, with the least dangerous working conditions. So the alternatives are worse.

The problem, once again, is that we judge the Third World according to our own material standard of living. The fact is that child employment was widespread in the West just a few generations ago. It has existed in all societies. In preindustrial France, parents were forbidden *not* to send their children to work. Children in a poor country do not become workers because their parents are cruel but because the family needs their earnings to survive. So we cannot prohibit child labor in these countries just like that, and still less can we forbid the countries concerned to export things to us. If we did, then pending an improvement in material conditions, the children would be forced into even worse occupations—at the very worst, into crime and prostitution. In 1992 it was revealed that Wal-Mart was buying garments that had been manufactured by child workers in Bangladesh. Congress then threatened to prohibit imports from countries with child labor. As a result of that threat, many thousands of children were fired by the Bangladeshi textile industry. A follow-up by international organizations showed that many of the children had moved to more dangerous, less well-paid jobs, and in several cases had become prostitutes.[4] A similar boycott of the Nepalese carpet industry, according to UNICEF, resulted in more than 5,000 girls being forced into prostitution.

The Swedish NGO Save the Children (Rädda Barnen) is one of the organizations that have tried to instill a degree of moderation and sense into the debate on child labor:

> *In most cases the Swedish Save the Children says no to boycotts, sanctions, and other trade-related measures against the employment of children. Experience has shown that the children who have to leave their jobs as a consequence of such measures risk finding themselves in more difficult situations and more harmful occupations.*

Half of child workers work part time, and many do so to finance their schooling. If they were to lose their jobs, as a result of prohibitions or boycotts, a difficult situation would be made even worse. To tackle the problems, we have to distinguish which problems—prostitution and the enslavement of children, for example—must be fought by every available means, and which can only be counteracted through economic improvements and rising living standards. Save the Children, Sweden, continues:

> *General assertions that child labor is a good or bad thing serve little purpose. . . . To regard all occupations as equally unacceptable is to simplify a complicated issue and makes it more difficult to concentrate forces against the worst forms of exploitation.*[5]

Child labor in Sweden was primarily eliminated not by prohibitions but by the economy growing to such an extent that parents were able to give their children education instead—thereby maximizing the children's incomes in the longer term. In addition, mechanization made the simplest manual labor less profitable. That development eventually enabled Sweden to legally prohibit such child labor as remained, not the other way around. The same recipe can reduce child labor in developing countries today. The ILO has noted that the number of workers aged 10–14 is declining substantially with the growth of the Asian economies. In India, the proportion of child workers has fallen from 35 percent fifty years ago to 12 percent today. In East and Southeast Asia, child labor is expected to have vanished completely by 2010. In the poorest developing countries, the proportion of children in the workforce has fallen in the past 40 years from 32 to 19 percent, and in the medium income group it has fallen from 28 to 7 percent.[6]

Everyone must have access to education, and that education must yield a return. It must be capable of leading to a better paying job than could have been obtained without schooling. Only then will it become possible, and remunerative, for parents to save their children from work. It is not enough for education to be universally available. Schools also have to be of good quality. In many countries the schools are appalling, and children attending them are badly treated, even subjected to physical violence. This is in part a function of the schools' status as public institutions whose teachers are almost impossible to fire. Part of the solution lies in freedom of choice, enabling families to take control of schools from staff and national authorities, perhaps through a voucher system, as in Sweden.

It is always open to discussion whether, in a particular situation, temporary trade sanctions are a feasible way of bringing down an exceptionally cruel dictatorship, for example one that practices apartheid or slavery, makes war, or massacres civilians. But even in cases like these, it is important to bear in mind that sanctions will quite probably harm the country's population and may even, if prolonged, strengthen the position of the rulers. Trade generally tends to make the maintenance of centralized power difficult, because it gives rise to more international contacts and to power centers other than the sovereign. If all countries participate in sanctions against a dictatorship, perhaps some useful purpose can be served in certain cases. Symbolic sanctions, such as the freezing of diplomatic relations or boycotts on sporting events, can be particularly useful against dictatorships, because they do not harm the population in the same way as a suspension of trade. But the important thing here is that sanctions of this kind should not in any way be mixed up with sanctions imposed on countries merely because they are still poor.

The best policy is to bring pressure to bear in other contexts and in political forums, instead of proceeding to dismantle what is perhaps the most effective solution—trade. Our politicians and organizations should never cease criticizing other countries if they violate human rights, practice censorship, persecute dissidents, or prohibit associations—trade unions, for example. The desire to give the populations of other countries a chance to develop by trading freely must never be confused with a benevolent attitude towards their governments. Western politicians who cozy up to dictatorial regimes for the purpose of ensuring that their export enterprises are able to sell to those countries are in practice legitimizing their oppression. If governments are anti-liberal, their oppression should never be passed over in silence. "Injustice anywhere is a threat to justice everywhere," as Martin Luther King Jr. put it.

But what about us?

"All right then," certain critics of globalization reply, "it may be good for the developing countries, our trading with them in spite of their being poor, but it's bad for us." For if the developing countries pay lower wages, do not protect their environment, and have insufferably long working hours, then won't their cheap output eliminate our higher paying jobs, forcing us to lower our standards and our wages? We will have to keep working harder and longer to keep up. Firms and capital quickly migrate to where the lowest wages and the worst working conditions exist. It will be a "race to the bottom." The one with the lowest social standard will win and will corner the investments and export revenues.

Theoretically this seems a tough case to answer. The only trouble is that it has no foundation in reality. The world has not witnessed a deterioration of working conditions or wages in the past few decades, but precisely the opposite. And the explanation is simple. Consumers aren't looking to buy goods from people who are poorly paid; they just want products that are good and as inexpensive as possible, whoever makes them. The reason wages are lower in developing countries is that firms there are less productive, that is, they produce less per employee.

If wages rise because productivity does so, there is no problem, and consumers have no reason to seek out whatever has been produced by the cheapest labor. In 30 years, Japanese wages rose from one-tenth of the American level to a level higher than

America's. But that did not make Japanese workers less competitive, because their productivity rose at the same rate. Firms are not primarily looking for cheap labor either. If they were, the world's aggregate production would be concentrated in Nigeria. Firms are more interested in getting as much as possible out of the capital they have committed. Wages in poor countries are low because, relatively speaking, manpower there provides less of a return to businesses—a result of workers there being less skilled and having access to less efficient machinery. As investments, educational standards, and prosperity rise in the developing countries, wages also go up. This means that we can expect to see progress in the developing countries rather than deterioration in the industrialized world. Indeed, that is exactly what the facts demonstrate. In 1960, the average Third World worker had about 10 percent of an American industrial worker's wage. Today this has risen to 30 percent, in spite of the American wage level also having risen. If competition had kept wages down in affluent countries, the proportion of national income going to wages ought to diminish, but it is not doing so.[7]

The populist presidential candidate Ross Perot argued skillfully against the NAFTA agreement with Mexico and Canada. If it came into force, ran one of his more memorable pieces of rhetoric, the people would hear a "giant sucking sound" as all U.S. jobs were vacuumed up by Mexico. In fact, since this particular free trade agreement came into force in 1995, employment in the United States has risen by 10 million jobs. The U.S. labor force is the world's best paid. If U.S. firms were solely intent on paying low wages, they would leave en masse for various African countries. And yet 80 percent of American investments go to high-wage countries like the United Kingdom, Canada, the Netherlands, and Germany, all of which have equivalent or higher social standards and regulatory levels. What firms are mainly looking for,

Third World wages are rising

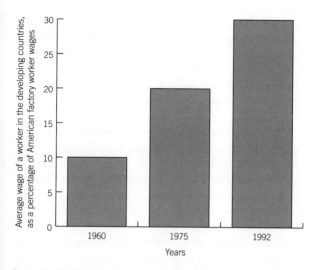

Source: Gary Burtless, Robert Lawrence, and Robert Shapiro, *Globaphobia: Confronting Fears about Open Trade* (Washington: Brookings Institution, 1998).

then, is social and political stability, the rule of law, secure property rights, free markets, good infrastructure, and skilled manpower. When countries compete to offer those things, there is a race to the top, rather than to the bottom.

It is commonly supposed that we in the United States and Western Europe are having to work harder and harder and put in progressively longer hours to cope with competition from the Third World and from increasingly efficient machinery. Some people do indeed work more than is healthy, and there is a widespread feeling of higher demands and faster tempo at work.

But this does not stem from Third World competition. Historically, it has always been the case that the poor worked far longer hours than the affluent. Yet researchers for the Bureau of Labor Statistics found that now people in higher income brackets are actually working several hours longer on average than low-income workers in the United States.[8]

The time we all spend working has diminished with rising prosperity, for the simple reason that growth enables us to do less work for the same pay—if we want to. Compared with our parents' generation, most of today's workers go to work later, go home earlier, have longer lunch and coffee breaks, longer vacations, and more public holidays. In the United States, working hours today are only about half of what they were a hundred years ago, having diminished by about 10 percent since as recently as 1973—a reduction equaling 23 days per year. On average, American workers have acquired five extra years of waking leisure time since 1973. This is also because we have begun working progressively later in life, are retiring earlier, and are living longer. A Western worker in 1870 had only two hours off for each hour worked, spread out over a lifetime. By 1950 that figure had doubled to four hours off, doubling again to the present figure of about eight hours off for each hour worked. Economic development, thanks partly to trade enabling us to specialize, makes it possible for us to reduce our working hours considerably and also to raise our material living standard. We have never needed less time to earn our living.

Even so, it is natural for us in the affluent Western world today to talk a lot about stress. This is partly caused by something basically positive, the fantastic growth of options available to us. Pre-industrial citizens, spending all their lives in one place and perhaps meeting a hundred people in a lifetime, were unlikely to feel that they did not have time for everything they wanted to

Americans are working less and less in the course of a lifetime

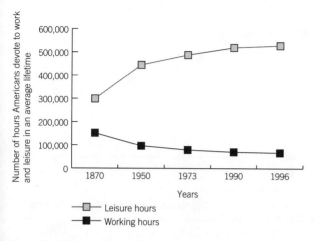

Source: Michael W. Cox and Richard Alm, *Myths of Rich and Poor: Why We're Better Off Than We Think* (New York: Basic Books, 1999), chap 3.

do. People spent a lot of their nonworking time sleeping. Today, we can travel the world, read newspapers, see films from every corner of the globe, and meet a hundred people every day. We used to go to the mailbox and wait for the postman. Now the mail is in our inbox, waiting for us. We have a huge entertainment industry that offers an almost infinite number of ways to pass the time if we get bored. No wonder that the result is a certain frustration over not finding time for everything. Compared with the problems people have had in all ages, and most people in developing countries still have today, this kind of worry should be recognized for what it is—a luxury.

Working hours are diminishing

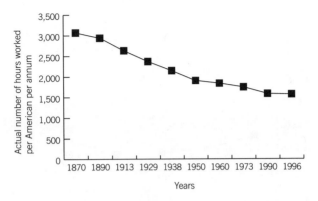

Source: Michael W. Cox and Richard Alm, *Myths of Rich and Poor: Why We're Better Off Than We Think* (New York: Basic Books, 1999), chap 3.

Stress and burnout at work are real problems, but in many ways those are new words for old phenomena. At the same rate as more and more people are experiencing burnout, fewer seem to be getting diagnosed with neck disorders and mental problems. This matter also has to be viewed in perspective. Every age and place tends to think that its own particular problems are worst. Often this is due to ignorance or to a tendency to romanticize the past. It can be a problem, being so ardent about one's work as to overdo things, but isn't it no less of a problem that so many people are bored to death by their work? We must not forget that the big problem still is that so many people have jobs that offer them neither challenges nor development.

The essential point when discussing burnout and capitalism concerns the possibility of getting a hold on one's situation—and which system gives one the best opportunity of doing so.

There are problems with employees who work too hard and employers who demand too much or are too vague about what they expect from workers. But capitalism enables people to give priority to what they consider important. They can choose to take things easier if they feel that they are working too much; they can pressure their employers for better conditions through such means as unions, and the employer can review the work situation. Each individual can opt out of certain things so as not to feel permanently at the beck and call of others. You don't have to check your e-mail over the weekend, and there is no law against turning on the answering machine.

Big is beautiful

In the anti-globalists' worldview, multinational corporations are leading the race to the bottom. By moving to developing countries and taking advantage of poor people and lax regulations, they are making money hand over fist and forcing other governments to adopt ever less restrictive policies. On this view, tariffs and barriers to foreign investment become a kind of national defense, a protection against a ruthless entrepreneurial power seeking to profiteer at people's expense. The alternative is an empire of enormous multinationals ruling the world, regardless of what people think or want. The fact that 51 out of the world's 100 biggest economies are corporations is repeated like an ominous mantra. The problem, though, is not that corporations are growing, but that more national economies are not doing the same. Big corporations are no problem—they can achieve important economies of scale—as long as they are exposed to the threat of competition should they turn out products inferior to or more expensive than those of other firms. What we have to fear is not size but monopoly.

Free trade is often said to give businesses more power. But enterprises in a liberal society have no coercive power. State power is based on the right of coercion, backed up as a last resort by the police. The only "power" corporations have to get people to work for them or to pay for their products is based solely on offering something that people want—jobs or products. Even if you have to accept a job from someone or other to survive, no employer has coerced you or made your situation worse. On the contrary, the employer has given you a better alternative to a bad situation. Corporations can, of course, do a great deal of harm—for example, by moving out of a small community—but only because they had previously offered some benefit that they later retract. Offices and factories, however, might not have opened up in the first place if companies knew that they would be required to keep them running whether or not they were profitable.

What has happened in the age of globalization is not that corporations have acquired more power through free trade. They used to be far more powerful—and still are—in dictatorships and controlled economies. Large, powerful corporations have always been able to corrupt public institutions by colluding with rulers and hobnobbing with them on luncheons and dinners. They have been able to obtain protection through monopolies, tariffs, and subsidies just by placing a phone call to political leaders. Free trade has exposed corporations to competition. Above all, consumers have been made freer, so that now they can ruthlessly pick and choose even across national borders, rejecting those firms that don't measure up.

Historical horror stories of companies governing a society de facto have always come from regions where there has been no competition. People living in isolation in a small village or a closed country are dependent on the enterprises existing there, and are forced to buy what they offer at the price they demand, enriching a tiny clique at consumers' expense. Sometimes capitalism is accused of having created monopolies and trusts, enormous associations of businesses that flourish, not by being best, but by being biggest and squelching competition. But this is not brought about by capitalism. On the contrary, free trade and competition are the best guarantees of a competitor penetrating the market if the dominant firm misbehaves. It says much that the first monopolies appeared, not in 19th century Britain, whose policy was almost one of laissez faire, but in the United States and Germany, which became industrialized later and protected their markets with tariffs. Sugar monopolies in European countries live on today because of the EU's sugar tariffs, as a result of which a lump of sugar costs two or three times as much in the EU as in the rest of the world.

Capitalists are seldom great adherents of capitalism: often, they have the biggest interest of all in legally protected monopolies and exclusive privileges. Introducing a market economy and free trade is one way of taking these things away from them, of forcing them to offer the best possible goods and services in return for a share of our resources. Free trade gives enterprises the freedom to offer more consumers what they want, but it does not confer privilege of coercive power on anyone. The freedom of a business in a free market economy is like a waiter's freedom to offer the menu to a restaurant patron. And it entitles other waiters—foreign ones, even!—to come running up with rival menus. The loser in this process, if anyone, is the waiter who once had a monopoly.

The things that many critics of the market call for—firms that are less intent on profit, markets that are less free, restructuring that is less hectic, and so on—could be seen in post-communist Russia, where government-owned enterprises were in practice given away, instead of being privatized through an open auction. In many cases, that giveaway resulted in the management and employees taking over the old firm free of charge, without having to raise money for the venture through a modernization of production to yield future profits. Because that would require major structural changes and heavy job losses, which would be troublesome for everyone working there, the whole modernization of the private sector is being stalled, and growth is not accelerating. Instead, many of the owners are simply helping themselves to corporate resources. Many of these firms were snapped up by people with strong political contacts. They have been more concerned with expanding their own spheres of influence and plundering the businesses than with developing them for future profit, as people investing their own money in a project would have an interest in doing. In addition, it is more difficult for outsiders to compete with these old firms, because Russian business is subject to a battery of tariffs, licensing requirements, arbitrary regulations, feeble legal safeguards, and rampant corruption. After initial liberalization measures in 1992, the Russian process moved in the opposite direction. Paradoxically, lack of freedom for Russian business as a whole leads to enormous freedom for a handful of big businesses with political protection.[9]

Nothing forces people to accept new products. If they gain market share, it is because people want them. Even the biggest companies survive at the whim of customers and would have to close down tomorrow if they ceased thinking about those customers. Mega-corporation Coca-Cola has to adapt the recipe for its drinks to different regions in deference to varying local tastes. McDonald's sells mutton burgers in India, teriyaki burgers in Japan, and salmon burgers in Norway. TV mogul Rupert Murdoch has failed to create a pan-Asian channel and, instead, is having to build different channels to suit the local audiences.

Companies in free competition can grow large and increase their sales only by being better than others, and they can operate in international markets only by maintaining superior productivity. Companies that fail to do so quickly go bust or get taken over by others who can make better use of their capital, buildings, machinery, and employees. Capitalism is very tough—on firms offering old-fashioned, poor-quality, or expensive goods and services. Fear of old companies growing progressively larger and eventually becoming independent of the markets has absolutely no foundation in reality. Experience from one of the most capitalistic countries in the world, the United States, indicates exactly the opposite. Ever since the 1930s, critics of the market have been warning of the risk of domination by big corporations. Meanwhile, the market share of the 25 biggest corporations has steadily dwindled.

The critic of globalization asks why corporations grow even larger than nation states, backing up the question with one of the most widespread figures in the whole globalization debate: of the world's 100 largest economies, 51 are business corporations. This objection loses much of its credibility once we realize that the impressive figure of 51 out of a hundred is incorrect. It is based on a comparison of corporate *sales* with the aggregate production, or GDP, of nation states—but these are not comparable entities. GDP counts only the value a given nation has *added* to a product, whereas sales figures include the entire value of the product, from whatever source. A firm selling a house did not create the whole thing from scratch. To achieve the end product, it has outsourced any number of services and purchased components and materials. To estimate the firm's sales without deducting purchases and expenditures inevitably overestimates their size. If, instead, we try to calculate the value that the firm adds to the goods, we arrive at something like 25–35 percent of sales, and it suddenly becomes clear that only 37 of the world's 100 largest economies are business corporations. Those mostly come at the bottom of the list: of the 50 largest economies, only 2 are corporations. The impression that corporations in general are larger than countries fades when we discover that a small country like Sweden

214

is more than twice as large as the world's biggest corporation, Wal-Mart. France is more than 15 times bigger, the United States more than a hundred times. Practically all industrialized countries are bigger than all corporations. The 50 largest corporations in the world have a GDP equaling only 4.5 percent of that of the 50 biggest countries.[10]

It is true that corporations generally have grown in absolute size over the past two decades, but so too has the world economy—in fact, slightly faster. So these figures do not in any way show corporations to have grown bigger and more powerful than governments. In fact, corporations have grown smaller as compared with, for example, the countries in North America and East Asia, the very regions that have opened up markets and admitted business competition. By doing so, they have grown faster than the corporations themselves. Meanwhile countries that have had closed markets and have not received investment—most African countries, for example—have diminished relative to corporations. Trade and investment, then, do not make corporations bigger and more powerful than governments, but the absence of such globalization appears to do just that.

Freer, more efficient financial markets, which allow capital to spread to new entrepreneurs with fresh ideas, have made it progressively easier for small firms to compete with the big corporations. And things have been made easier still by advances in information technology. Between 1980 and 1993, the 500 biggest American firms saw their share of the country's total employment diminish from 16 to 11.3 percent. Even if we use the problematic measure of globalization's critics to determine the relative size of the 500 biggest firms—sales in relation to aggregate GDP—the myth is refuted, because that figure fell dramatically, from 59.3 to 36.1 percent. That's a drop of almost half in just 13 years.

During the same period, the average personnel strength of American firms fell from 16.5 to 14.8 persons, and the proportion of the population working in firms with more than 250 employees fell from 37 to 29 percent.[11]

By most standards, then, the dominance of the largest corporations diminishes in a free market, in favor of a host of more flexible undertakings. Half the firms operating internationally in the world today have fewer than 250 employees. Many of the biggest are being knocked out by competitors. Of the companies on the 1980 list of the 500 biggest enterprises in the United States, one-third had disappeared by 1990 and another 40 percent had gone five years later. In certain capital-intensive industries, such as pharmaceuticals, motor manufacturing, and aerospace, size matters more, owing to the cost of developing new products. But big mergers among those companies are a sign, not of their power over consumers, but of their inability to survive otherwise. True, the biggest brand logos are always being flashed before our eyes, but we forget that they are constantly being joined by new ones and are losing old rivals. How many people recall that Nokia, just a few years ago, was a small Finnish firm manufacturing motor tires and boots?

Companies starting up in foreign countries would not have a market if no one wanted to do business with them, and they would not get any workers if they failed to offer good terms. When a company is more productive than others, it produces cheaper goods. Because, consequently, its workers are worth more to it, the company can afford to pay them more and have better working conditions than other firms do. This becomes extraordinarily clear if we compare the conditions of people employed in American-owned factories and offices in developing countries with those of people employed elsewhere in the same country. Critics

216

Big corporations are becoming less dominant

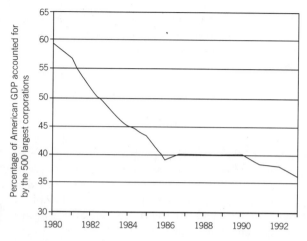

Source: Sebastian Edwards, *Openness, Productivity and Growth.* NBER Working Paper 5978 (Cambridge, Mass.: National Bureau of Economic Research, 1997).

observe, quite rightly, that employees in developing countries have far worse conditions than we have in the affluent world, but that is an unfair comparison, because workers in the developed world have far higher productivity. The interesting comparison, the one that decides whether foreign firms in a developing country are a good thing, is how well off those employees are compared with other workers in the same country. In the poorest developing countries, the average employee of an American-affiliated company makes eight times the average national wage! In middle income countries, American employers pay three times the national average. Even compared with corresponding modern jobs in the same country, the multinationals pay about 30 percent

217

higher wages. Foreign firms in the least developed countries pay their employees, on average, twice as much as the corresponding native firms. Marxists maintain that the multinationals exploit poor workers. But if "exploitation" means many times greater wages, then is that such a bad alternative?

The same marked difference can be seen in working conditions. The International Labor Organization (ILO) has shown that the multinationals, especially in the footwear and garment industries, are leading the trend toward better workplace and working conditions. Because of the low standards of suppliers' factories in the Third World, Nike has long been vilified by anti-globalists. But the truth is that Nike is one of the companies offering employees the best of conditions, not out of generosity, but with an eye to profit. These companies can pay more because their productivity is higher, and they are more responsive to popular opinion. Nike, consequently, has demanded a higher standard of its suppliers, and native firms have to follow suit.

Zhou Litai, one of China's foremost labor attorneys, has pointed out that it is Western consumers who are the principal driving force behind the improvement of working conditions, because they are making Nike, Reebok, and others raise standards: "If Nike and Reebok go," Zhou points out, "this pressure evaporates. This is obvious."[12]

When multinational corporations accustom workers to better wages and better-lit, cleaner factories without dangerous machinery, they raise the general standard. Native firms then also have to offer better conditions, otherwise no one will work for them. This trend is easiest to quantify in terms of Third World wages, which, as we have already seen, have risen from 10 percent to 30 percent of American wages over the past 40 years.

Nike has seen to it that its subcontractors also open up their factories to impartial inspection. Systematic interviews of anonymous employees by the Global Alliance for Workers and Communities show, of course, that there are complaints, but above all that employees are glad to have gotten jobs in the first place, and they consider them to be good jobs. At Indonesian factories, 70 percent of employees had traveled long distances to get their jobs. Three-quarters were satisfied with relations with their superiors and felt that they were free to put forward ideas and suggestions. The latter group roughly equals the proportion of Swedish national government employees who feel free to communicate viewpoints to their employer, which puts the answers into perspective, even though the situations, of course, are not comparable. At Vietnamese factories, 85 percent wanted to go on working for at least another three years, and the same number felt secure with their working conditions and the machinery. At the Thai factories only 3 percent felt that they were on poor terms with their superiors, and 72 percent considered themselves well paid. The provision by companies of free medicines, health care, clothing, food, and transport for their workers was particularly appreciated.

One of the few Western participants in the globalization debate to have actually visited Nike's Asian subcontractors to find out about conditions there is Linda Lim of the University of Michigan. She found that in Vietnam, where the annual minimum wage was $134, Nike workers were getting $670. In Indonesia, where the minimum wage was $241, Nike's suppliers were paying $720.[13] Once again, it is vital to remember that these conditions should not be compared with those found in the affluent countries, but with the alternatives open to these people. If Nike were to withdraw, on account of boycotts and tariff walls from the Western world, the suppliers would have to shut down, and the employees would be put out of work or would move to more dangerous jobs with lower, less steady wages in native industry or agriculture.

Many developing countries have what are called economic "free zones," also known as export-processing zones, mainly for export industries. There, firms are allowed to start up with especially advantageous tax conditions and trade regulations. Anti-globalists characterize the free zones as havens for slave-driving and inhuman working conditions. There are indeed abuses and scandals in some quarters, and resolute action is needed to prohibit them. Mostly, abuse and scandal happen in poor dictatorships, and so, instead of freedom having "gone too far," it has not gained a foothold. In her book *No Logo*, which quickly became popular in anti-capitalist circles, Canadian activist Naomi Klein claims that Western companies have created terrible working conditions in such zones. But she does not offer any proof. She has only heard a few rumors of bad conditions in one Philippine export-processing zone, which she admits having traveled to only because it was one of the worst. When the OECD tried to obtain an overall picture of these zones, it found that they had multiplied job opportunities for the poor, and that wages there were higher than in the rest of the country. In the great majority of the thousand or so small zones, the same labor legislation applied as elsewhere in the country. In addition, more and more free zones are observing that cheap labor is not the full recipe for successful competition, and are encouraging firms to invest in and educate their work forces. In the same study, the OECD pointed out that there was a positive relation between fundamental rights for the employees (prohibition of slavery and abuses, freedom to negotiate and to form trade unions) and more investment and higher growth.[14]

Multinationals, by virtue of their size, are able to finance research and long-term projects. According to the OECD, these corporations reinvest some 90 percent of their profits in the country where they operate. Operating as they do in several countries, they serve as channels for know-how, more-efficient organizational structures, and new technology. Complaining about the existence of multinationals means complaining about better wages, lower prices, and greater prosperity. It is such enterprises that are leading the international race to the top. And it is not only in the developing countries that multinationals offer better conditions. Foreign firms in the United States pay about 6 percent higher wages than native American firms, and they are expanding their personnel strength twice as fast. Foreign businesses account for 12 percent of R&D investment in the United States and for no less than 40 percent in the United Kingdom.[15]

Of course, that is not to say that all firms behave well, any more than all people do. There are rogues among entrepreneurs, just as there are in politics. We can find plenty of instances of companies treating their employees, the population, or the environment badly. In the raw materials industry especially, there is a tendency to cozy up to the regime of the country where the business operates, no matter how dictatorial and oppressive it may be. Otherwise, the firms might not be allowed to operate there. But bad behavior by some is no reason for banning large corporations or preventing them from investing, any more than we should disband the police because we find instances of police brutality, or eject all immigrants because some of them are criminals. Instead, bad behavior is a reason to prosecute firms if they break the law and to criticize and boycott those firms that conduct themselves badly.

The big problems generally concern states permitting or even inducing firms to behave irresponsibly. There has to be a strict distinction between the public and private sectors. Governments must establish firm regulatory codes, and corporations must produce and trade in the best possible way within those codes. If firms comply with bad regulatory codes, then the remedy should be to reform the codes and criticize the corporation, not to impede business as such. The solution lies in democratizing governments and creating fair laws establishing that one party's freedom ends where the other party's begins.

The presence of multinational corporations in oppressive governments can very often be an aid to the pursuit of democracy, because those corporations are sensitive to pressure from Western consumers, which has a direct impact on sales. It can be easier to influence Nigerian politics by boycotting Shell than by trying to bring pressure to bear on the Nigerian government. This is hinted at in the subtitle of Naomi Klein's book *No Logo: Taking Aim at the Brand Bullies.* Klein points out that the big corporations have tried to create a special positive aura for their trademarks through many decades of advertising and goodwill. But by doing so they have also shot themselves in the foot. The trademarks, being their biggest asset, are hugely sensitive to adverse publicity. It can take a company decades to build up a trademark but only a few weeks for activists to demolish it. Really, though, Klein ought to see this as an argument for capitalism, because the corporate giants can be pressured if they behave badly in any respect. A street vendor can cheat you because you will never see him again, but the big trademarks, as a matter of survival, have to behave respectably. They have to turn out good, safe products and treat employees, customers, and the environment well so as not to lose their goodwill. Negative attention spells huge losses.[16]

The magazine *The Economist* has also observed that corporate morality is often superior to that of the average government. Most companies formulate guidelines and define requirements for dealing with environmental problems and sexual harassment, even in countries where such expressions do not exist in the local vocabulary. Most companies would feel compelled to fire a board chairman publicly implicated in corruption scandals, as Germany's former federal chancellor Helmut Kohl was, or in sexual harassment and dubious financial dealings, like former president

Bill Clinton. And yet these were heads of state in two of the most democratic and stable of Western countries.[17]

The Bangladeshi garment industry provides a prime example of foreign enterprises channeling knowledge and new ideas that can revolutionize an economy. During the 1970s local entrepreneur Noorul Quader established cooperation with the South Korean company Daewoo. Daewoo sold sewing machines to Quader and trained his workers. When his firm started up in Bangladesh, Daewoo assisted him for just over a year longer with marketing and advice on new methods of production, in return for 8 percent of earnings. One hundred thirty skilled workers and two engineers from South Korea inaugurated production in Bangladesh in 1980, and garment exports were accepted by the authorities as an island of free trade in an otherwise protectionist economy. Output almost doubled every year, and by 1987 the company was already selling 2.3 million sweaters, worth $5.3 million. By then, 114 of the 130 original workers had already started up garment firms of their own, and all of a sudden, Bangladesh, which until now had not had a single garment-export enterprise, had 700 of them. Today there are more than three times that number, making garment manufacturing Bangladesh's biggest industry, accounting for some 60 percent of the country's exports. The factories have more than 1.2 million employees, about 90 percent of them women, who have moved in from the impoverished countryside in search of more secure, better-paying jobs. Another five million are employed in industry as a whole. Although working conditions are bad, the new jobs have often meant new opportunities of choice and higher wages, even in the traditional occupations, which are now having to exert themselves to attract workers.[18]

223

"Gold and green forests"*

Although multinational corporations and free trade are proving good for development and human rights in the Third World, there still remains the objection that globalization harms the environment. Factories in the Western world, the argument runs, will relocate to poorer countries with no environmental legislation, where they can pollute with impunity. The West has to follow suit and lower its own environmental standards in order to stay in business. That is a dismal thesis, with the implication that when people obtain better opportunities, resources, and technology, they use them to abuse nature. Does there really have to be a conflict between development and the environment?

The notion that there has to be a conflict runs into the same problem as the whole idea of a race to the bottom: it doesn't tally with reality. There is no exodus of industry to countries with poor environmental standards, and there is no downward pressure on the level of global environmental protection. Instead, the bulk of American and European investments goes to countries with environmental regulations similar to their own. There has been much talk of American factories moving to Mexico since NAFTA was signed. Less well known, however, is that since free trade was introduced Mexico has tightened up its environmental regulations, following a long history of complete nonchalance about

---

* "Gold and green forests" is a Scandinavian figure of speech. It means to promise that you will produce whatever someone wants, even if it is practically impossible.

environmental issues. This tightening up is part of a global trend. All over the world, economic progress and growth are moving hand in hand with intensified environmental protection. Four researchers who studied these connections found "a very strong, positive association between our [environmental] indicators and the level of economic development." A country that is very poor is too preoccupied with lifting itself out of poverty to bother

Prosperity brings more environmental regulations

(Correlation between prosperity and environmental regulation in 31 studied countries)

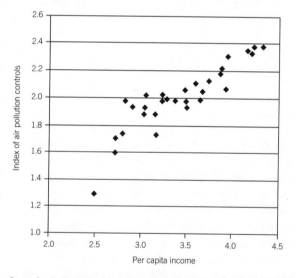

Source: Sumita Dasgputa, Ashoka Mody, Subhendu Roy, and David Wheeler, *Enviromental Regulation and Development: A Cross-Country Empirical Analysis.* World Bank Working Paper (Washington, D.C.: World Bank, March 1995).

about the environment at all. Countries usually begin protecting their natural resources when they can afford to do so. When they grow richer, they start to regulate effluent emissions, and when they have still more resources they also begin regulating air quality.[19]

A number of factors cause environment protection to increase with wealth and development. Environmental quality is unlikely to be a top priority for people who barely know where their next meal is coming from. Abating misery and subduing the pangs of hunger takes precedence over conservation. When our standard of living rises we start attaching importance to the environment and obtaining resources to improve it. Such was the case earlier in western Europe, and so it is in the developing countries today. Progress of this kind, however, requires that people live in democracies where they are able and allowed to mobilize opinion; otherwise, their preferences will have no impact. Environmental destruction is worst in dictatorships. But it is the fact of prosperity no less than a sense of responsibility that makes environmental protection easier in a wealthy society. A wealthier country can afford to tackle environmental problems; it can develop environmentally friendly technologies—wastewater and exhaust emission control, for example—and begin to rectify past mistakes.

Global environmental development resembles not so much a race for the bottom as a race to the top, what we might call a "California effect." The state of California's Clean Air Acts, first introduced in the 1970s and tightened since, were stringent emissions regulations that made rigorous demands on car manufacturers. Many prophets of doom predicted that firms and factories would move to other states, and California would soon be obliged to repeal its regulations. But instead the opposite happened: other states gradually tightened up their environmental stipulations.

Because car companies needed the wealthy California market, manufacturers all over the United States were forced to develop new techniques for reducing emissions. Having done so, they could more easily comply with the exacting requirements of other states, whereupon those states again ratcheted up their requirements. Anti-globalists usually claim that the profit motive and free trade together cause businesses to entrap politicians in a race for the bottom. The California effect implies the opposite: free trade enables politicians to pull profit-hungry corporations along with them in a race to the top.

This phenomenon occurs because compliance with environmental rules accounts for a very small proportion of most companies' expenditures. What firms are primarily after is a good business environment—a liberal economy and a skilled workforce—not a bad natural environment. A review of research in this field shows that there are no clear indications of national environmental rules leading to a diminution of exports or to fewer companies locating in the countries that pass the rules.[20] This finding undermines both the arguments put forward by companies against environmental regulations and those advanced by environmentalists maintaining that globalization has to be restrained for environmental reasons.

Incipient signs of the California effect's race to the top are present all over the world, because globalization has caused different countries to absorb new techniques more rapidly, and the new techniques are generally far gentler on the environment. Researchers have investigated steel manufacturing in 50 different countries and concluded that countries with more open economies took the lead in introducing cleaner technology. Production in those countries generated almost 20 percent less emissions than the same production in closed countries. This process is being

227

driven by multinational corporations because they have a lot to gain from uniform production with uniform technology. Because they are restructured more rapidly, they have more modern machinery. And they prefer assimilating the latest, most environmentally friendly technology immediately to retrofitting it, at great expense, when environmental regulations are tightened up.

Brazil, Mexico, and China—the three biggest recipients of foreign investment—have followed a very clear pattern: the more investments they get, the better control they gain over air pollution. The worst forms of air pollution have diminished in their cities during the period of globalization. When Western companies start up in developing countries, their production is considerably more environment-friendly than the native production, and they are more willing to comply with environmental legislation, not least because they have brand images and reputations to protect. Only 30 percent of Indonesian companies comply with the country's environmental regulations, whereas no fewer than 80 percent of the multinationals do so. One out of every 10 foreign companies maintained a standard clearly superior to that of the regulations. This development would go faster if economies were more open and, in particular, if the governments of the world were to phase out the incomprehensible tariffs on environmentally friendly technology.[21]

Sometimes one hears it said that, for environmental reasons, the poor countries of the South must not be allowed to grow as affluent as our countries in the North. For example, in a compilation of essays on *Environmentally Significant Consumption* published by the National Academy of Sciences, we find anthropologist Richard Wilk fretting that:

> *If everyone develops a desire for the Western high-consumption lifestyle, the relentless growth in consumption, energy use, waste, and emissions may be disastrous.*[22]

228

But studies show this to be colossal misapprehension. On the contrary, it is in the developing countries that we find the gravest, most harmful environmental problems. In our affluent part of the world, more and more people are mindful of environmental problems such as endangered green areas. *Every day* in the developing countries, more than 6,000 people die from air pollution when using wood, dung, and agricultural waste in their homes as heating and cooking fuel. UNDP estimates that no fewer than 2.2 million people die every year from polluted indoor air. This result is already "disastrous" and far more destructive than atmospheric pollution and industrial emissions. Tying people down to that level of development means condemning millions to premature death every year.

It is not true that pollution in the modern sense increases with growth. Instead, pollution follows an inverted U-curve. When growth in a very poor country gathers speed and the chimneys begin belching smoke, the environment suffers. But when prosperity has risen high enough, the environmental indicators show an improvement instead: emissions are reduced, and air and water show progressively lower concentrations of pollutants. The cities with the worst problems are not Stockholm, New York, and Zürich, but rather Beijing, Mexico City, and New Delhi. In addition to the factors already mentioned, this is also due to the economic structure changing from raw-material-intensive to knowledge-intensive production. In a modern economy, heavy, dirty industry is to a great extent superseded by service enterprises. Banks, consulting firms, and information technology corporations do not have the same environmental impact as old factories.

According to one survey of available environmental data, the turning point generally comes before a country's per capita GDP has reached $8,000. At $10,000, the researchers found a positive connection between increased growth and better air and water quality.[23] That is roughly the level of prosperity of Argentina, South Korea, or Slovenia. In the United States, per capita GDP is about $36,300. Here as well, the environment has consistently improved since the 1970s, quite contrary to the picture one gets from the media. In the 1970s there was constant reference to smog in American cities, and rightly so: the air was judged to be unhealthy for 100–300 days a year. Today it is unhealthy for fewer than 10 days a year, with the exception of Los Angeles. There, the figure is roughly 80 days, but even that represents a 50 percent reduction in 10 years.[24] The same trend is noticeable in the rest of the affluent world—for example, in Tokyo, where, a few decades ago, doomsayers believed that oxygen masks would in the future have to be worn all around the city because of the bad air.

Apart from its other positive effects on the developing countries, such as ameliorating hunger and sparing people the horror of watching their children die, prosperity beyond a certain critical point can improve the environment. What is more, this turning point is now occurring progressively earlier in the developing countries, because they can learn from more affluent countries' mistakes and use their superior technology. For example, air quality in the enormous cities of China, which are the most heavily polluted in the world, has steadied since the mid-1980s and in several cases has slowly improved. This improvement has coincided with uniquely rapid growth.

Some years ago, the Danish statistician and Greenpeace member Bjørn Lomborg, with about 10 of his students, compiled statistics and facts about the world's environmental problems. To his astonishment, he found that what he himself had regarded as self-evident, the steady deterioration of the global environment,

230

Prosperity goes easier on the environment

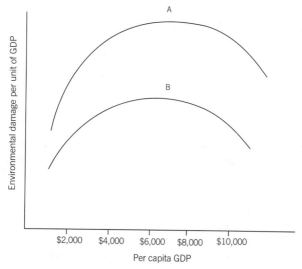

A = Cross-sectional data for countries, 1960
B = Cross-sectional data for countries, 2000

Note: As can be seen, wear and tear on the environment diminishes not only with increased prosperity but at all income levels over time.

Source: World Bank, *World Development Report 1992: Development and the Environment* (Washington: World Bank, 1992).

did not agree at all with official empirical data. He found instead that air pollution is diminishing, refuse problems are diminishing, resources are not running out, more people are eating their fill, and people are living longer. Lomborg gathered publicly available data from as many fields as he could find and published them in the book *The Skeptical Environmentalist: Measuring the Real State of the World.* The picture that emerges there is an important corrective to the general prophesies of doom that can so easily be imbibed from newspaper headlines.

Lomborg shows that air pollution and emissions have been declining in the developed world during recent decades. Heavy metal emissions have been heavily reduced; nitrogen oxides have diminished by almost 30 percent and sulfur emissions by about 80 percent. Pollution and emission problems are still growing in the poor developing countries, but at every level of growth annual particle density has diminished by 2 percent in only 14 years. In the developed world, phosphorus emissions into the seas have declined drastically, and E. coli bacteria concentrations in coastal waters have plummeted, enabling closed swimming areas to reopen.

Lomborg shows that, instead of large-scale deforestation, the world's forest acreage increased from 40.24 million to 43.04 million square kilometers between 1950 and 1994. He finds that there has never been any large-scale tree death caused by acid rain. The oft-quoted, but erroneous statement about 40,000 species going extinct every year is traced by Lomborg to its source—a 20-year-old estimate that has been circulating in environmentalist circles ever since. Lomborg thinks it is closer to 1,500 species a year, and possibly a bit more than that. The documented cases of extinction during the past 400 years total just over a thousand species, of which about 95 percent are insects, bacteria, and viruses. As for the problem of garbage, the next hundred years worth of Danish refuse could be accommodated in a 33-meter-deep pit with an area of three square kilometers, even without recycling. In addition, Lomborg illustrates how increased prosperity and improved technology can solve the problems that lie ahead of us. All the fresh water consumed in the world today could be produced by a single desalination plant, powered by solar cells and occupying 0.4 percent of the Sahara Desert.

It is a mistake, then, to believe that growth automatically ruins the environment. And claims that we would need this or that number of planets for the whole world to attain a Western standard of consumption—those "ecological footprint" calculations—are equally untruthful. Such a claim is usually made by environmentalists, and it is concerned, not so much with emissions and pollution, as with resources running out if everyone were to live as we do in the affluent world.

Clearly, certain of the raw materials we use today, in present-day quantities, would not suffice for the whole world if everyone consumed the same things. But that information is just about as interesting as if a prosperous Stone Age man were to say that, if everyone attained his level of consumption, there would not be enough stone, salt, and furs to go around. Raw material consumption is not static. With more and more people achieving a high level of prosperity, we start looking for ways of using other raw materials. Humanity is constantly improving technology so as to get at raw materials that were previously inaccessible, and we are attaining a level of prosperity that makes this possible. New innovations make it possible for old raw materials to be put to better use and for garbage to be turned into new raw materials. A century and a half ago, oil was just something black and sticky that people preferred not to step in and definitely did not want to find beneath their land. But our interest in finding better energy sources led to methods being devised for using oil, and today it is one of our prime resources. Sand has never been all that exciting or precious, but today it is a vital raw material in the most powerful technology of our age, the computer. In the form of silicon—which makes up a quarter of the earth's crust—it is a key component in computer chips.

There is a simple market mechanism that averts shortages. If a certain raw material comes to be in short supply, its price goes up. This makes everyone more interested in economizing on that resource, in finding more of it, in reusing it, and in trying to find substitutes for it. The trend over the last few decades of falling raw material prices is clear. Metals have never been as cheap as they are today. Prices are falling, which suggests that demand does not exceed supply. In relation to wages, that is, in terms of how long we must work to earn the price of a raw material, natural resources today are half as expensive as they were 50 years ago and one-fifth as expensive as they were a hundred years ago. In 1900 the price of electricity was eight times higher, the price of coal seven times higher, and the price of oil five times higher than today.[25] The risk of shortage is declining all the time, because new finds and more efficient use keep augmenting the available reserves.

In a world where technology never stops developing, static calculations are uninteresting, and wrong. By simple mathematics, Lomborg establishes that if we have a raw material with a hundred years' use remaining, a 1 percent annual increase in demand, and a 2 percent increase in recycling and/or efficiency, that resource *will never be exhausted*.

If shortages do occur, then with the right technology most substances can be recycled. One-third of the world's steel production, for example, is being reused already. Technological advance can outstrip the depletion of resources. Not many years ago, everyone was convinced of the impossibility of the whole Chinese population having telephones, because that would require several hundred million telephone operators. But the supply of manpower did not run out; technology developed instead. Then it was declared that nationwide telephony for China was physically impossible because all the world's copper wouldn't suffice for installing heavy gauge telephone lines all over the country. Before that had time to become a problem, fiber optics and satellites began to supersede copper wire. The price of copper, a commodity that people believed would run out, has fallen continuously and is now only about a tenth of what it was 200 years ago.

People in most ages have worried about important raw materials becoming exhausted. But on the few occasions when this has happened, it has generally affected isolated, poor places, not open, affluent ones. To claim that people in Africa, who are dying by the thousand every day from supremely real shortages, must not be allowed to become as prosperous as we in the West because we can find theoretical risks of shortages occurring is both stupid and unjust.

The environmental question will not resolve itself. Proper rules are needed for the protection of water, soil, and air from destruction. Systems of emissions fees are needed to give polluters an interest in not damaging the environment for others. Many environmental issues also require international regulations and agreements, which confront us with entirely new challenges. Carbon dioxide emissions, for example, tend to increase rather than diminish when a country grows more affluent. When talking about the market and the environment, it is important to realize that efforts in this quarter will be facilitated by a freer, growing economy capable of using the best solutions, from both a natural and a human viewpoint. In order to meet those challenges, it is better to have resources and advanced science than not to have them.

Very often, environmental improvements are due to the very capitalism so often blamed for the problems. The introduction of private property creates owners with long-term interests. Landowners must see to it that there is good soil or forest there

235

tomorrow as well, because otherwise they will have no income later on, whether they continue using the land or intend to sell it. If the property is collective or government-owned, no one has any such long-term interest. On the contrary, everyone then has an interest in using up the resources quickly before someone else does. It was because they were common lands that the rain forests of the Amazon began to be rapidly exploited in the 1960s and 1970s and are still being rapidly exploited today. Only about a 10th of forests are recognized by the governments as privately owned, even though in practice Indians possess and inhabit large parts of them. It is the absence of definite fishing rights that causes (heavily subsidized) fishing fleets to try to vacuum the oceans of fish before someone else does. No wonder, then, that the most large-scale destruction of environment in history has occurred in the communist dictatorships, where all ownership was collective.

A few years ago, a satellite image was taken of the borders of the Sahara, where the desert was spreading. Everywhere, the land was parched yellow, after nomads had overexploited the common lands and then moved on. But in the midst of this desert environment could be seen a small patch of green. This proved to be an area of privately owned land where the owners of the farm prevented overexploitation and engaged in cattle farming that was profitable in the long term.[26]

Trade and freight are sometimes criticized for destroying the environment, but the problem can be rectified with more efficient transport and purification techniques, as well as emissions fees to make the cost of pollution visible through pricing. The biggest environmental problems are associated with production and consumption, and there trade can make a positive contribution, even aside from the general effect it has on growth. Trade leads to a country's resources being used as efficiently as possible. Goods are produced in the places where production entails least expense and least wear and tear on the environment. That is why the amount of raw materials needed to make a given product keeps diminishing as productive efficiency improves. With modern production processes, 97 percent less metal is needed for a soft drink can than 30 years ago, partly because of the use of lighter aluminum. A car today contains only half as much metal as a car of 30 years ago. Therefore, it is better for production to take place where the technology exists, instead of each country trying to have production of its own, with all the consumption of resources that would entail. It is more environmentally friendly for a cold northern country to import meat from temperate countries than to waste resources on concentrated feed and the construction and heating of cattle pens for the purpose of native meat production.

If governments really believed in the market economy, they would stop subsidizing energy, industry, road construction, fisheries, agriculture, devastation of forests, and many other things. Those subsidies have the effect of keeping alive activities that otherwise would not exist, or else would have been performed by better methods or in other places. The Worldwatch Institute maintains that taxpayers the world over are forced to pay about $650 billion every year toward environmentally destructive activities. Cessation of those subsidies, the institute claims, would allow a global tax reduction of 8 percent. In the United States alone that would mean every family paying $2,000 less in taxes each year.[27]

The example of EU meat production shows that not only the environment but animals as well are made to suffer by unproductive industries. Subsidies for inefficient livestock management in the EU have meant cruel conditions for animals with severely cramped transport conditions and, at times, the feeding of carcass meal to livestock. A better idea would be to abolish agricultural tariffs and import meat from South America, where the animals can roam great tracts of land, grazing freely, until they have to be rounded up. But that solution is prevented today by sky-high tariffs. During the mad cow disease crisis, for example, McDonald's wanted to avoid the hazards of using EU meat for its hamburgers in some of its European franchises, but was not permitted to import from South America. The forequarter meat from which the hamburger is ground is excluded by tariffs of several hundred percent.

VI

Irrational, international capital?

The leaderless collective

Opponents of capitalism argue that the market machinery may, after prolonged effort, elevate a country to the heights of prosperity, only to see everything blown to pieces a month later. They paint a picture of irrational speculators investing wildly and then making off with their capital when the herd changes direction. Nearly $1.5 trillion cross national boundaries every day, they complain, as if this fact were a problem in itself. Globalization critic Björn Elmbrant describes the financial market as "a leaderless collective staggering about and tripping over its own feet."[1]

Anxiety about financial markets is easily created. They seem abstract because so few people have any direct contact with them. We only feel their effects, and so it is easy to make a mystery of them. The force involved prompted President Clinton's campaign manager, James Carville, to say: "[In the next life] I would like to come back as the bond market. You can intimidate everybody." People who are hostile to markets love pointing to patterns of stock market behavior that seem odd if one cannot understand the reasons for them. In this way suspicion is cast on the market. A firm's shareholders, for example, are pleased when the firm axes jobs. But this does not mean that they love the sight of unemployment. What appeals to them is the greater productivity and reduced expenditure that can result.

But the American stock market generally takes an upward turn when unemployment does so. Is not this reaction a sign of rejoicing in the misfortune of others? No, it is a sign of investors knowing that the Federal Reserve takes rising unemployment as a sign of a downturn and a reduced risk of inflation and that, therefore, the Federal Reserve is likely to lower the interest rate. What the stock market loves is not unemployment but the economic lubricant of lower interest rates. This phenomenon is no stranger than that of the stock market sometimes leaping upward when the trade cycle indicators point downward and growth decelerates. "Great," investors say to themselves, "that must mean another interest rate cut on the way at last."

But stock market fluctuations are increasing; no one can deny that. Do these fluctuations at least mean that investors have become less long term in their thinking and are just following the crowd? There may be a grain of truth in this. Of course, the market is not perfectly rational in every situation, whatever that would mean. The roller-coaster movement in recent years, especially of dot-com share prices, shows exaggerated hopes and mistaken pricing to be a natural part of a market that is about the future. But it also shows that the exaggerations will not survive indefinitely. Exaggerated hopes cannot make up for lack of real substance in an enterprise.

Part of the reason for the fluctuations is not short-term thinking, but rather the stock market's having become even more focused on the long term. With the old type of industrial enterprise, future performance can be easily judged from historical data concerning investments and sales. So the market's valuation of the enterprise was fairly stable. But in new, more research-intensive sectors with less certain sales prospects, long-term sales can be harder to predict. It is less easy now to tell whether the firm is going to boom or bust. How are we to know that firms developing new mobile phones today will also be front-runners in 10 years' time? When we do not know, every little indication regarding a company's future prospects gives rise to rapid changes. The same applies to the entire stock market when it is unclear which way the economy is going to move. Every hint of future upturns or downturns will be felt swiftly.

Imagine, then, what it is like with companies focusing entirely on the future—those engaging in pharmaceutical research, for example. Possibly they will no longer exist in 10 years' time, but perhaps they will find that vaccine for HIV, in which case their shareholders will become millionaires. "Bubbles" can then occur for perfectly rational reasons. Even if a horse is unlikely to win the race, given high enough odds there may be cause to put some money on it. If we look at the market's behavior as a whole, though, share price fluctuations do *not* appear to have increased where traditional firms are concerned.

Now, many critics of the market say that they have nothing against national financial markets. "Hypercapitalism" is the problem—capital without boundaries ravaging all over the world without even having to present a passport at the border. This, we are told, is impatient capital that cares more about the next quarter's profits than about long-term development and technical renewal.

The defense of the mobility of capital is a question of freedom. This is not a matter of "the freedom of capital," as the critics complain, because capital is not a person capable of being free or unfree. It is a matter of *people's* freedom to decide what to do with their own resources—the freedom, for example, to invest their pension savings wherever they believe it is best to do so. Pension funds are in fact the most important investors in the international market. More than half of all American households now own stock shares, either directly or through retirement funds. They are the market.

There is also a question of businesses being at liberty to seek financing from other countries. Factories and offices do not build

242

themselves—it takes capital. The notion that speculators throttle long-term development is contradicted by the facts: development has proceeded hand in hand with more and more investment in research and innovation. This growing freedom has been important for global development in recent years, making it possible for capital to be invested where it yields the biggest return and, accordingly, where it is used as efficiently as possible.[2]

This is easy to understand if we think of narrower boundaries than national ones. Suppose you have a thousand dollars you want to lend out, and you can do this only within your own town. You might have a choice between investing the money with a used book dealer or with the owner of a small café. Maybe you believe in the café owner, and so decide to give the loan to her. With it, she can buy a new espresso machine and replace a few old tables, but because demand for mochaccinos in a small town is still relatively limited, she will make only a small profit on this investment, so she can pay you only 2 percent interest on the money. But since the book dealer would pay only 1 percent, the café owner need have no fear that you'll take your money elsewhere.

If instead you have the whole state to choose from, there will be more people competing for your capital. A factory enabled by your money to purchase some new machinery could raise its earnings considerably and is therefore able to pay twice as much interest as the café proprietor. You earn more this way, but so does the whole economy, because the resources are used more efficiently than they would be by the other alternatives. This is even more true, of course, if you are allowed to invest your money nationwide or worldwide. In that case, all potential investments are compared with each other. Still more firms will then be after your money, and those capable of using it best are prepared to pay most for it. Money, loans, and share capital are generally invested where they are expected to yield the biggest return. In this way capital is used efficiently and boosts productivity, which develops the economy in which it is invested and gives the biggest return to the investor.

Because each entrepreneur has to compete with everyone else, it may sound as if the wealthiest firms will attract all the capital, because they can offer the highest returns. But capital is also obtainable from all the different countries, and so the supply increases. And it is not the wealthiest who bid most, but those who can make most out of the money. Why, after all, would an established firm pay an especially high rate of interest for money it doesn't really need? The biggest profits, as a rule, are not made in industries where there has already been ample investment, but in new enterprises that are unable to finance exciting projects. Capital markets are most important of all to those with good ideas but no capital. As we saw earlier, free capital markets appear to augment a society's economic equality. These markets cause people and businesses with a lot of capital to profit by placing the capital in the hands of those who have none but seem capable of using it more efficiently. And so they enable small firms to set up in competition with established ones. The more flexible the market and the fewer the impediments, the more easily capital flows to those who can make best use of it.

The affluent countries have large quantities of capital, while the poor countries of the South are short of it. So free movement of capital means investments moving toward more capital-starved countries with better investment opportunities. The developing countries receive more than a quarter of the world's combined investments in businesses, projects, and land. Thus, there is an enormous private transfer of capital from industrialized to developing countries. The flow of direct investments to the developing countries is now running at about $200 billion, on net, each year. This amount is more than 4 times the figure a decade ago and 15 times the figure 20 years ago, thanks to freer capital markets and improved information technology. This development is something fantastic for countries that have always been held back by shortage of capital. As mentioned earlier, in 10 years the poor countries of the world have obtained a trillion dollars in foreign direct investments—slightly more than all the development assistance they have received, worldwide, in the past 50 years. So the leaderless collective, allegedly staggering about and tripping over its own feet, has been more than five times cleverer than the governments and development aid establishments of the affluent countries at channeling capital to the developing countries.

Progressively larger share of investments goes to the developing countries

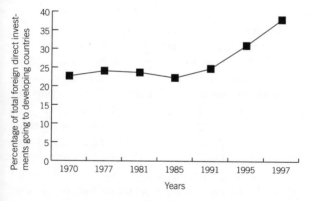

Source: Ajit K. Ghose, *Trade Liberalization and Manufacturing Employment.* Employment Paper 2000/3 (Geneva: International Labour Office, 2000).

The developing countries get increasingly more capital

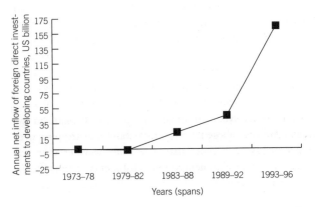

Source: Barry Eichengreen, Michael Mussa, et al., *Capital Account Liberalization: Theoretical and Practical Aspects* (Washington: IMF, 1998).

As critics of globalization point out, only about 5 percent of all economic transfers comprise real trade in goods and services. The remaining financial trade is concerned with "making money out of money," which some of the critics seem to think adds nothing of value to the economy. But there is nothing so productive as financing improvements in production. Doing so provides resources for production and spurs technical progress.

An international financial market enlarges the volume of investments. When there are large and efficient financial markets with the ability to buy and sell risks through derivatives, it becomes possible to finance bigger projects and take bigger risks than were previously viable. This is what accounts for the bulk of the turnover in the financial market. With billions of dollars circling the globe every day, a very small portion of the money actually changes hands: most of the transactions are due to firms and investors reallocating their investments, so as to guard against risks. It is only since this reallocation became possible that the developing countries have gained proper access to international flows of capital.

Through access to international finance we can spread our risks, simply by investing in different places. If one country's economy did badly, then in the past this would have meant that not enough money was available for things like old age pensions. If the same thing happened today, there would be enough money to go around as long as the country's people had been allowed to spread their savings between different countries. Sweden's new pension system has enabled me personally—and before this I had neither stock shares nor trust funds—to invest part of my future pension in new markets in Latin America and Asia, instead of tying the money up in Sweden. The financial markets also make it possible for households, businesses, and even governments to borrow when their incomes are low and to repay when their incomes are higher. This becomes a way of alleviating downturns without being forced to cut down on one's consumption as drastically as would otherwise be necessary.

In its Capital Access Index, the Milken Institute has shown that economies develop best when capital is readily available and cheap and is distributed openly and honestly. They manage least well when capital is in short supply, expensive, and arbitrarily distributed. Broad, free financial markets with many players create development, while a system of "state-directed capital flows concentrated in a small number of financial institutions and corporations hampers growth." Studies have generally shown that the functional development of financial markets in a certain country provides a good indication of that country's growth for coming years. There are studies showing no connection between freedom from capital regulations and growth, but in those studies no attempt has been made to measure the intensity of the regulations in different countries. One survey tried to take account of that intensity, looking at 64 industrialized and developing countries and eliminating (to the extent possible) the effect of other factors. That survey pointed to a clear aggregate connection between freedom of capital movements and economic growth, as well as suggesting that countries with freedom for capital receive far more tax revenue from businesses. Freedom causes resources to go where they can be used most productively, which makes it easier for businesses to start up and facilitates international trade.[3]

Regulate more?

The problems associated with the mobility of capital are that it can suddenly flee countries that get into economic difficulties or that a currency can be subjected to destabilizing speculation. Many lenders and investors have no specific knowledge of a particular country's economy, so if large numbers begin to leave it, others may take this trend as an indication that something is wrong and follow the tide. Panic and a herd mentality set in. Credit vanishes, projects have to be discontinued, firms lose all their resources, and the economy slams on all the brakes.

One of the reasons that short-term capital transactions grow faster than long-term investments or commodity trade is that the latter are very severely regulated in all states of the world. If these markets were to be properly liberalized, we would get different proportions. Some feel that the level of regulation must be equalized, but in the wrong direction, by also regulating the financial market by means of controls of different kinds. Malaysia, for example, introduced strict exchange controls as a temporary measure during the "Asian crisis" of the late 1990s. Even if such measures could alleviate the immediate problem, they have the long-term effect of causing investors to avoid the country in the future. If investors might be prevented from leaving the country when they want to, they will demand a higher return for coming there in the first place, and the country will risk a capital shortage. All empirical data show that allowing capital to flow freely *out* of a country freely increases the amount flowing in. The immediate result of imposing controls in this instance was that Malaysia's neighbors—Indonesia, for example—suffered a swifter exodus of capital, because of widespread fears that it would follow the Malaysian example of controls. In the long term, this effect recoiled against the Malaysia itself by lowering investor confidence. One investor in Asian funds recently said of Malaysia:

A market that used to have up to 18 percent of weighting in most funds is now totally ignored.[4]

That economic isolation has coincided with the country's movement toward political isolation.

One alternative is a more permanent regulation of short-term capital flows. If quick capital does not enter in the first place, it reduces the risk of the country suffering an exodus of capital later on. Chilean rules have often been looked on as exemplary in this respect, since that country has avoided major crises. Chile has insisted that capital entering the country remain there for a certain length of time and that a certain portion of it be deposited at very low interest with the central bank. This type of regulation seems to work better than alternative controls, but Chile's reason for introducing such rules was that savings were so high that it did not *want* to have more capital in the country. This situation is hardly the same as the one afflicting developing countries starved for capital and investments. Even in capital-rich Chile, the policy led to financial problems. Big companies operating internationally circumvented the controls and got hold of capital anyway, while small businesses coped less well and had to pay interest rates many times higher.

The perspective of these rules is excessively short term. Chile *was* hit by a real economic crisis in 1981–82, with bank failures and a 90 percent devaluation. That crisis happened at the same time as its capital controls were at their most rigorous, when inflows of capital were prohibited unless the capital remained in the country for at least five and a half years. Wise from the crisis, Chile decided to reform and consolidated its chaotic banking sector, which is probably the main reason why it has avoided further crises. (Incidentally, Chile's decision to cancel its capital regulations came at the height of the Asian crisis.)[5]

Capital controls often serve as a means of lulling investors and politicians into a false sense of security. A looming crisis covered up by market-distorting regulations only hits harder once the underlying problems are finally exposed. Only months before the Asian crisis hit South Korea, local politicians and international investors believed the country's restrictions on capital mobility would save it from an exchange crisis. In 1997, Goldman-Sachs judged South Korea's banks and central bank to be in bad shape, but since the country had capital regulations, they declared that investors could disregard the risks this implied. The investors took the advice and ignored the risks. The Asian crisis then struck hardest against Indonesia, South Korea, and eventually Russia, which had the stiffest capital regulations in any growth market. Those with the lightest regulations—Hong Kong, Singapore, and Taiwan—fared far better.[6] Brazil too was hard hit; politicians there had thought that restrictions against short-term capital would steer them clear of the crisis.

Sooner or later, mismanaged policy leads to crisis. And if capital controls make politicians believe that they are free to pursue any policy they like, the odds are that they will aggravate the crisis. In theory, temporary capital controls in a crisis could give the country breathing room to modernize its banking and finance sector, iron out problems in the budget, and liberalize the economy. Often, though, regulations are put to the opposite use, as a means of avoiding painful reforms. One sign of this avoidance is that countries with capital regulations have, on average, bigger budget deficits and higher inflation than those without. This is also why liberal economies with freer financial markets emerge from their crises more quickly. We can compare the rapid recovery of many Asian states after the Asian crisis with Latin America's crisis of the early 1980s, after which Latin American countries imposed controls on capital outflows and refrained from liberal reforms. The result was a lost decade of inflation, prolonged unemployment, and low growth. Compare Mexico's rapid recovery after the "Tequila crisis" of 1995 with the same country's prolonged depression after the debt crisis of 1982.

Another problem with capital controls is that they are hard to maintain in a world of ever-improving, ever-faster communication. They are in practice an invitation to crime, and a great deal of investors' time is devoted to circumventing the regulations. The longer a regulation has been in force, the less effective it becomes, because investors then have time to find ways around it. Besides, most regulations have their exceptions for particularly important or vulnerable enterprises. So in most countries controls become an incentive for corruption, and different people are treated differently by the law.

Tobin tax

One proposed capital regulation that has achieved popularity in recent years is the so-called Tobin tax, named after Nobel laureate economist James Tobin, who first suggested it. The Tobin tax is a low tax of 0.05–0.25 percent on all currency exchange, which is advocated by the ATTAC movement among others. The idea is to slow down capital movements and make investors think twice before allowing capital to cross currency exchange boundaries. It's argued that in this way harmful speculation and major exchange crises could be avoided. Criticism of the Tobin tax has focused on the impossibility of introducing it. In practice, all countries would have to agree on it; otherwise transactions would go through nonsignatory countries. And if it could be introduced, more and more trade would go to the major currencies in order to avoid transaction costs. Perhaps nearly the entire world economy would end up using U.S. dollars. But there is a more serious objection to the Tobin tax: even if it were possible to introduce, it would be harmful.

This tax would actually be more harmful to the financial market than regulations by individual countries. The only effect of the latter is to reduce inflow in the country opting for them, whereas a Tobin tax would reduce turnover and the possibility of external financing all over the world, even for countries in great need of such financing. Obstacles to the movement of capital fence it in where it is already—in the affluent countries—and the Third World is the loser. The Tobin tax, therefore, is not really a tax on capital but a tariff that makes trade and investment more expensive. Advocates of the Tobin tax claim that it need not have this effect, because it is so low. For long-term investments the cost will be negligible. But the problem is that an investment is not just one transaction. An investor may perhaps partially finance a project, recoup some of the money in profits, increase the investment if it is successful, transfer earnings to other parts of the operation, add capital, buy components from abroad, and so on. With every little transaction taxed, the total cost of the Tobin tax will be many times greater than the low cost suggested by the percentage figure on paper, and so doing business in one's own currency and in one's own region will be more profitable. This will lead to a general reduction of the return on capital, and it will cause capital-starved countries to have less access to capital and, consequently, fewer investments. Interest rates will rise, and borrowers will have to pay more for their loans.

The adherents of the Tobin tax say that what they really want to get at is sheer currency speculation, not productive investment. But the idea that there is some hard and fast boundary between useful investments and "useless speculation" is completely wrong. Derivatives, which the critics usually regard as sheer speculation, are necessary in order for investments to work. In a world of changing prices and exchange rates, a firm's forecasting can be completely overturned if it does not have the type of insurance that derivatives afford. Suppose a company extracts a metal and the price of that metal suddenly falls dramatically; earnings fail to materialize and bankruptcy threatens. Instead of devoting a large part of its activity to wondering how markets are going to develop, the firm can buy a right to sell the raw material at a predetermined price later on—a sale option. The purchaser of this option takes over the risk and the responsibility of predicting market developments. The metal company can quietly concentrate on extracting the metal, and the risk is willingly taken over instead by people who specialize in observing developments and apportioning the risks—in a word, speculators.

Because exchange rates are rapidly changeable, firms encounter the same risk if, for example, the currency in which they are paid quickly depreciates. If a metal company has trouble predicting the future course of its own market, it is far more difficult for it to keep track of economic developments in the currency and exchange risks over a period of several months or years. This uncertainty makes it still more important to be able to trade in currency derivatives of different kinds, so that a company can, for example, purchase the right to sell the currency it will be receiving at a predetermined price. But it is this very "speculation" that a Tobin tax would prevent. And, just like an ordinary investment, it involves more than one single transaction. If a speculator took over only complete risks, he would be very vulnerable. The speculator must always be able to reapportion his risks according to developments in order to balance his total portfolio of risk. This ability is guaranteed by a large secondhand market that enables one to trade in these derivatives almost immediately. This "speculation" is how the insurance is made as cheap as possible for the company, allowing it to invest in spite of risks. And it is essentially the same way the secondhand market for shares, the stock market, gives people the courage to finance new businesses by participating as shareholders.

The structure of the Tobin tax is aimed at this very market. It would result in fewer speculators being ready to take on risks and in their demanding much more payment for doing so. The insurance, then, would be much more expensive for companies and investors, with the result that they would not invest in countries and currencies with a greater element of risk. Once again, it is the more capital-starved and risk-laden regions—poor developing countries—that would be the losers. Investors would place their capital only where it seemed secure and where they knew the market. During the past decade, the developing countries have received over a quarter of all foreign direct investment. This figure would fall dramatically if a Tobin tax were introduced. It would be more difficult for people and businesses in poor countries to obtain loans, and they would be forced to pay higher rates of interest.

There is a serious risk, then, that financial markets would be disrupted by a Tobin tax. But that tax would not be capable of preventing exchange crises. In practice, the tax would establish only a low barrier to impede everyday trading. If exchange transactions *above* that threshold suddenly became profitable, there would be drastic fluctuations. The problems of currency speculation and capital exodus would not be averted. When speculators realize that they have a chance of breaking a fixed exchange rate (for example, sterling and the Swedish krona in 1992), they stand to make such enormous amounts of money that a tax of a fraction of the gain would not deter them. If they can make 20 or 50 percent on an exchange rate, they will not be put off by a tax of 0.05 percent. The same applies when confidence in a country fails and gigantic losses can be avoided by getting out fast, as in the Asian crisis of 1997. The small tax that is sufficient to disrupt the everyday, healthy functioning of the financial market would not be sufficient to prevent these crises.

High turnover in the exchange market reduces the risk of temporary shortages and distorted pricing. A bigger market also reduces the risk of individual players and transactions decisively affecting prices. In this way free exchange markets prevent the occurrence of violent exchange rate fluctuations, something that, paradoxically, the Tobin tax could augment by reducing the liquidity of the exchange market. Constant equalizations and adjustments would be replaced by big periodic jolts. Currency, market shocks, and volatility have not increased since the 1970s, despite the widespread liberalization of markets and a quadrupling of volume. The fact is that countries with severe capital regulations have far more erratic exchange rates than those with fewer restrictions.[7]

But for all these shortcomings, the Tobin tax still has one advantage: it would yield tremendous revenues. The ATTAC movement counts on $100 billion a year—some say $10 billion to $50 billion a year. However, the question is whether this money could ever be collected. Collection would require an immense bureaucracy keeping track of all transactions throughout the world and empowered to collect the money. We are talking here about transactions taking place in computers all over the globe, including in countries that in practice have neither accounting systems nor an effective administration. In other words, there would have to be some kind of world government, the bureaucracy of which would presumably eat up a large part of the revenues collected. How is this bureaucracy to be governed? By the United Nations, where dictatorships have the same power as democracies? Who would stop this world government from swerving into an orgy of corruption? Who would prevent abuses of its expansive power? And who would get the money?

Nevertheless, the Tobin tax would in theory mean several billion dollars that, for example, could be used to help the Third World. But if we are convinced that a capital transfer of this kind would be helpful, why can't we achieve it by other means? Why not abolish the tariffs against these countries or dismantle the EU's destructive agricultural policy, which is holding them back?

Why not augment development assistance or introduce a global charge on polluting activity? Why should we necessarily procure revenue by sabotaging the financial market? Unless that is the true motive. . . .

The Asian crisis

To find out how crises can be prevented, we ought to study earlier crises and their causes. The Asian crisis of 1997–98 is often said to have come like a bolt from the blue, with healthy economies suddenly hit by speculative assaults and capital flight. It wasn't like that at all. The grain of truth in that version of events is that these countries would not have suffered an exodus of capital if they had not liberalized movements of capital, because then the capital would never have come to them in the first place. What created the crisis, though, was a combination of factors, among which speculation was not the triggering factor but rather the drop that made an already full glass run over.[8]

The economies affected by the Asian crisis had been showing clear signs of trouble ahead for some time, and these signs grew stronger during 1996 and early 1997. Those economies had received enormous inflows of capital during the 1990s, especially through short-term borrowing abroad, which was encouraged by their governments. The proportion of the debts of Thai banks and institutions borrowed from abroad rose from 5 to 28 percent between 1990 and 1995. Thailand's central bank, along with various banking regulations, created high domestic interest rates, making it lucrative to borrow abroad. Much of that borrowed money was then re-lent at higher rates of interest at home. Governments encouraged these loans with fixed exchange rates and tax subsidies. At the same time they discriminated against long-term capital. South Korea tried to exclude it completely by prohibiting

259

foreign direct investments and purchases of shares and securities. Short-term loans were the only possible way of raising capital from abroad.

A South Korean bank could borrow dollars or yen for a very short term—money that it would soon have to pay back. Meanwhile, it lent this money at a higher rate of interest for long-term investments in South Korea. Banks counted on always being able to renew the foreign loans, since otherwise they would suddenly be left without money to meet their other obligations. Capital was channeled through banks and finance companies that were unprepared for such enormous inflows. They were not exposed to competition, and they were often allied with the ruling regime and with strong economic interests. Many of the resources in South Korea, Malaysia, Thailand, and Indonesia went to favored firms and prestige projects. Outsiders had no reason to be apprehensive, because they knew that the ruling powers would never allow their favorites to go under. This principle applied to the national banks, but also to private firms like the *chaebols*—South Korea's super-corporations—or the business empire operated by Suharto's acquaintances in Indonesia. Besides, foreign creditors knew for sure that the IMF would intervene and save them from losses if the region as a whole ran into problems. And so the foreigners lent unlimited amounts, resulting in overinvestment in low-yield heavy industry and real estate, instead of in more dynamic enterprises.

All the countries destined to be hit by the crisis had enormous short-term debts relative to their reserves. At the same time, they all had fixed or controlled exchange rates. This situation created a number of eventually devastating problems. Usually, one does not dare to borrow huge sums abroad and then lend them only slightly more expensively at home if exchange rates are constantly fluctuating. One can lose on even very small exchange rate move-ments unless one is insured against the risk. But with the govern-ment professing to guarantee a fixed exchange rate, this risk appeared to vanish, and everyone was able to borrow like mad. In addition, regulation meant that the local currency was overval-ued (by about 20 percent), not least because the dollar, to which many of these currencies were pegged, rose. This overvaluation helped make exporting more difficult. Thai exports, which had risen by 25 percent in 1995, actually started to decline in the following year. In 1996, the year before the crisis that allegedly struck like a bolt from the blue, the Thai stock market index lost one-third of its value.

Because exchange rates were higher than the market believed they ought to be, the currencies became a prey to speculators, as happened to several currencies that were part of the European Monetary System (EMS) in 1992–93. If anyone is prepared to pay more for something than it is worth, speculators are, of course, eager to cash in on it. Speculators can borrow fantastic sums of money in local currency and exchange them at the maximum rate in the central bank. As a result, the countries affected by the Asian crisis in 1997 were forced to use their currency reserves to defend their excessive exchange rates.

The exodus of capital, then, was not just mindless panic, but quite rational. Confidence in the countries' economy and future growth had begun to evaporate. What was worse, so had belief in the ability of their economies to weather a crisis. It was known that they did not have viable legal institutions, such as bankruptcy legislation. Now they had also exhausted the reserves that guaran-tee foreign loans and the whole of the financial system. If everyone pulled out, the reserves would not be sufficient. Individual invest-ors realized that they would have to recover their capital quickly in order to get it out in time. Faith in the government's ability to save every business that got into trouble began to wobble. The first ones to get rid of their local currency holdings were not speculators but native enterprises that needed to pay off their loans quickly. When the countries were forced to abandon their exchange rates after huge losses, confidence in them declined still further. Capital fled, loans were not renewed, and firms were suddenly left without financing. The crisis was on.

Undoubtedly, investors influenced one another, and something of a herd mentality ensued, but again, this reaction was not a matter of blind panic. Countries with healthy economies and solid institutions, such as Taiwan, Singapore, and Australia, coped well when their neighbors were knocked sideways. And so the term "Asian crisis" is not all that accurate. Upon reflection, it becomes clear that national policy decided how greatly a country was affected by the crisis. Two researchers who studied the course of the crisis summed it up as follows:

> We found no evidence of contagion, in which the currency difficulties of one country were transferred to other countries. All of the countries that suffered the most serious financial difficulties did so because each had real economic difficulties, associated in large part with an excessive growth of bank credit and bank loan and insolvency issues.[9]

The effects of the crisis were felt all over the world, but in an integrated world it is natural for events in one quarter to affect others—and not because of an irrational herd mentality. Shortage of liquidity—that is, having one's money tied up in investments when some ready cash is needed—means that investors have to repatriate capital from other risk-laden countries. It should be

262

expected that U.S. companies and banks, and thus the U.S. economy, would be affected by one of their most important markets being plunged into a profound crisis. Asian banks in crisis have to withdraw resources from Russia, which makes problems for Brazilian banks and fund operators who have lent money in that direction, and so on. But international effects run both ways. Positive events in one country can produce positive effects elsewhere. The previous upturn in Latin America and Asia contributed to good times in Europe and the United States. And very possibly it was the subsequently strong economy of the United States that saved the world from depression in connection with the Asian crisis and quickly pulled the Asian economies up again.

Claims by Naomi Klein and others that all the progress achieved in East Asia was obliterated by the crisis are sheer nonsense. One country that was very badly hit, South Korea, saw its per capita GDP, adjusted for purchasing power, decline in 1998 to just over the 1995 level, which in turn was more than twice the level 10 years earlier. And only a year later, in 1999, South Korean GDP registered an all-time high. Certain aspects of the crisis have also been hugely exaggerated by activists on the left. Some went so far as to maintain that the crisis plunged 50 million Indonesians into absolute poverty (earning less than a dollar a day). This figure is over four times the number who were even temporarily reduced to absolute poverty *in the whole of Southeast Asia*. Official WB figures show the increase in Indonesia to have been less than a million up to 1999, a number that has since declined.[10]

Instead of crisis

There are various methods for avoiding financial and exchange rate crises, but the most essential of them is simply for a country to have a healthy economic policy. The very first people to move their savings away from a country that subsequently experiences a massive exodus of capital are usually its own citizens, who have a front-row view and most often know best which economic problems their rulers are attempting to conceal. This suggests that lack of confidence is brought about by real problems, not by ignorance and follow-the-leader behavior. The top priority for crisis avoidance is for the government to have control of its finances and inflation. Galloping budget deficits and high inflation were not the problem during the Asian crisis, but they are definitely the fastest and most common ways of ruining confidence in an economy.

The most important long-term commitments for new economies are reforms of legal and financial institutions. Countries should liberalize their domestic financial markets and their trade policy before opening up to foreign capital. Otherwise, capital will not be channeled in harmony with the wider market, leading to malinvestment. Supervision and regulation of the financial sector have to be reformed, and competition must be permitted. Corruption and nepotism must be weeded out and superseded by the rule of law and capital yield requirements. Given the tendency of ignorance to cause panic in critical situations, much depends on reliable information and transparency in national and corporate dealings, something that many Asian governments had deliberately obstructed. Credit valuation and bankruptcy laws, which in reality have been lacking in many Asian countries, have to be introduced. The global community could provide effective counseling on the strengthening of national financial markets. Accounting rules and capital coverage requirements can be coordinated, and agreements can be introduced on the consistent management of financial crises—management that until now has been pretty arbitrary.

It is true that the liberalization of financial markets has sometimes been followed by financial crises. The trouble, however, is not liberalization as such but the absence of the necessary institutions to go with it. Economist Jagdish Bhagwati is among those who have pointed out that liberalization of capital flows can create problems if it precedes other important reforms. He suggests as a solution, not capital controls, but that countries first create political stability, free trade, and domestic reforms, such as privatization, before attempting to liberalize their financial markets.[11] In practice, though, liberalization of financial markets comes easier, and so it has often preceded domestic reforms, which can take far longer to implement and must overcome opposition from vested interests. The IMF bears much of the blame for deregulations previously having occurred without the necessary preconditions being in place. Two journalists for *The Economist* have compared the IMF's advocates of capital mobility to an unscrupulous salesperson in a pet shop declaring that a dog is wonderful company, while forgetting to explain that in order to survive it must be fed and taken for walks.[12]

Nowadays the IMF devotes more effort to advising countries on how to create good institutions in the long term, and governments have become interested listeners. This task is an important one, but such reforms demand long-term work of a decidedly unglamorous nature. Shouting for capital controls and a Tobin tax, while misguided, can appear easier and more exciting than the arduous process of institution building. The one rational, quick-fix reform that could be implemented in this spirit is the abolition of controlled exchange rates. James Tobin, the originator of the tax that bears his name, has himself pointed to fixed exchange rates as perhaps the principal cause of the Asian crisis.[13]

Fixed exchange rates are what give speculators something to speculate against. As soon as economic problems, suspicion of a looming devaluation, or indications of an inflationary policy occur, the exchange rate is perceived as too high. The market decides that the currency is not worth the price that the government has put on it. With a fixed exchange rate, speculators can earn vast amounts by borrowing in the currency and selling it to the central bank. When the country has been forced to devalue the currency by lowering its exchange rate, the speculator can repay the loan, which by then has substantially depreciated. An excessive exchange rate in relation to supply and demand, and to what the currency will be worth after the likely devaluation, amounts to a huge subsidy for speculation. The government is, in effect, buying itself an exchange crisis. Inaccurate pricing is incompatible with openness to movements of capital—the only question is whether it's the prices or the movements of capital that are wrong. Speculators selling local currency when the central bank pays an inflated price for it is no stranger than thousands of Europeans growing sugar beets when the EU pays too much for them.

When the fixed exchange rate is too high, it is already too late, whatever governments may do next. They can defend the exchange rate at colossal expense, emptying their reserves and raising interest rates as a result, which will put a stranglehold on the economy. Alternatively, they can let the value of their currency fall steeply to the market level, in which case the country's industries will be unable to repay the big loans that they took on at the higher exchange rate. Either way, crisis will follow. In one study, two economists point out that practically all fixed exchange rate arrangements, sooner or later, have run into exchange rate crises. This was what happened to the EMS countries in 1992, to Mexico in 1997, to Russia in 1998, to Brazil in 1999, and to Argentina in 2001. Two other analysts point out the flip-side:

We are not aware of an example of a significant financial or currency crisis in an emerging market with fully flexible exchange rates.[14]

The dictatorship of the market?

There is one objection to free financial markets that transcends economics. Critics of globalization see them as a threat to democracy. With free markets, capital and businesses can quickly move across national boundaries if they are dissatisfied with the policy any one country pursues. If taxes climb too high, corporations may flee to an offshore tax shelter. If a country, especially a small one, begins having high budget deficits, it may be punished with higher interest rates. *New York Times* columnist Thomas Friedman coined the term "the golden straitjacket" to describe the way globalization affects governments: policy flexibility is constrained by the need to avoid scaring away increasingly mobile businesses. All those things, the critics reason, imply that markets are beginning to steer politics, and they go so far as to speak of "market fascism" or a "dictatorship of the market."

The latter slogan is a grotesque distortion, one that trivializes the crimes of real dictatorships and attempts to equate two phenomena that are utter opposites, not variations on the same theme. Probably the first country to introduce a nonconvertible currency—that is, one its citizens were not allowed to exchange for other currencies—was the extremely protectionist Nazi Germany. The communist governments actually regarded dictatorship as a precondition for the command economy. Shifts of power and free debate would upset long-term government planning and were compatible only with the liberal market, in which individuals decide for themselves. In contrast, new democracies invariably choose, as one of their first actions, to open up their markets and liberalize their economies.

The converse also applies. In the long run it is hard for dictatorships, once they have accepted economic freedom, to avoid introducing political liberty as well. In country after country in recent decades, we have seen rulers who granted their citizens the right to choose goods and invest freely soon thereafter forced to give them a free choice of government. This is precisely what happened to the Southeast Asian and Latin American dictatorships. Mexico's single-party state collapsed a few years after the country had opted for free trade. Suharto's Indonesian dictatorship fell like a house of cards in the wake of the Asian crisis. Now we can see some of the first democratic power shifts in Africa, in the very states that have committed themselves to more open markets.

It is widely assumed that the Arab states, marked by gender inequity and oil-focused planned economies, can never be democratized. But a couple of Arab states—Qatar and Bahrain—have embarked on liberal economic reforms, resulting in growth. This growth has been accompanied by a process of political reforms. Qatar has dismantled its press censorship, and the Al-Jazeera satellite channel operates freely—*too* freely, in the opinion of the Americans during the war with the Taliban in Afghanistan and with Saddam Hussein's regime in Iraq. The United States tried to prevail on the government of Qatar to take control of the channel, only to be told that this could not be done in a country where there was freedom of expression. Qatar has also had democratic local elections in which women have been allowed to both vote and stand for office. Bahrain's new leader has released political prisoners, and dissidents have returned from exile to take part in the political dialogue. In 2002, the country held both municipal and national parliamentary elections that saw women and men alike in the voting booth and on the ballot. People who grow richer, are better educated, and are accustomed to choice will not acquiesce in others' deciding matters on their behalf, and so the market economy often leads to democracy just as democracy consolidates the market economy. When groups that were previously excluded acquire a political voice, it becomes less easy for the elite to feather its nest at their expense. This leads to more economic liberalization measures, which reduce poverty and, consequently, strengthen democracy. A decentralized economic system makes possible the establishment of groups independent of the political power, which in turn provides a basis for political pluralism. International surveys of economic freedom have shown that citizens who are entitled to trade internationally are roughly four times more likely to enjoy political democracy than those who do not have this right. This is one reason that democratic activists in China were so eager for their country to join the World Trade Organization: with the benefits of membership come pressure for transparency and decentralization. A dictatorship that has always acted tyrannically and arbitrarily must now conform to an impartial international code in at least one sphere. Shortly before China's accession, an imprisoned dissident said of the prospect of greater openness: "Before the sky was black. Now there is a light. This can be a new beginning."[15]

The 20th century clearly showed that no economic system but capitalism is compatible with democracy. Any talk of a "dictatorship of the market" is not only insulting but also abysmally ignorant.

It is true that a debtor is, in some sense, unfree. By contracting a budget deficit and debts, a country incurs the market's suspicion. Reforms have to be introduced to restore confidence in the national economy, otherwise the outside world will demand higher rates of interest on additional loans or else simply stop lending. A modern state can thus find itself "in the hands of the market," but the government is to blame for this outcome, not the market. If the government mismanages its finances and will not finance its expenditure out of its own funds, but with the market's, then it has decided to make itself dependent on the market.

The international financial markets were actually created by welfare states wishing to borrow for their expenditures during the crises of the 1970s. In this way they increased their scope for maneuver. Without financial markets, the government would be forced to live within its means, while with financial markets the need to raise revenue can be put off until later. Hence, states with a credible and stable policy have a much wider range of options available than they would have before financial markets existed. But lenders have good historical reasons for distrusting states with a large national debt. Often those states have unilaterally reduced the amounts lenders can claim by means of high inflation or devaluation, which reduce the value of a currency. So financial markets have cause to keep a watchful eye on the doings of governments and not to grant such favorable terms to those that don't seem to be making ends meet. But creditors lending money on their own terms cannot be likened to dictatorship. Governments are still at liberty to mismanage their economies; they are deprived only of the ability to force others to finance their mismanagement.

> "When national debts have once been accumulated to a certain degree, there is scarce, I believe, a single instance of their having been fairly and completely paid. The liberation of the public revenue, if it has ever been brought about at all, has always been brought about by a bankruptcy; sometimes by an avowed one, but always by a real one, though frequently by a pretended payment."
> Adam Smith, 1776[16]

Capitalism and democracy go hand in hand

(Degree of economic freedom and democratic rights in 46 studied countries)

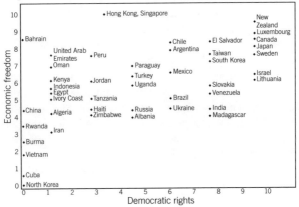

Source: Roger Donway, "Lands of Liberty," *Navigator,* no. 4, 2000.

The market's assessment is often progressive. The Latin American dictatorships fell during the 1980s when the market abandoned their deeply indebted, crisis-ridden economies. Post-crisis, most of the Asian states are committed to openness and democratization. Because they need information and the rule of law, investors hate secretiveness and corruption like poison. There is no better way of driving capital out of a country than to foster suspicions of malfeasance among the political elite, and there are few attractions so powerful as transparency and illumination in the public sphere.

To some people, the very idea of the market passing judgment on politics is undemocratic. Lenders, as they see it, should keep quiet and willingly make their money available, even if governments look as though they may blow it all through inflation. By

272

the same token, there is nothing undemocratic about taxpayers placing their savings abroad. Reacting to politics in order to protect one's interests is only anti-democratic if one equates democracy with total governmental control and implicit deference to the rulers of the nation. If *that* is democracy, public dissent and journalistic scrutiny are also undemocratic. Such a "democracy" sounds more like a dictatorship that insists on total submission.[17]

What critics really find threatened by the market is not democracy but the policies they want democracies to introduce—policies involving greater government power over people's economic decisionmaking. But saying that the market threatens government control of our economic actions is less exciting than calling it a threat to democracy. Why should it be "more democratic" for a democratic government to have more powers of decisionmaking over us? Would the United States, by this logic, be made more democratic if the government were to decide whom we could marry, what work we could do, or what we were entitled to write in a newspaper? Of course not. A majority of the people should elect their political representatives; that doesn't mean they should also decide by vote how individuals run their lives. Democracy is a way to rule the state, not a way to rule society.

If policy has to be changed under pressure from the market, such changes can sound like a threat to democracy. Suppose, for example, that the U.S. government has to abolish double taxation of capital gains because otherwise companies would leave the United States. This view again presupposes that people must always comply with political decisions and that the political process must be influenced by nothing beyond the conscious decisionmaking of Congress. But the normal state of affairs is that inspiration and challenges to the status quo often come from outside, not from the politicians themselves. Democracy exists partly in order to adapt a country's policies to changing circumstances, and this adaptation, when it happens, is not undemocratic. If it were, then any factors increasing the tax burden and public spending more than political parties had promised would also be undemocratic. There are any number of such factors, including the demands of pressure groups (Green protesters, for example); the expansion by bureaucrats of their activities; and efforts by politicians to keep their own party faithful happy. I have yet to hear anyone speak on this account of "the dictatorship of public spending."

The notion that the market forces countries to adopt certain policies has, it seems to me, been created by craven politicians. Lacking the energy or the ability to justify the choice to adopt a policy of fiscal restraint or to liberalize, politicians declare such measures necessary, forced upon them by globalization. This is a handy cop-out, and a denigration of the market economy into the bargain.

There is reason to challenge the very premise of the argument that markets compel a market-liberal policy. The players in the market do not demand a liberal ideology in order to "reward" a country with their decisions about where to locate or send capital, but they do require a well-ordered economy that is not on the verge of collapse. The market's reaction to policy is one reason for the welcome proliferation of diminishing budget deficits, low inflation, and low rates of interest in countries once characterized by the opposite. You would hardly put your money into a pension fund that invested according to an ideology rather than by economic criteria. If the economy is equally well ordered, investors will not treat a social democratic welfare state any differently from a libertarian nightwatchman state. One of the world's most globalized countries is Sweden, which also happens to have the world's highest taxes.

The past two decades of globalization have witnessed an expansion of government machinery. Between 1980 and 1995, taxation in all the countries of the world rose from 22.6 to 25.9 percent of their GDP, and public spending rose from 25.7 to 29.1 percent of GDP.[18]

The fact that people and businesses are able to move freely does not necessarily entail that they will immediately relocate where taxes are lowest. They will move to wherever they feel that they get best value for their tax money. If citizens feel that they are getting security and service that are worth the money they pay in taxes, they will not leave a country. If businesses feel that they are getting research, education, and infrastructure worth the money they pay in taxes, they will not leave the country either. It is only if taxes are used inefficiently or on things that people do not value (something that has been known to happen from time to time) that they will cause problems in a world where we can move about more freely. It will be more difficult to maintain taxes that people feel give nothing in return. Which isn't exactly undemocratic, is it?

It may even be that globalization makes it easier to maintain the political system voters want, even if their choice is in favor of high taxes and a large public sector. This is because globalization and free trade make it easier for us to obtain the things our system disfavors by exchange from countries with other systems. If the government health care monopoly in Britain or Canada discourages the development of new technology and science in the medical sector, it remains possible to import these things from countries where the medical sector is more dynamic. If high taxes impede the emergence of domestic financial markets, companies can procure capital in other countries. Globalization enables countries to afford things they are not good at. Problems remain for certain policies,

275

of course. If a country's own citizens are denied opportunities or incentives for education and production, it will have nothing to trade with. But the main point is that the nature of our own political system is still something we, the electorate, decide on the basis of our own values.

VII

Liberalize, don't standardize

The right to choose a culture

If children were forced to discover everything for themselves, they would develop very slowly. Happily, they have parents who transmit their experience and knowledge. In this way, children can rapidly acquire far more information than they could have acquired on their own—what can be eaten, what is poisonous, how to find the center of town, and how to swim. One of the biggest advantages of globalization is that young economies can learn from the older ones. Developing countries are not children, and the industrialized countries are certainly not parents, but the economies of the industrialized nations have passed through the transformations that the developing countries have ahead of them. The growth of those countries need not take as long as it did for the Western world. Instead, they can take shortcuts and learn from our mistakes. Development that took the West 80 or 100 years to accomplish has been successfully replicated by Taiwan in 25 years.

The developing countries can skip intermediate stages of development and benefit directly from the technology being produced, for example, in Europe and the United States. Mobile phones are a case in point. The developing countries need not incur the cost of constructing permanent telephone lines; they can leap directly to wireless technology. Mobile phones can now be used even by the poor to find out about prices of their goods. Many developing countries now have phone rental companies, and villagers often pool their funds for a mobile phone. This advance has meant steadier prices across larger markets, as well as less wasted food because of more exact delivery times.

Halima Khatuun is an illiterate woman in a Bangladeshi village. She sells eggs to a dealer who comes by at regular intervals. She used to be compelled to sell at the price he proposed, because she did not have access to other buyers. But once, when he came and offered 12 taka for four eggs, she kept him waiting while she used the mobile phone to find out the market price in another village. Because the price there was 14 taka, she was able to go back and get 13 from the dealer. Market information saved her from being cheated.[1]

New information technology is now revolutionizing old economic activities the world over. Hundreds of artisans—many of them women—in Morocco, Tunisia, Lebanon, and Egypt who never had access to international markets before can now sell their products through an Internet network called Virtual Souk.[2] Sales are climbing, and they are now able to retain a larger share of the earnings than was possible in the old markets.

People in poor countries can perform service tasks for Western companies by being connected to the head office via satellite and the Internet, and they can also obtain information. Thanks to the Internet, reliable medical advice and advanced education are no longer reserved for those living in the world's metropolitan cities. People may complain about the slowness of progress, with only about 5 percent of the world's population, mostly in the affluent Western countries, having access to the Internet, but such complaints ignore the historical perspective. The Internet as we know it is about 3,500 days old and has already reached nearly one out of every 10 people on earth. This is the fastest spread of technology in world history. The telephone has existed for 125 years, but until only a few years ago, half the world's inhabitants had never made a phone call. This time things are moving with infinitely greater rapidity, and globalization is the reason. One out of every 10 families in Beijing and Shanghai has a computer, and within a few years, Chinese will be the Web's biggest language.

The ability of the developing countries to take shortcuts in development leads some to imagine a common destination at the end of the road, one that all societies will be converging on. That picture troubles many people. They fear a "McDonaldization" or "Disneyfication" of the world, a creeping global homogeneity that leaves everyone wearing the same clothes, eating the same food, and seeing the same films. But this portrayal does not accurately describe the globalization process. Anyone going out in the capitals of Europe today will have no trouble finding hamburgers and Coca-Cola, but they will just as easily find kebab, sushi, Tex-Mex, Peking Duck, Thai, French cheeses, or cappuccino. We know that Americans listen to Britney Spears and watch Adam Sandler films, but it's worth remembering that the United States is also a country with 1,700 symphony orchestras, 7.5 million annual trips to the opera, and 500 million museum visits a year.[3] Globalization doesn't just send the world shlocky reality TV and overplayed music videos, but also classic films on numerous movie channels; documentaries on Discovery and the History Channel; and news on CNN, MSNBC, or any of their many competitors. The masterpieces of music and literature are now just a few clicks away on the Web, and the classics of cinema history are available in the video store around the corner.

With many reservations, one can say that developments are moving toward a common objective, but that objective is not the predominance of a particular culture. Instead it is pluralism, freedom to choose from a host of different paths and destinations. People's actual choices will then vary. Globalization and greater exchange result, not in all the different countries choosing the same thing, but in a far wider variety of options suddenly finding room in one country. When markets broaden and become international, this globalization increases the prospects of even very narrow cultural manifestations surviving and flourishing. Perhaps not all that many people in any given place are in the market for experimental electronic music or film versions of novels by Dostoevsky, and so the musicians and filmmakers concerned could never produce anything if they had only a local audience to rely on. But even very narrow customer segments acquire purchasing power when combined with similar tastes in other countries. Globalization can increase our chances of gaining access to exactly what we want, no matter how isolated we may feel in our liking for it. Moroccan folk art and French Roquefort cheese acquire better survival prospects when demand for them is aggregated from consumers across the world. The supply of goods and culture grows larger, with demand coming from all around the globe. This internationalization is, ironically, what makes people believe that differences are vanishing. When you travel abroad, things look much the same as in your own country: the people there also have goods and chain stores from different parts of the globe. This phenomenon is not due to uniformity and the elimination of differences but, on the contrary, is caused by a growth of pluralism everywhere. Americans are cultural leaders because they have been accustomed to producing commercially for a very large public, a function of having a large country with a common language. Now other countries are being given the same chance.

This opportunity can be negative in certain situations, admittedly. When traveling to another country, we want to see something unique. Arriving in Rome and finding Hollywood films,

Chinese food, Japanese Pokemon games, and Swedish Volvos, we miss the local color. And national specialties like pizza, pasta, and espresso are already familiar to us because we have them at home, too. A few pizzerias in Rome even promise Chicago-style pizza. What we gain by being free to choose everything at home is that this opportunity makes it hard to find any place that feels really authentic, at least on the main tourist routes. This is a problem, but it's another one of those luxury problems. A man from Prague was sometimes visited by Czech friends who had settled abroad. They deplored McDonald's having come to Prague, because it threatened the city's distinctive charm. This response made the man indignant. How could they regard his home city as a museum, a place for them to visit now and then in order to avoid fast food restaurants? He wanted a real city, including the convenient and inexpensive food that these exile Czechs themselves had access to. A real, living city cannot be a "Prague summer paradise" for tourists. Other countries and their populations do not exist in order to give us picturesque holiday experiences. They, like us, are entitled to choose what they think suits them.[4]

Cultures change, and the greater the number of options, the faster change will be. If one can read about other lifestyles and values in the newspaper and see them on television, adopting them may no longer seem like as big a step to take. Basically, though, there's nothing new about cultures changing, colliding with each other, and cross-pollinating. They've always done these things. Culture means cultivation, and change and renewal are an inherent part of that. If we try to freeze certain cultural patterns in time and highlight them as distinctively American or Thai or French or Swedish or Brazilian or Nigerian, they cease to be culture. They cease to be a living part of us and instead become museum relics and folklore. There is nothing wrong with museums—they can be pleasant places to spend an afternoon—but we can't live in one.

In coming to terms with the idea of isolated and preserved culture, the Norwegian social anthropologist Thomas Hylland Eriksen has pointed out that culture is a process, not a static object, and therefore essentially unlimited:

> *When the government is to be the guarantor of the population's cultural identity, culture has to be defined and codified in the rigid administrative language of the bureaucracy. It ceases to be living, dynamic, changeable and manifold and becomes a package, a completed jigsaw puzzle from which none of the pieces can be removed without spoiling the picture.*[5]

Even the traditions we think of as most "authentic" have generally resulted from cultural imports.[6] Foreigners often find it hard to believe, but one of the most sacred Swedish traditions is watching Donald Duck on TV on Christmas Eve, while another, 11 days earlier, involves celebrating an Italian saint by adorning the hair of blond girls with lighted candles. The Peruvian author Mario Vargas Llosa claims to have learned one thing from his lifelong studies of culture, French culture especially, which French politicians wish to protect with tariffs and subsidies:

> *And the most admirable lesson that I received . . . was the knowledge that cultures do not need to be protected by bureaucrats or police, confined behind bars, or isolated by customs officials to be kept alive, because that provincializes and stifles them. They need to live in freedom, exposed to exchanges with different cultures, thanks to which they renew and enrich themselves.*

283

It is not the dinosaurs of "Jurassic Park" that are threatening the culture that gave the world Montaigne and Flaubert, Debussy and Cezanne, Rodin and Marcel Carne, but the band of demagogues who talk about culture as if it were a mummy that cannot be taken out into the air of the world because freedom would destroy it.[7]

The cultural encounters of globalization reduce the risk of people being trapped in one culture. This may come as bad news to the guardians of tradition, but many people can imagine no greater triumph than escaping from the stereotypes and constraints of their own cultures. Globalization may be necessary in order to escape hidebound gender roles, to be allowed to live according to one's own values, or to break the family tradition and enter a career of one's own choosing. Having other cultural expressions to refer to can help. How can the elite maintain that their own way of life is the only possible one when television and the Internet carry so much information about an infinite number of alternatives? How can politicians pander to homophobia while simultaneously negotiating trade agreements with openly gay officials from other countries? Regularly meeting people who do not think and live like oneself is an effective antidote to narrow-mindedness, parochialism, and smug complacency.

The British sociologist Anthony Giddens provides a striking illustration from his own recollections of how oppressive the one and only solution of tradition can be:

If ever I am tempted to think that the traditional family might be best after all, I remember what my great aunt once said to me. She must have had one of the longest marriages of anyone, having been with her husband for over 60 years. She once confided that she had been deeply unhappy with him the whole of that time. In her day there was no escape.[8]

There is no universal formula to show how much modernization one must accept and how many traditions are to be preserved. Every balance has to be struck by people choosing for themselves. This can mean, but need not mean, that earlier forms of culture fade away. Now that other people who weren't born to the culture can gain access to it, its survival prospects are augmented in a different way—instead of being sustained by force of habit, it can spread by deliberate choice. The author Salman Rushdie has remarked that it is trees, not human beings, that have roots.

The onward march of freedom

Openness to new influences makes it easy for the most tempting and convincing ideas to spread. That is why the idea of freedom and individualism has attained such tremendous force in the age of globalization. There are few ideas as inspiring as that of self-determination. When it is discovered that people in other countries have that right, it becomes almost irresistible. A taste of the freedom to receive new ideas, images, and sounds, the freedom to choose, quickly leads people to demand more choice, more power to decide for themselves. That is why people who are allowed to enjoy economic freedom demand political democracy as well, and why those attaining democracy demand individual liberty. The idea of human rights is traveling around the globe. If there is any elimination of differences in progress throughout the world, it has been the convergence of societies on democracy, on people being allowed to live as they please. The similarity consists in more and more people being allowed to be dissimilar.

> "That contempt in which lower castes used to be held is almost disappearing completely. Now it is obvious for me to know that everyone, untouchables included, is a human being, with the same human dignity as myself. We all have the same color blood."
> *Indian farmer Ram Vishal, himself of intermediate caste.*[9]

So much for the racist idea that certain peoples cannot "cope" with freedom, that they need a period of strong leaders, or that people in one country can have nothing to say about another country's policies. If other governments oppress or exterminate their own citizens, we are entitled, perhaps even duty bound, to combat such actions. The notion of human dignity meaning different things on different sides of the border has been badly dented. Even though it did not result in prosecution, a milestone was reached when a Spanish prosecutor prevailed on the British authorities to arrest former Chilean dictator Augusto Pinochet while he was visiting the United Kingdom. It was also logical that Cuban dictator Fidel Castro was furious over the decision, even though he has a very different political complexion. He appreciated that the world now held fewer hiding places for dictators. Today, despots and mass murderers who as little as a decade ago could freely travel the world now risk being hauled in front of war crimes tribunals and international courts. This development, in turn, has spurred the activity of national judicial systems, which shows that the international measures supplement rather than supersede local law. In the future, perhaps crimes against humanity will not pay.

The future is not predetermined. There is no single path, and there is nothing forcing us to accept globalization. The anti-globalists are perfectly right about that. Capital can be locked up, trade flows blocked, and borders barricaded. This happened at least once before, following the globalization of the late 19th century. The world had then experienced several decades of democratization and greater openness. People could cross borders without passports and find jobs without work permits. They could easily become citizens wherever they settled. But after decades of anti-liberal propaganda and nationalistic saber-rattling, this openness was replaced at the beginning of the 20th century by centralization and closed borders. Countries that had been part-ners in trade and in the creation of new values began seeing one another as enemies, to be fought in the name of old values. Markets were to be conquered by force, not through free competition. The outbreak of World War I in 1914 marks the end of that period's globalization. Protectionism and passport requirements were introduced for the first time in several generations.

Globalization brings with it a number of effects upon which it is easy to cast suspicion—old economic forms disrupted, interests undermined, cultures challenged, and traditional power centers eroded. When boundaries become less important, people, goods, and capital move more freely—but so too can crime, fanaticism, and disease. Advocates of globalization have to show that greater freedom and greater opportunities counterbalance such problems. They must point to possible ways of dealing with them, perhaps more effectively than before. Otherwise, there is a serious risk that anti-globalist ideas will take root in the Western world, in which case a downturn or a trivial tariff war, for example, could evoke a powerful protectionist reaction. After the Wall Street Crash of 1929, the United States switched to a drastic policy of protectionism; thereafter all it exported for many years was depression. Other governments responded in kind, and world trade collapsed, diminishing by two-thirds in just three years. A national crisis led to worldwide depression. The return of protectionism today would mean stagnation in the affluent world and deeper poverty in the developing countries. At worst, it would once again lead to conflict, to countries regarding each other as enemies. When governments turn in upon themselves, regarding what is foreign as a threat rather than an opportunity, the simplest and coarsest forms of nationalism will gain ground.

There is less risk of globalization crashing and burning in the same way today. Imperialist ambitions have been dashed, and globalization has taken hold in an unprecedented number of democratic countries. Ideas of democracy and human rights are becoming more and more influential, and Asia and Latin America are on the whole more closely integrated with the world economy than ever, by their own choice. Most countries aim for regulated, mutual trade agreements within, say, the WTO, so that powerful governments will not be able to crush free trade on a whim. But even if democracy and the market should continue to spread, there is no single path for everyone. Countries like Burma and North Korea show that it is possible to cut oneself off from the global environment, as long as one is prepared to pay heavily for doing so in terms of oppression and poverty. Nor is there anything forcing the EU to liberalize our markets, if we are prepared to take the losses of freedom and prosperity that liberalization implies—and if we are prepared to let the poor of the developing countries suffer through our decision to retain tariff walls. It is not "necessary" to follow the globalization trend; it is merely desirable. Globalization will not keep moving under its own steam if no one stands up for it, if no one challenges isolationism.

All change arouses suspicion and anxiety, sometimes justifiably so; even positive changes can have troublesome consequences in the short term. Decisionmakers are unwilling to shoulder responsibility for failures and problems. It is preferable to be able to blame someone else. Globalization makes an excellent scapegoat. It contains all the anonymous forces that have served this purpose throughout history: other countries, other races and ethnic groups, the uncaring market. Globalization does not speak up for itself when politicians blame it for overturning economies, increasing poverty, and enriching a tiny minority, or when entrepreneurs say that globalization, rather than their own decisions, is forcing them to pollute the environment, cut jobs, or raise their own salaries. And globalization doesn't usually get any credit when good things happen—when the environment improves, the economy runs at high speed and poverty diminishes. Then there are plenty of people willing to accept full responsibility for the course of events. Globalization does not defend itself. So if the trend toward greater globalization is to continue, an ideological defense will be needed for freedom from borders and controls.

In 25 years' time there are likely to be 2 billion more of us on this planet, and 97 percent of that population increase will occur in the developing world. There are no automatic, predetermined processes deciding what sort of a world they will experience and what their opportunities will be. Most will depend on what people like you and me believe, think, and fight for.

***

In the Chinese village of Tau Hua Lin, Lasse Berg and Stig Karlsson meet people who describe the change that has occurred in ways of thinking since they were last there: "The last time you were here, people's thoughts and minds were closed, bound up," Yang Zhengming, one of the farmers, explains. But when they acquired power over their own land, they became entitled, for the first time, to decide something for themselves. Even a modest freedom like that was revolutionary. They were forced to think for themselves, to think along new lines. They were allowed to start thinking more about themselves and their loved ones instead of the leader's dictates. Individuals are not means to a higher end; they are the ends in themselves. Yang goes on to say that "a farmer could then own himself. He did not need to submit. He decided himself what he was going to do, how and when. The proceeds of his work were his own. It was freedom that came to us. We were allowed to think for ourselves." Author Lasse Berg sums up his impressions in a more universal observation:

It is not only inside the Chinese that a Chinese wall is now being torn down. Something similar is happening all over the world, in Bihar, East Timor, Ovamboland. Human beings are discovering that the individual is entitled to be his own. This has by no means been self-evident before. The discovery engenders a longing, not only for freedom but also for the good things in life, for prosperity.[10]

This new mindset, all reservations notwithstanding, must inspire optimism. We have not traveled the full distance: coercion and poverty still cover large areas of our globe. Great setbacks can and will occur. But people who know that living in a state of oppression and ignorance is not natural or necessary will no longer accept this as the only conceivable state of affairs. People who realize that they are not merely the tools of society and the collective but are ends in themselves will not be submissive. People who have acquired a taste for freedom will not consent to be shut in by walls or fences. They will work to create a better existence for themselves and to improve the world we live in. They will demand freedom and democracy. The aim of politics should be to give them that freedom.

NOTES

Introduction

1. Benjamin R. Barber, "Globalizing Democracy," *The American Prospect* 11, no. 20, September 11, 2000, p. 16.
2. Anders Ehnmark, *Minnets hemlighet: en bok om Erik Gustaf Geijer* (Stockholm: Norstedts, 1999), p. 60.
3. Lasse Berg and Stig T. Karlsson, *I Asiens tid: Indien, Kina, Japan 1966–1999* (Stockholm: Ordfront, 2000), chap. 1.
4. John Gray, *False Dawn: The Delusions of Global Capitalism* (New York: The New Press, 1998) pp. 39–43.
5. See, for example, Human Rights Watch, *The Price of Oil: Corporate Responsibility and Human Rights Violations in Nigeria's Oil Producing Communities* (New York: Human Rights Watch, 1999), http://www.hrw.org/reports/1999/nigeria/index.htm.

Chapter 1

1. Wulfstan is quoted in Anthony Giddens, *Runaway World: How Globalisation Is Reshaping Our Lives* (London: Profile Books, 1999), p. 1. The quotation from Pope John Paul II is from his "Homily in the José Martí Square of Havana," delivered January 25, 1998. An English transcript is online at http://www.vatican.va/holy_father/john_paul_ii/travels/documents/hf_jp-ii_hom_25011998_lahavana_en.html.
2. Unless otherwise indicated, the facts and figures quoted in this chapter come from the United Nations Development Program (UNDP) and the World Bank, especially the respective annual publications of these two institutions, *Human Development Report* and *World Development Report*, and the compilation *World Development Indicators 2000*. Figures, it should be noted, sometimes vary from one source to another, because of differences in the methods of measurement, and so care must be taken to use the same method when studying a certain change over time.

   In this book, when contrasting developing countries with industrialized countries, I refer to the commonly accepted definition of developing (or underdeveloped) countries as those suffering, for example, from a low standard of living, poor public health and education, low productivity, shortage of capital, heavy economic dependence on agriculture and raw materials, and instability and dependence on the international arena. Compare Michael P. Todaro, *Economic Development*, 6th ed., (Reading, Mass.: Addison Wesley Longman, 1997), p. 38. By this definition, about 135 of the poorest states are counted as classic developing countries, with another group of thirty-odd countries heading away from developing country status. It is important to remember that the differences between these countries are so great that it is hard to speak of them as one group. The concept lumps together dictatorships and democracies; war zones and growth markets; abysmally poor, famine-wracked countries and countries heading for the ranks of the industrialized nations.

3. Published in Sweden as *I Asiens tid: Indien, Kina, Japan 1966–1999.*

4. Berg and Karlsson, p. 96.

5. Arne Melchior, Kjetil Telle, and Henrik Wiig, *Globalisering och ulikhet: Verdens inntektsfordeling og levestandard, 1960–1998* (Oslo: Royal Norwegian Ministry of Foreign Affairs, 2000). Also available in an abridged English version: *Globalization and Inequality: World Income Distribution and Living Standards, 1960–1998*, Studies on Foreign Policy Issues, Report 6:B, 2000, chap. 2, http://xodin.dep.no/ud/engelsk/publ/rapporter/032001-990349/index-dok000-b-n-a.html.

6. UNDP, *Human Development Report 1997* (New York: Oxford University Press for the United Nations Development Program, 1997), "Overview," p. 12.

7. Surjit S. Bhalla, *Imagine There's No Country: Poverty, Inequality, and Growth in the Era of Globalization* (Washington: Institute for International Economics, 2002).

8. Berg and Karlsson, p. 300.

9. Indur M. Goklany, "The Globalization of Human Well-Being," Cato Institute Policy Analysis no. 447, 2002, p. 7, http://www.cato.org/pubs/pas/pa447.pdf.

10. *Forbes*, November 16, 1998, p. 36; World Bank, *World Development Report 2000/2001: Attacking Poverty* (New York: Oxford University Press/World Bank, 2000), p. 184, http://www.worldbank.org/poverty/wdrpoverty/report/index.htm.

11. Amartya Sen, *Development as Freedom* (New York: Anchor Books, 1999), chap. 7.

12. Freedom House, *Freedom in the World 2002* (New York: Freedom House, 2002), http://www.freedomhouse.org/research/freeworld/2002/web.pdf.

13. Berg and Karlsson, p. 202.

14. "How Women Beat the Rules," *The Economist*, October 2, 1999.

15. Deon Filmer, "The Structure of Social Disparities in Education: Gender and Wealth," World Bank Policy Research Working Paper 2268 (Washington: World Bank, 1999), http://econ.worldbank.org/docs/1021.pdf.

16. Oxfam. "The Clothes Trade in Bangladesh." Oxford: Oxfam (http://www.oxfam.org.uk/campaign/clothes/clobanfo.htm) accessed May 1, 2001.

17. Shuije Yao, "Economic Development and Poverty Reduction in China over 20 Years of Reform," *Economic Development and Cultural Change* 48, no. 3 (2000), pp. 447–74. World Bank, "Does More International Trade Openness Increase World

Poverty?" vol 2 of Assessing Globalization (Washington: World Bank/PREM Economic Policy Group and Development Economics Group, 2000), http://www.worldbank.org/economicpolicy/globalization/ag02.html.

18. Berg and Karlsson, chap. 4.

19. Nirupam Bajpai and Jeffrey Sachs, "The Progress of Policy Reform and Variations in Performance at the Sub-National Level in India," Development Discussion Paper no. 730 (Cambridge, Mass.: Harvard Institute for International Development, 1999).

20. Central Intelligence Agency, *CIA World Factbook 2002*, http://www.cia.gov/cia/publications/factbook.

21. Michael W. Cox and Richard Alm, *Myths of Rich and Poor: Why We're Better Off than We Think* (New York: Basic Books, 1999), pp. 14ff.

22. Melchior, Telle, and Wiig. This development toward greater equality will be even faster in coming decades, with the world's workforce growing older and thus earning more equally; see Tomas Larsson, *Falska mantran: globaliseringsdebatten efter Seattle* (Stockholm: Timbro, 2001), p. 11f, http://www.timbro.se/bokhandel/pejling/pdf/75664801.pdf.

23. Xavier Sala-i-Martin, "The Disturbing 'Rise' of Global Income Inequality," National Bureau of Economic Research Working Paper no. 8904, http://www.nber.org/papers/w8904.

24. Bhalla.

25. World Bank, *Making Transition Work for Everyone: Poverty and Inequality in Europe and Central Asia* (Washington: World Bank, 2000).

26. Larsson, *Falska mantran: globaliseringsdebatten efter Seattle,* p. 11f.

27. UNICEF, "Children Orphaned by AIDS: Front-Line Responses From Eastern and Southern Africa," http://www.unicef.org/pubsgen/aids.

Chapter 2

1. Clyde Wayne Crews, *Ten Thousand Commandments: An Annual Snapshot of the Federal Regulatory State* (Washington: Cato Institute, 2003).

2. Sen 1999, p. 276.

3. See, for example, Jonathan Kwitny, *Endless Enemies: The Making of an Unfriendly World* (New York: Congdon and Weed, 1984), pp. 286–300, 380–81.

4. These charts, of course, do not distinguish between cause and effect. They are compatible with countries first growing rich and then starting to liberalize the economy. This is a material factor, but looking at the countries represented by these figures, one finds that the relation mainly operates in the other direction: liberalization measures are accompanied by growth. Nothing I say here should be taken to imply that history, culture, and other factors are irrelevant to national development. On the contrary, I believe that people's ideas and convictions are of momentous import for economic development, but I have concentrated here on the political factors, which, of course, also affect people's incentives.

295

5. Mabel C. Buer, *Health, Wealth, and Population in the Early Days of the Industrial Revolution, 1760–1815* (London: Routledge and Sons, 1926) p. 88.

6. Angus Maddison, *Monitoring the World Economy 1820–1992* (Paris: Development Center of the Organization for Economic Cooperation and Development, 1995).

7. The view of growth as an end in itself is absurd. If that were right, the important thing would be just producing as much as possible. That kind of growth is easily created by the state taking everyone's money and starting up an enormous output of things that people don't want, as in the case of steel and munitions in the former Soviet Union. Growth has to take place on people's terms, by producing things that people are demanding. That is why, fundamentally, it is only in a market economy, where demand affects prices and production, that growth can really take place in ways that benefit people.

8. Berg and Karlsson, p. 245.

9. David Dollar and Aart Kraay, *Growth Is Good for the Poor* (Washington: World Bank, April 2001) http://econ.worldbank.org/files/1696wps2587.pdf. For a balanced review of the debate on this report, see Jonas Vlachos, *Är ekonomisk tillväxt bra för de fattiga?: en översikt över debatten* (Stockholm: Globkom, 2000), http://www.glob-kom.net/rapporter/vlachos.pdf. Reports corroborating these findings include John Luke Gallup, Steven Radelet, and Andrew Warner, "Economic Growth and the Income of the Poor," CAER II Discussion Paper no. 36 (Cambridge, Mass.: Harvard Institute for International Development, 1998), http://www.hiid.harvard.edu/caer2/htm/content/papers/confpubs/paper36/paper36.htm. The authors suggest that, in proportional terms, the poor actually benefit more than do other groups from growth.

10. John Stuart Mill, *Principles of Political Economy: Books IV and V* (London: Penguin, 1985), Book V, chap. 2.

11. See, for example, Eric Engen and Jonathan Skinner, "Taxation and Economic Growth," *National Tax Journal* 49, no. 4 (1996): 617–642. Martin Feldstein, "Tax Incidence in a Growing Economy with Variable Factor Supply," *Quarterly Journal of Economics*, no. 88 (November 1974): 551–73; "The Welfare Cost of Capital Income Taxation," *Journal of Political Economy* 86, no. 10, pt. 2 (1978): S29–51. The digest of research presented in Sofia Leufstedt and Fredrik Voltaire, *Vad säger empirin om skatter och sysselsättning?* (Stockholm: Svensk Handel, September 1998), http://www.svensk-handel.se/Filer/empiri.pdf, suggests that a 10 percent increase in the size of the public sector reduces growth by about 1.5 percentage points.

12. Cox and Alm, chap. 4. Some have argued that this social mobility is greater in more egalitarian countries, such as Sweden, despite heavier tax burdens, but this is probably due to a confusion of concepts. It is easier to enter a new income bracket in Sweden because pay differentials are so small there. On the other hand, it is more difficult to raise the absolute amount of one's earnings.

13. Concerning equality of assets versus equality of income, see Klaus Deininger and P. Olinto, *Asset Distribution, Inequality, and Growth*, World Bank Policy Research Paper no. 2375 (Washington: World Bank, 2000). For the connection with democracy,

see Klaus Deininger and Lyn Squire, "New Ways of Looking at the Old Issues: Asset Inequality and Growth," *Journal of Development Economics* 57 (1998): 259–87.

14. Simon Kuznets, "Economic Growth and Income Inequality," *American Economic Review* 45 (March 1955): 26.

15. World Bank, *Income Poverty: Trends in Inequality* (Washington: World Bank, 2000), http://www.worldbank.org/poverty/data/trends/inequal.htm. The data refuting Kuznets are presented in Deininger and Squire, pp. 259–287. For a review of the research, see Arne Bigsten and Jörgen Levin, *Tillväxt, inkomstfördelning och fattigdom i u-länderna* (Stockholm: Globkom, September 2000), http://www.globkom.net/rapporter.phtml.

16. G. W. Scully, *Constitutional Environments and Economic Growth* (Princeton, N.J.: Princeton University Press, 1992).

17. Niclas Berggren, "Economic Freedom and Equality: Friends or Foes?" *Public Choice*, vol. 100 (September 1999): 203–23.

18. "Measuring Globalization," Foreign Policy, January/February 2001. According to the third edition of this index, the most globalized countries are Ireland and Switzerland. The United States comes in 11th, but this is somewhat misleading because the United States is so large that it accommodates far more long-distance travel, trade and communication within its frontiers than can small countries.

19. Compare David Dollar and Aart Kraay, *Property Rights, Political Rights, and the Development of Poor Countries in the Post-Colonial Period* (Washington: World Bank, 2000), http://www.worldbank.org/research/growth/pdfiles/dollarkraay2.pdf and *Growth Is Good for the Poor*. Concerning the importance of property rights for economic development, see Nathan Rosenberg and L. E. Birdzell, *How the West Grew Rich: The Economic Transformation of the Industrial World* (New York: Basic Books, 1986).

20. Hernando de Soto, *The Mystery of Capital: Why Capitalism Triumphs in the West and Fails Everywhere Else* (London: Bantam Press, 2000).

21. James Gwartney, Robert Lawson, Chris Edwards, Walter Park, Veronique de Rugy, and Smita Wagh, *Economic Freedom of the World 2002* (Vancouver: Fraser Institute, 2002), http://freetheworld.com; Gerald P. O'Driscoll, Edwin J. Feulner, and Mary Anastasia O'Grady, *The 2003 Index of Economic Freedom* (Washington: Heritage Foundation and Wall Street Journal, 2002), http://www.heritage.org/index/2003.

22. Christer Gunnarsson and Mauricio Rojas, *Tillväxt, stagnation, kaos: en institutionell studie av underutvecklingens orsaker och utvecklingens möjligheter* (Stockholm: Studieförbundet Näringsliv Samhälle, 1997), pp. 50ff.

23. Berg and Karlsson, p. 93f. Quotation from World Bank *World Development Report 2000/2001*, p. 85.

24. World Bank, *The East Asian Miracle: Economic Growth and Public Policy* (New York: Oxford University Press/World Bank, 1993), p. 6. See also Gunnarsson and Rojas.

25. Jeffrey Sachs and Andrew Warner, "Economic Reform and the Process of Global Integration," Brookings Papers on Economic Activity, no. 1, 1995, pp. 26–32, 72–95.

26. Jeffrey Sachs and Andrew Warner, "Sources of Slow Growth in African Economies," *Journal of African Economies* 6, no. 3 (1997): 335–76; Arthur Goldsmith, "Institutions and Economic Growth in Africa," African Economic Policy Papers, Discussion paper no. 7, (Cambridge, Mass.: Harvard Institute for International Development, July 1998), http://www.eagerproject.com/discussion7.shtml. A confused interpretation considers Africa *more* integrated than other continents with the world economy, because exports from the African countries are unusually large in proportion to GDP. However this is not due to their being unusually export heavy, but simply to the native economies being so extraordinarily weak and small. See also George B. N. Ayittey, *Africa in Chaos* (New York: St. Martin's, 1999).

27. Gwartney et al.

28. "The Zimbabwean Model," *The Economist*, November 30, 2002.

29. Sachs and Warner, "Sources of Slow Growth in African Economies."

Chapter 3

1. The most common criticism of free trade is that certain tariffs and quotas are needed for the protection of particular industries. It is less common for anyone today to believe in self-sufficiency as a policy, but the belief lives on in groups more critical of modern civilization, such as the Green political parties. Advocates also include the French anti-globalist ATTAC movement. Its chairman, Bernard Cassen, makes self-sufficiency an argument against reducing tariffs for developing countries: "I'm very surprised by the argument that poorer countries, undeveloped countries, must have more market access to developed ones. What does that mean, in reality? That means that you expect undeveloped countries to export. To export what? To export commodities that they need for their own internal market ... we must return to self-centered economies, and not to export-led economies that have proved a real failure." Bernard Cassen, "Who Are the Winners, and Who Are the Losers of Globalization?" speech presented at The Amis UK Conference "Globalization in Whose Interest?" Conway Hall, London, June 17, 2000.

2. James Mill, *Elements of Political Economy*, 3d ed. (London: Baldwin, Cradock and Joy, 1826), chap. V, sec. 3.

3. Adam Smith, *An Inquiry Into the Nature and Causes of The Wealth of Nations* (Indianapolis: Liberty Classics, 1981), p. 488f.

4. Tomas Larsson predicted the collapse of the Seattle meeting for precisely this reason in his excellent book *The Race to the Top: The Real Story of Globalization* (Washington: Cato Institute, 2001) originally published in Swedish in 1999 as *Världens klassresa*.

5. Brink Lindsey and Daniel Ikenson, "Antidumping 101: The Devilish Details of 'Unfair Trade' Law," Cato Trade Policy Analysis no. 20, 2002, http://www.freetrade.org/pubs/pas/tpa-020es.html.

6. Daniel Ikenson, "Steel Trap: How Subsidies and Protectionism Weaken the U.S. Steel Industry," Cato Trade Briefing Paper no. 14, 2002, http://www.freetrade.org/pubs/briefs/tbp-014es.html.

7. Sachs and Warner, "Economic Reform and the Process of Global Integration."
8. The critics include free traders T. N. Srinivasan and Jagdish Bhagwati, "Outward-Orientation and Development: Are Revisionists Right?" (paper written for the Professor Anne Krueger Festschrift, September 1999), http://www.columbia.edu/~jb38/Krueger.pdf. Francisco Rodriguez and Dani Rodrik, "Trade Policy and Economic Growth: A Skeptic's Guide to The Cross-National Evidence," Working Paper Series no. 7081 (Cambridge, Mass.: National Bureau of Economic Research, 1999) are leading trade skeptics, but even they point out (p. 62): "We do not want to leave the reader with the impression that we think trade protection is good for economic growth. We know of no credible evidence—at least for the post-1945 period—that suggests that trade restrictions are systematically associated with higher growth rates. . . . The effects of trade liberalization may be on balance beneficial on standard comparative advantage grounds; the evidence provides no strong reason to dispute this." One of Dani Rodrik's arguments against free trade is that countries with high tariffs, such as China and India, have faster growth than the EU and the United States, which have low tariffs. But he forgets that China and India have achieved these growth figures by liberalizing their economies. It is when countries begin reducing their tariffs from high initial levels that they achieve the biggest growth gains, because workers then switch to occupations in which they have the biggest advantages. The United States and the EU acquired similar impetus when their trade was liberalized. Besides, China and India have such large populations that trade liberalization within the country means free trade on a far bigger scale than is implied by the ordinary regional free trade agreements in the rest of the world.
9. Sebastian Edwards, "Openness, Productivity and Growth," National Bureau of Economic Research Working Paper 5978, (Cambridge, Mass.: National Bureau of Economic Research, 1997); Haåkan Nordström, "The Trade and Development Debate: An Introductory Note with Emphasis on WTO Issues," (Stockholm: Kommittén om Sveriges politik för global utveckling, Globkom, March 2000), http://www.globkom.net/rapporter/nordstrom.pdf.
10. Jeffrey Frankel and David Romer, "Does Trade Growth Cause Growth?" *American Economic Review* 89, no. 3 (June 1999): 379–399.
11. David Dollar and Aart Kraay, "Trade, Growth and Poverty," World Bank Working Paper 2615 (Washington: World Bank, 2001), pp. 5, 35.
12. Dollar and Kraay, "Trade, Growth and Poverty," p. 26.
13. Percy Barnevik, *Global Forces of Change*, lecture presented at the 1997 International Industrial Conference, San Francisco, September 29, 1997, p. 4.
14. This finding is generally confirmed by Daniel Ben-David and L. Alan Winters, "Trade, Income Disparity and Poverty," World Trade Organization Special Study No. 5 (Geneva: World Trade Organization, 1999), http://www.wto.org/english/res_e/booksp_e/disparity_e.pdf. It is also supported by Alberto F. Ades, and Edward L. Glaeser, "Evidence on Growth, Increasing Returns, and the Extent of the Market," *Quarterly Journal of Economics* 114, no. 3 (August 1999). One argument against free trade

bringing growth is that growth was higher during the early postwar decades than it is today, in the age of globalization. But this objection ignores the fact that growth is quicker when huge tariffs begin to come down. Growth is also generally fastest when the starting point is poverty, with any number of opportunities of obtaining a big return on investments, owing to the shortage of capital and disastrous political affairs formerly prevailing—as, for example, after a war. As countries become more fully developed and invested, the economy reverts to a more normal growth curve. Furthermore, the argument cannot in any way explain why, in this case, it is the very countries that opt for free trade that have the fastest growth today, whereas protectionist states are lagging further and further behind.

15. Mauricio Rojas, *Millennium Doom: Fallacies about the End of Work* (London: Social Market Foundation, 1999).

16. Paul Krugman, "The Accidental Theorist: All Work and No Play Makes William Greider a Dull Boy," *Slate*, January 24, 1997, http://slate.msn.com/id/1916.

17. Susan George in an interview by Bim Clinell, "Dom kallar oss huliganer," *Ordfront* 12 (2000).

18. Steven J. Matusz and David Tarr, "Adjusting to Trade Policy Reform," World Bank Working Paper 2142 (Washington: World Bank, 2000), http://www.worldbank.org/html/dec/Publications/Workpapers/wps2000series/wps2142/wps2142.pdf.

19. Cox and Alm, p. 65ff and chap. 1.

20. Anders Åslund, "Därför har Estland lyckats," *Svenska Dagbladet*, August 2, 2000; Razeen Sally, "Free Trade in Practice: Estonia in the 1990s," *Central Europe Review* 27 (2000), http://www.ce-review.org/00/27/sally27.html.

21. *Cato Handbook for Congress: 108th Congress* (Washington: Cato Institute, 2002), pp. 631–641.

22. Julian Simon, *The Economic Consequences of Immigration*, 2nd ed. (Ann Arbor: University of Michigan Press, 1999), p. 368, see also chaps. 5–6, 17.

Chapter 4

1. Patrick Low, Marcelo Olarrega, and Javier Suarez, "Does Globalization Cause a Higher Concentration of International Trade and Investment Flows?" World Trade Organization Staff Working Paper: Economic Research and Analysis Division (Geneva: World Trade Organization, 1998). Many states are closed to some extent. Of 161 developing countries investigated, 131 still have regulations opposing foreign direct investment.

2. Thomas W. Hertel and Will Martin, "Would Developing Countries Gain from Inclusion of Manufactures in the WTO Negotiations?" presented at the World Trade Organization/World Bank Conference on "Developing Countries in a Millennium Round," September 20–21, 1999 in Geneva at the WTO's Center William Rappard, p. 12, http://www.itd.org/wb/hertel.doc.

3. Ronnie Horesh, "Trade and Agriculture: The Unimportance of Being Rational," *New Zealand Orchardist* (April 2000), also available at http://www.geocities.com/socialpbonds/orchard2.html.

4. ATTAC Chairman Bernard Cassen maintains that "every country or group of countries has the absolute right to protect its agriculture," in an interview with Lars Mogensen, "ATTAC lider af børnesygdomme," *Danish Information*, February 23, 2001. In the international platform defining its essential issues, ATTAC declares its intention of combating the forces within the EU that are conducting a "free trade crusade" and, among other things, are seeking to "dismantle the common agricultural policy." This fact, however, is apparently so embarrassing to Swedish ATTAC adherents that they endeavor to conceal it. In the Swedish translation of this very section in Bim Clinell's adulatory book *ATTAC: gräsrötternas revolt mot marknaden,* trans. by Margareta Kruse (Stockholm: Agora, 2000), pp. 75–78, this is reduced to a mere complaint about those who "are pushing development towards new fields of deregulation," without any mention of the CAP.

5. Kym Anderson, Bernard Hoekman, and Anna Strut, "Agriculture and the WTO: Next Steps," (Washington: World Bank/Centre for Economic Policy Research, 1999), http://wbweb4.worldbank.org/wbiep/trade/papers_2000/ag-rie-sept.pdf.

6. Joseph François, Hans H. Glismann, and Dean Spinange, *The Cost of EU Trade Protection in Textiles and Clothing* (Stockholm: The Ministry for Foreign Affairs, March 2000); Leif Pagrotsky, "Varför en ny WTO-runda?" speech at the EU committee's WTO hearing, November 25, 1999.

7. Patrick Messerlin, *Measuring the Costs of Protection in Europe* (Washington: Institute for International Economics, 2001).

8. Eli Heckscher, "Vaårt tullsystems framtid III. Industri- och agrartullar," *Svensk Handelstidning*, August 25, 1918.

9. "White Man's Shame," *The Economist*, September 25, 1999; Clare Short, *Eliminating World Poverty: Making Globalisation Work for the Poor,* White Paper on International Development (London: Her Majesty's Stationery Office, December 2000), http://www.globalisation.gov.uk.

10. The description of Latin American conditions is based on Gunnarsson and Rojas.

11. Milton Friedman and Rose Friedman, *Two Lucky People: Memoirs* (Chicago: University of Chicago Press, 1998), chap. 24.

12. Sachs and Warner, "Economic Reform and the Process of Global Integration," pp. 52–55.

13. Aaron Lukas, "WTO Report Card III: Globalization and Developing Countries," Cato Trade Briefing Paper no. 10, 2000, p. 11, http://www.freetrade.org/pubs/briefs/tbp-010.pdf.

14. Bruce Bartlett, "The Truth about Trade in History," in *Freedom to Trade: Refuting the New Protectionism*, edited by Edward L. Hudgins (Washington: Cato Institute, 1997).

15. Hertel and Martin, pp. 4ff.

16. Andrei Illarionov, "Russia's Potemkin Capitalism," in *Global Fortune: The Stumble and Rise of World Capitalism*, edited by Ian Vásquez (Washington: Cato Institute, 2000), p. 209.

17. Goldsmith, p. 11.

18. Lionel Demery and Lyn Squire, "Macroeconomic Adjustment and Poverty in Africa: An Emerging Picture," *The World Bank Research Observer* 11, no. 1 (February 1996): 39–59; Jeffrey Sachs, "External Debt, Structural Adjustment, and Economic Growth," paper addressed to the G-24 Research Group in Washington, September 18, 1996, Geneva.

19. World Bank, *World Development Report 2000/2001*, p. 202.

20. William Easterly, "How Did Highly Indebted Countries Become Highly Indebted? Reviewing Two Decades of Debt Relief," World Bank Working Paper no. 2225 (Washington: World Bank, 1999), http://econ.worldbank.org/docs/952.pdf.

21. World Bank, *Assessing Aid: What Works, What Doesn't, and Why* (New York: Oxford University Press/World Bank, 1998), http://www.worldbank.org/research/aid/aidtoc.htm; Craig Burnside and David Dollar, "Aid, Policies and Growth," *American Economic Review* 90, no. 4 (September 2000): 847–868.

22. World Bank *World Development Report 2000/2001*, pp. 182f.

23. Brian Doherty, "WHO Cares?" *Reason Magazine*, January 2002, http://reason.com/0201/fe.bd.who.shtml.

Chapter 5

1. The same phenomenon is associated with the concept of "globalization." When international anti-globalists were staging a demonstration in Prague, it was organized by the umbrella organization "Initiative Against Economic Globalization," but the Swedish variant, knowing globalization to have a positive connotation in Sweden, styled itself "Globalization from Beneath" instead. Bernard Cassen, chairman of French ATTAC, says that he has "tried to find a single advantage with globalization, but in vain." See Bernard Cassen, interview by John Einar Sandvand. "Globalizering kun til besvær," Norwegian *Aftenposten*, March 2, 2001. At the same time, the Swedish ATTAC movement say that they are not at all opposed to globalization, they just want different rules for it.

2. Cit. Steven Greenhouse and Joseph Kahn, "Workers' Rights: U.S. Effort to Add Labor Standards to Agenda Fails," *New York Times*, December 3, 1999. Adherents eagerly point out that the International Confederation of Free Trade Unions favors social clauses, but it does so in spite of vociferous opposition from its members in the South. The other international union organization, the World Federation of Trade Unions, with 110 million members in 130 different countries, has argued against the inclusion of social clauses in WTO trade agreements.

3. Lukas, p. 11.

4. Carol Bellamy, *The State of the World's Children 1997* (New York: UNICEF, 1997), p. 23, http://www.unicef.org/sowc97.

5. Rädda Barnen: "Faktablad om barnarbete," http://www.rb.se, accessed May 1, 2001.

6. Concerning the ILO, see Berg and Karlsson, p. 64. Global figures can be found in Goklany p. 8.

7. Gary Burtless, Robert Z. Lawrence, Robert E. Litan, and Robert Shapiro, *Globaphobia: Confronting Fears about Open Trade* (Washington: Brookings Institution, 1998), chap. 4.

8. Philip L. Rones, Jennifer Gardner, and Randy E. Ilg, "Trends in Hours of Work since the Mid-1970s," *Monthly Labor Review* (April 1997): 3–14.

9. Illarionov 2000.

10. Paul De Grauwe and Filip Camerman, "How Big Are the Multinational Companies?" *Mimeo* (January 2002), http://www.degrauwe.org/publicatie.php?pub=globalisering/multinationals.htm.

11. James Rolph Edwards, "The Myth of Corporate Power," *Liberty* (January 2001).

12. Lukas, p. 6.

13. The surveys can be accessed at http://www.theglobalalliance.org. Concerning Lim, see Liza Featherstone and Doug Henwood, "Clothes Encounters: Activists and Economists Clash over Sweatshops," *Lingua Franca* 11, no. 2 (March 2001). For Swedish national government employees, see Gunnar Aronsson and Klas Gustafsson, "Kritik eller tystnad: en studie av arbetsmarknads-och anställningsförhaållandens betydelse för arbetsmiljökritik," *Arbetsmarknad and Arbetsliv* 5, no. 3 (1999): 189–206.

14. Organization for Economic Cooperation and Development, *International Trade and Core Labor Standards* (Paris: Organization for Economic Cooperation and Development, 2000).

15. "Foreign Friends," *The Economist*, January 8, 2000. Organization for Economic Cooperation and Development, *Survey of OECD Work on International Investment*, Working Paper on International Investment (Paris: Organization for Economic Cooperation and Development, 1998), http://www.oecd.org/pdf/M000013000/M00013315.pdf.

16. Naomi Klein, *No Logo: Taking Aim at the Brand Bullies* (New York: Picador USA, 2000). Klein finds it repugnant that firms exploit people's need to belong, to share in a group identity. But if this is a basic need, then surely it is a good thing that an identity should be freely chosen from among a range of options, rather than merely inherited. I would rather see people arguing about whether a Mac or a PC is best than about whether being black or white is best. Surely the very triviality of the issue makes it preferable for people to feel superior for having Adidas trainers rather than for being heterosexual.

17. "The World's View of Multinationals," *The Economist*, January 27, 2000. Even a critic like Björn Elmbrant maintains that the world's enterprises are not growing worse "but that continued exploitation is more and more becoming mingled with responsible entrepreneurship." Björn Elmbrant, *Hyperkapitalismen* (Stockholm: Atlas 2000), p. 79.

303

18. Clive Crook, "Third World Economic Development," in *The Fortune Encyclopedia of Economics*, edited by David Henderson (New York: Warner Books, 1993).
19. Susmita Dasgupta, Ashoka Mody, Subhendu Roy, and David Wheeler, "Environmental Regulation and Development: A Cross-Country Empirical Analysis," World Bank Policy Research Working Paper 1448 (Washington: World Bank, 1995).
20. Adam B. Jaffe, Steven R. Peterson, Paul R. Portney, and Robert Stavins, "Environmental Regulation and the Competitiveness of U.S. Manufacturing: What Does the Evidence Tell Us?" *Journal of Economic Literature* 33, no. 1 (March 1995): 132–163.
21. Investments and the environment: David Wheeler, "Racing to the Bottom? Foreign Investment and Air Pollution in Developing Countries," World Bank Policy Research Working Paper 2524 (Washington: World Bank, 2000), http://econ.worldbank.org/view.php?type = 5andid = 1340. Steel production: D. Wheeler, M. Huq, and P. Martin, "Process Change, Economic Policy and Industrial Pollution: Cross Country Evidence from the Wood Pulp and Steel Industries," (paper presented at the annual meeting of the American Economic Association, Anaheim, Calif., 1993).
22. Richard R. Wilk, "Emulation and Global Consumerism," in *Environmentally Significant Consumption*, edited by Paul C. Stern, Thomas Dietz, Vernon W. Ruttan, Robert H. Socolow, and James L. Sweeney (Washington: National Academy Press, 1997), p. 110.
23. Gene M. Grossman and Alan B. Krueger, "Economic Growth and the Environment," National Bureau of Economic Research Working Paper 4634 (Cambridge, Mass.: National Bureau of Economic Research, 1994); Marian Radetzki, *Den gröna myten: ekonomisk tillväxt och miljöns kvalitet* (Stockholm: Studieförbundet Näringsliv Samhälle, 2001).
24. Stephen Moore and Julian L. Simon, *It's Getting Better All the Time: 100 Greatest Trends of the Last 100 Years* (Washington: Cato Institute, 2000), section XIV.
25. Ibid., section XV.
26. The example is cited in Ingemar Nordin, *Etik, teknik och samhälle* (Stockholm: Timbro, 1992), p. 154.
27. David Roodman, "Worldwatch Proposes $2,000 Tax Cut per Family to Save the Planet," Worldwatch Briefing (Washington: Worldwatch Institute, 1998), http://www.worldwatch.org/alerts/pr980912.html.

Chapter 6

1. Elmbrant, pp. 89f.
2. A good introduction to the subject is Klas Eklund's "Globala kapitalrörelser," in *Välfärd, politik och ekonomi i en ny värld* (Stockholm: Arbetarrörelsens Ekonomiska Raåd, 1999). A rather more theoretical approach is provided by Barry Eichengreen and Michael Mussa, et al., *Capital Account Liberalization: Theoretical and Practical Aspects* (Washington: IMF, 1998).
3. This study, and those conflicting with it, are summarized in Eichengreen et al., p. 19. See also Glenn Yago and David Goldman, *Capital Access Index Fall 1998: Emerging and Submerging Markets* (Santa Monica, Calif.: Milken Institute, 1998).

4. Sheila McNulty, "Investors Lose Faith in Malaysia's Weak Reforms," *Financial Times*, January 17, 2001.
5. Sebastian Edwards, "A Capital Idea? Reconsidering a Financial Quick Fix," *Foreign Affairs* 78 (May/June 1999): 18–22.
6. John Micklethwait and Adrian Wooldridge, *A Future Perfect* (New York: Random House, 2000), p. 55.
7. Eichengreen and Mussa, p. 18.
8. Steven Radelet and Jeffrey Sachs, "What Have We Learned, So Far, From the Asian Financial Crisis," CAER II Discussion Paper no. 37 (Cambridge, Mass.: Harvard Institute for International Development, 1999), http://www.hiid.harvard.edu/caer2/htm/content/papers/paper37/paper37.htm; Tomas Larsson, "Asia's Crisis of Corporatism," in Vásquez.
9. Yago and Goldman.
10. Klein, chap. 9; Elmbrant, p. 85f; World Bank *World Development Report 2000/2001*, p. 163.
11. Jagdish Bhagwati, "Why Free Capital Mobility May Be Hazardous to Your Health: Lessons from the Latest Financial Crisis, paper presented at the NBER conference on capital controls, Cambridge, Mass., November 7, 1998, http://www.columbia.edu/~jb38/papers/NBER_comments.pdf.
12. Micklethwait and Wooldridge, p. 178.
13. James Tobin in an interview with Radio Australia, November 17, 1998, http://www.abc.gov.au/money/vault/extras/extra14.htm. For example: "My own feeling is that it's a great mistake for developing economies to try to have fixed exchange rates. ... The three big currencies—the dollar, the yen and the Deutsche Mark (soon to be the Euro)—have floating rates, and we don't have exchange rate crises among them. I don't know why we insist on having fixed exchange rates for Korea and Thailand and so on. But that creates crises ..." See also James Tobin, "Financial Globalization: Can National Currencies Survive?" (paper presented at the Annual World Bank Conference on Development Economics, April 20–21, 1998, Washington), http://www.worldbank.org/html/rad/abcde/tobin.pdf.
14. Concerning variable exchange rates, see Radelet and Sachs, p. 13. Fixed exchange rates: Maurice Obstfeld and Kenneth Rogoff, "The Mirage of Fixed Exchange Rates," *Journal of Economic Perpectives* 9, no. 4 (Fall 1995): 73–96.
15. In China the advocates of WTO membership were critics of the regime, reformists and liberals, while the opponents were to be found among the big corporations, the security service, and the army. John Pomfret and Michael Laris, "Chinese Liberals Welcome WTO Bid," *Washington Post*, November 18, 1999. Concerning opposition from old forces, see John Pomfret, "Chinese Are Split over WTO Entry," *Washington Post*, March 13, 2000.
16. Smith, p. 929f.
17. Mattias Svensson, *Mer demokrati—mindre politik* (Stockholm: Timbro, 2000), http://www.timbro.se/bokhandel/pejling/pdf/75664666.pdf.
18. Larsson, *Falska mantran: globaliseringsdebatten efter Seattle*, p. 44.

Chapter 7

1. World Bank *World Development Report 2000/2001*, p. 73.
2. See http://www.peoplink.org/vsouk.
3. Moore and Simon, p. 218f.
4. Jonah Goldberg, "The Specter of McDonald's: An Object of Bottomless Hatred,"*National Review*, June 5, 2000.
5. Thomas Hylland Eriksen, *Kulturterrorismen: en uppgörelse med tanken om kulturell renhet* (Nora, Sweden: Nya Doxa, 1999), p. 46.
6. For numerous examples of "indigenous" cultural products made possible by cultural contact and trade, see Tyler Cowen, *Creative Destruction: How Globalization Is Changing the World's Cultures* (Princeton, N.J.: Princeton University Press, 2002).
7. Mario Vargas Llosa, "Can Culture Be Exempt from Free Trade Agreement?" *Daily Yomiuri*, April 25, 1994.
8. Giddens, p. 66.
9. Berg and Karlsson, p. 51.
10. Berg and Karlsson, pp. 162–171.

Index

Page references followed by an *f* or *n* denote references to figures and footnotes respectively.

Absolute poverty, 21, 26
  China, 48
  East Asian countries, 99–100
  Nigeria, 108
Adjustment costs versus welfare gains, 142
Africa
  AIDS/HIV, 60
  contrasted to East Asian countries, 104–11
  democratic power in, 269
  development aid dependency, 105–6
  development assistance, 184–85
  education, 36
  free trade and open economies in, 109–10
  girls attending school, 45
  "green revolution," 33
  growth, 99, 108–9, 130
  hunger and suffering, 32, 105
  impact of politics and leaders on development, 104–7
  internecine conflicts, 41
  isolation and regulation, 155
  "lion economies," 109–11
  long-lived leaders, 106
  medicine, 187
  openness, 103
  oppression, corruption, and protectionism, 105–6, 107
  standard of living, 104
  structural adjustment programs, 181
  women, 44
  See also specific countries
Africa Growth and Opportunity Act, 161
Agricultural tariffs, on meat, 238
Agriculture
  East Asia, 101
  protectionism and, 157–62
  regulation of, 95–96
AIDS. *See* HIV/AIDS
Air pollution and emissions, 228, 229, 232
Air quality, 230
Al-Jazeera satellite channel, 269
Amazon rain forests, 236
American stock market, 240–41
"Anarchist Front," 8, 10
Anarchists/anarchy, 7–10
  liberty and, 16
Annan, Kofi, 155
Anti-discrimination, India, 53
Anti-globalism, 287–89
Antidumping measures, 125–26, 160
Arab states, 269

Argentina
  dependency theory, 163
  economic crisis of 2002, 167
  exchange rate crisis, 267
  reduced inflation and poverty, 96
Asia
  absolute poverty, 21
  poverty, 25
  in world economy, 289
Asian crisis, 259–63
  exchange controls and, 249–50
  IMF recommendations and,
    178–79
  South Korea and, 251
"Asian tigers." See East Asia
ATTAC, 139, 253, 257
Australia
  Asian crisis and, 262
  employment, 137
Autonomy, personal, 23
Ayittey, George, 106

Bahrain, 269–70
Balance of trade, 121–22
Bangladesh
  child labor, 199
  garment industry, 223
  liberalization and poverty
    reduction, 132
  poverty line, 54
Barber, Benjamin, 11
Basic assets, people's need for, 85
Bastiat, Frédéric, 41
Bauer, Peter T., 185
Berg, Lasse, 21–23, 29, 290–91
Berggren, Niclas, 89
Bhagwati, Jagdish, 265

Bhalla, Surjit S., 26–27, 56
Bill and Melinda Gates Health Fund,
  189
Birth control, 46
Birthrates, availability of
    contraception and, 46
Borders, 287
  internationalization and, 9
  open, 10
  "the ox made peace" saying, 41
Botswana
  free trade, 109
  starvation, 34
Boutros-Ghali, Youssef, 193
Boycotts, 199–200, 201
Brazil
  air pollution control, 228
  Asian crisis and, 251
  dependency theory, 163
  exchange rate crisis, 267
  failed government industrial
    initiatives, 174
  growth and income differences, 86
Bureau of Labor Statistics, 206
Burma
  exclusion from global
    environment, 289
  human rights violations, 40
  lack of growth and poverty, 132
  protectionist policy and controlled
    economy, 103
Bush, George H. W., 146
Bush, George W., 146
Business and politics, 16

California, Clean Air Acts, 226–28
"California effect," environmental
    protection and, 226–28

Cambodia, starvation, 34
Canada, employment, 137
CAP. *See* European Union, Common Agricultural Policy
Capital Access Index, 247–48
Capital controls, 249–52, 266
Capital markets, 242–48
Capitalism, 17
  democratization and, 268–76
  and freedom, 16-17, 242-48
  medical advances and, 186–89
  myopic focus on imperfections, 98
  negative example, 98
  "neo-liberal" market and policy, 14–15
  philanthropic, 189
  progress and, 98
  reducing the world's problems, 61
  unequal distribution in developing countries, 152–55
  uneven distribution of wealth due to uneven distribution of, 154
  what it is and is not, 16–18
Carbon dioxide emissions, 235
Carville, James, 240
Caste system, India, 53
Castro, Fidel, 287
Catholicism, democracy and, 40
Centralization, 41–42, 287
Chaebols, Asian crisis and, 260
Change in economic activity, efficiency-related, 140–44
Cheap imports, avoiding, 120–22
Child labor, 193, 198–202
Children
  AIDS orphans, 60
  education, 45–46

Chile
  dependency theory, 163
  development and economic policy, 168
  economic crisis, 250–51
  liberalization and poverty reduction, 132
China, 47–50
  absolute poverty, 26, 48
  agriculture investment, 47
  air pollution control, 228
  Berg and Karlsson in, 21–22, 290–91
  democracy in, 270
  equality/inequality, 133
  foreign trade, 48
  growth and income differences, 86
  labor-intensive industries, 172
  opening markets, 72
  starvation, 34
  telephony example, 234–35
  women, 43
Chinese Exclusion Act of 1882, 146
Clean Air Acts, California, 226–28
Clinton, Bill, 146, 193, 223
Cold War, 38
Colombia, equality in, 86
Colonialism, wealth and poverty and, 152
Common Agricultural Policy (CAP) *See* European Union
Communication, capital controls, 252
Communism, China, 49
Comparative advantage, 117–18, 170
Competition and competitive markets
  absence or lack of, 165, 167

with developing countries, 205
free, 16
"infant industry tariffs" and,
    173–74
multinational corporations,
    213–14
unfair competition, 125–26
Computer chips, sand/silicon and,
    233
Computers, China, 280
Concorde, failure of, 174
Confidence in an economy, 264, 270
    Asian crisis and, 261–62
Congo, 99
Consumers
    efficiency and gains for, 141, 142
    globalization consisting of everyday
        actions of, 12–14
    multinational corporations and,
        213
Consumption, environment and,
    228–37
Contraception/birth control, 46
Copper, China's telephony example,
    234–35
Corruption
    Africa, 105–6, 107
    controls and, 252
    economic freedom and, 70–71
    world government possibilities,
        257
Costa Rica, 132-33
Crimes against humanity, 287
Criminal syndicates, immigration
    schemes, 147
Cuba
    equality in, 86

human rights violations, 40
Cultural choice, 278–85
Cultural identity, 283
Cultural imports, traditions
    considered "authentic," 283
Cultural innovation, 150
Culture, 17
    change and renewal in, 282–84
    cultural encounters of globalism,
        281–85
    freedoms and voluntary relations
        in, 17, 283–84
    global homogeneity, 280–82
    isolation and preservation, 283
    as a process, 283
Currency exchange, Tobin tax and,
    253–58
Currency overvaluation, Asian crisis
    and, 261
Currency speculation, 254–57, 261,
    266

Daewoo, 223
de Soto, Hernando, 91–95
"Dead capital," 93
Debt
    developing countries, 177–85
    freedom and, 270–72
    national debts, 271
    short-term, 260–61
Debt cancellation, 181–84
Decentralization, 270
Deforestation, 232
Deliberate choice, 285
Demand, worldwide, 281
Democracy, 17, 289

310

demands that parallel debt
cancellation, 183
demands that parallel receipt of
aid, 185
multinational corporations'
presence in oppressive countries,
222
reducing the world's problems, 61
representative democracy as
preferable form of government, 8
tasting and thus demanding, 286,
291
Democratization, 38–42, 268–76
East Asian countries, 100
Democratizing the World Bank and
International Monetary Fund,
177
Deng Xiaoping, 47
Dependency theory, 163–64
Derivatives, 254–55
Desalination, 35, 233
Developing countries
abolition of tariffs and quotas, 176
"catch-22" of trade conditions,
194–96, 197
deaths from polluted indoor air,
229
debt, 177–85
debt cancellation, 183–84
direct international investments in,
154–55
East Asia's distinguishing features
and, 100–101
elites and, 94
export dollars surpassing
development assistance, 162
foreign direct investment in, 256

free trade, 169–72
growth and openness, 129–32
growth in open poor economies
versus open affluent ones,
133–35
growth rates, 129, 130
hunger, 31–35
IMF recipients' unwillingness to
follow advice, 181
investment in, 154–55, 244–45,
256
labor organizations and transfer of
technology to, 196
Latin America, 163–68
life expectancy of women, 46
loss sustained by protectionism,
156–62
manufactured goods exports,
170–72
medicine and, 186–89
neo-colonist policymaking
controls, 193
potable drinking water, 34–35
property rights, 90–98, 92
repeat debt cancellations, 184
respect for patent and IP rights,
196–97
shortcuts to development, 278–80
stunting growth for sake of
environmental protection,
228–29
tariffs, 173–76
trade with other developing
countries, 175
unequal distribution of capitalism,
152–55
vaccinations for children in, 189

311

wage increases, 204, 205f, 218
wages paid by multinational
    corporations in, 216–18
See also Industrialized countries;
    specific countries
Development. *See* Growth and
    development
Development assistance
    Africa, 105–6, 184–85
    export dollars surpassing, 162
    India, 183
    Ivory Coast, 183
    political leaders and, 185
"Dictatorship of the market," 268
    See also Political systems,
        democratization
Diplomatic relations, freezing, 201
Direct international investments in
    developing countries, 154–55
Disease, cost of cures, 188
Dollar, David, 79, 96, 97
Domestic subsidies, as de facto trade
    barriers, 126–27
Dumping
    EU products, 159
    "price dumping," 125–26

East Asia
    absolute poverty, 26
    child labor, 200
    growth "miracle," 99–103
    hunger, 31
    impact of politics on development,
        99–103
    life expectancy, 100
    likened to flock of geese, 172

post-WWII production and
    prosperity, 119
Eastern Europe, inequality, 57
Eco-dumping, 193
Economic adjustments, 140–44
Economic and financial crises
    Asian crisis, 178–79, 249–50,
        251, 259–63, 264
    avoiding, 264–67
    confidence in an economy and,
        261–62
    crisis management, 265
    currency overvaluation and, 261
    International Monetary Fund and,
        260, 265
    Latin American crisis of 1980s,
        252
    reforms and, 252
Economic equality. *See* Equality
Economic free zones
    China, 48
    multinational corporations and,
        219–20
Economic freedom
    Africa, 107
    corruption and, 70–71
    equality increase and, 88f
    and growth and development,
        72–83
    prosperity and, 73
    and reduction in poverty, 95f
Economic Freedom of the World, 95
Economic growth
    China, 48
    free movements of capital and,
        248
    India, 51, 53, 77–78

inequality and, 84–89
Economic liberalism, 15
  rights of ownership and, 91
Economic liberalization, 61
  China, 48, 49
  effects of transition to, 88–89
  India, 52
Economic policy
  structural adjustment programs
    and, 180–81
  threatened by the market, 273–74
Economic reforms, 15
  promised reforms and IMF grants,
    179–80
Economic refugees, 147–48
Economic reversals, China, 48–49
Economies, long-term commitments
  for, 264–65
The Economist magazine, 222, 265
Economy
  freedoms and voluntary relations
    in, 17
  long-term commitments for
    economies, 264–65
Education, 36–37
  children, 45–46
  of children, 200–201
  East Asia, 100–101
  girls and women, 45–46
  India, 45, 53
Edwards, Sebastian, 131–32
Efficiency
  "creative destruction" and, 140–44
  in production, 137–40, 237
  in world economy, 172
EFTA. *See* European Free Trade
  Association
Egypt, registering property, 92

Ehnmark, Anders, 12
Elections, China, 49
Elmbrant, Bjørn, 240
Emigration. *See* Immigration/
  emigration
Emissions
  air pollution and, 228, 229, 232
  carbon dioxide, 235
  regulations, 226–28
Employment
  free trade and, 136–44
  NAFTA and, 204
  work hours and workday pace,
    205–6, 207f
Employment benefits, proportion of
  U.S. wages, 144
EMS. *See* European Monetary
  System
Enhanced Border Security and Visa
  Entry Reform Act of 2002,
  145–46
Environmental conditions,
  developing countries, 193–94
Environmental improvements, per
  capita GDP and, 229–30
Environmental protection, 193–94,
  224–38
Environmental regulations, prosperity
  and, 225–26
*Environmentally Significant
  Consumption,* 228
Equality, 84–89
  free capital markets and, 244
  results in trade-liberalizing
    countries, 133
Eriko, 78
Eriksen, Thomas Hylland, 283

Estonia, trade liberalization, 144
Ethiopia
  equality in, 86
  starvation, 34
EU. *See* European Union
Europe
  competition with developing
    countries, 205
  Eastern, inequality, 57
  mobility, 145
  spread of prosperity, 25
  work-related stress and burnout,
    206–9
  See also specific countries
European Commission, cost of EU
    trade barriers, 160
European Free Trade Association
    (EFTA), economic differences
    between countries, 135
European Monetary System (EMS),
    261, 267
European Union (EU)
  Common Agricultural Policy,
    158–60
  economic differences between
    countries, 135
  employment, 137
  Everything-but-Arms initiative,
    161
  meat subsidies, 237–38
  mobility, 145
  need for immigrants, 148
  subsidies, 158–61, 237–38
  summit in Gothenburg, Sweden,
    9–10
  trade barriers, 125
  See also specific countries

Everyday actions, globalization
    consisting of, 12–14
Everything-but-Arms initiative, 161
Exchange rates, 255, 256
  fixed or controlled, 260–61,
    266–67
Exhausting raw materials, 235
Expenditures, environmental
    compliance portion, 227
Export-processing zones. *See*
    Economic free zones
Export subsidies, 159

Facilitating economic change,
    141–42
Famine disasters, 33–34
Financial crises. *See* Economic and
    financial crises
Financial markets, 240–48
  attention to government finance
    management, 271
  Tobin tax and, 256
Finland, employment, 137
Food production, employment
    example, 137–38
Foreign direct investment, Tobin tax
    and, 256
Foreign Policy magazine, 89
Forest acreage increase, 232
Frankel, Jeffrey, 132
Fraser Institute, 107
Free markets, 17
  democracy and, 268–76
  "market fundamentalism" and, 15
  See also Capital markets
Free movements of capital
  determinant of equality, 89

314

economic growth and, 248
enabling the poor, 90
investment and, 244–48
See also Capital controls
Free trade
benevolent attitude and, 201–2
"catch-22" for developing
countries, 194–96, 197
determinant of equality, 89
developing countries, 169–72
employment and, 136–44
enabling the poor, 90
growth benefits of, 128–35
immigration/emigration and,
145–50
important imports, 120–27
information sharing and, 128–29
innovation and, 128–29
job creation/dissolution and,
136–44
mutual benefit, 114–19
rules governing genuine free trade,
192–93
skepticism of, 192–93
See also specific countries
Freedom
China, 47, 290–91
of choice, 11, 13–14, 18, 23,
278–85, 285. *See also* Pluralism
economic. *See* Economic freedom
efficient use of resources and
capital and, 128
of enterprise, 100, 101
expansion of, 40
of expression, 17
of migration/movement, 90. *See
also* Immigration/emigration

personal, 16. *See also* Individual
liberty
power over our own lives and, 11,
290–91
of the press, 17
self-determination and, 286–91
tasting and thus demanding, 286,
291
Freedom House, 39
French culture, 283–84
Friedman, Thomas, 268
Fugitives, numbers living as, 60
Fyodorov, Boris, 179

Garbage, problem of, 232
Gates, Bill, philanthropy in
developing countries, 189
GDP. *See* Gross domestic product
Geijer, Erik Gustaf, 12
Gender equity, prosperity and, 45
George, Susan, 139
Germany, 72
Ghana
equality/inequality, 133
liberalization, growth, and
development, 110
Giddens, Anthony, 284
"Gini coefficient" for measuring
inequality, 57
Girls
education, 45–46, 53
life expectancy in South Asia, 46
Global Alliance for Workers and
Communities, 218–19
Global economic institutions,
177–84

See also World Bank; International Monetary Fund

Global environmental problems, statistics and facts, 230–35

Global food production, 32–33

Global growth, past centuries, 76

Global homogeneity, 280–82

Global inequality, 54–59

Global misery, 20–24, 60–61

The Global Trap, 136

Globalism
  cultural encounters of, 281–85
  self-determination and, 286–91

Globalization, 9–14
  credit for the good that happens, 289–90
  criticism, 10–11, 14–15
  democratization of political systems and, 268–76
  freedom and, 286–91
  growth during 1990s, 135*f*
  of late 19th century, 287–88
  and local power relations and the poor, 90
  reservations about, 60–61
  as scapegoat, 289

Globalization index, 89

Gold and green forests, 224*n*

Goldman-Sachs, 251

Government
  administration and collection of Tobin tax worldwide, 257
  expansion of government machinery, 275
  industrial initiatives in developing countries, 174–75
  interventions in "miracle" economies, 100
  mismanagement of finances, 271
  need for, 8
  See also specific countries

Gray, John, 15

"Green revolution," 33

Greider, William, 136, 138–39

Gross domestic product (GDP)
  capitalism and inequality in, 153–54
  growth and, 76–77
  multinational corporations' sales in relation to, 214–16
  per capita GDP level and environmental improvements, 229–30
  trade increases and rise in per capita income, 132

Growth and development, 72–83
  broad, free financial markets and, 247–48
  child labor decline and, 200
  conflict between environment and, 224–38
  connected to better air and water quality, 230
  East Asian growth "miracle," 99–103
  economic freedom and, 72–83
  free trade and growth, 119*f*
  free trade benefits, 128–35
  GDP and, 76–77
  global growth in past centuries, 76
  government intervention and, 100, 102, 165–66, 174–75
  growth in open poor economies versus open affluent ones, 133–35

impact of African politics on,
104–11
impact of East Asian politics on,
99–103
pollution and, 229
stunting growth for sake of
environmental protection,
228–29
See also Developing countries;
Economic growth

Haiti
exports to EU, 161
registering property, 92
HDI. *See* Human Development
Index
Health care improvements, 29, 53
Heckscher, Eli F., 161
HIPCs. *See* Highly indebted poor
countries
High school education, 36
Highly indebted poor countries
(HIPCs), 182
HIV/AIDS
deaths, 60
lower-priced inhibitors for,
187–88
Honduras, stagnation and poverty,
132
Hong Kong
Asian crisis and, 251
freedom of enterprise, 101
"open" economy, 103
post-WWII production and
prosperity, 119
Human capital, 67

Human condition
historically, 73, 75
worldwide improvement, 28–29
Human development, 27
Human Development Index (HDI),
56, 57–58
Human Development Report 1997 of
UNDP, 25
Human Development Report of 1999
of UNDP, 55, 57–58
Human dignity, 287
Human nature, meeting our needs,
139–40
Human rights, 286, 289
Indian caste system, 53
violations, 16, 40
Humanism, 22–24
Hunger, 21, 31–35, 60
"Hypercapitalism," 10, 242
Hyperinflation, 96, 131, 167

Ignorance, 291
Illarionov, Andrei, 180
ILO. *See* International Labor
Organization
IMF. *See* International Monetary
Fund
Immigrants
dollar benefit to host country, 149
illegal, 149
need for, 148–50
welfare policy reform and, 149–50
Immigration/emigration, free trade
and, 145–50
Imperialism, wealth and poverty and,
152
Import barriers, 120

Import duties, reduction, 162
Import quotas, 120
Import substitution, 163
Import tariffs, 176
Income
    distribution in liberal economy,
        87–88
    gaps, 82–83
    high growth and income
        differences, 86
    living standards and, 77*f*
    trade increases and rise in per
        capita income, 132
    world income distribution, 1960,
        1980, and 2000, 58*f*
Indebtedness, freedom and, 270–72
Index of openness, 103
India, 51–53
    Berg and Karlsson in, 21–22
    child education, 36
    development assistance, 183
    education, 45, 53
    failed government industrial
        initiatives, 174
    "green revolution," 33
    growth and development, 51, 53,
        77–78
    relief for the poor, 97–98
    service sector jobs, 170
    starvation, 34
    women, 43
Individual decisionmaking and
    responsibility, 67
Individual liberty, 8, 11, 14, 16, 22,
    89, 290–91
    See also Freedom; *specific freedoms,
    liberties, and rights*

Indonesia
    absolute poverty, 99
    Asian crisis and, 250, 251, 260,
        263
    dictatorships, 269
    failed government industrial
        initiatives, 174
    government intervention, 100
    growth and income differences, 86
    "open" economy, 103
    water supply, 35
    worker satisfaction, 219
Industrial Revolution, standard of
    living improvement and, 60–61
Industrialized countries
    abolition of tariffs and quotas, 176
    annual growth rates, 129, 130
    competition with developing
        countries, 205
    learning from, 278–80
    size in relation to corporations,
        214–16
    work-related stress and burnout,
        206–9
Inequality
    distribution of capitalism in
        developing countries, 152–55
    economic growth and, 84–89
    "Gini coefficient" for measuring,
        57
    global, 54–59
    between persons versus between
        countries, 56–57
    results in trade-liberalizing
        countries, 133
"Infant industry tariffs," 173
Infant mortality, 29, 30*f*, 53

Infectious disease, WHO and, 188–89

Inflation, 96, 100
hyperinflation, 96, 131, 167

Information sharing, free trade and, 128–29

Information technology, 52–53, 170, 215, 279–80

Injustices, 21

Innovation
"creative destruction and," 140
cultural, 150
free trade and, 128–29
new garbage and old raw material uses, 233
saving and investment and, 76

Intellectual property (IP) rights, 196–97

International financial markets, 246–48
attention to government finance management, 271

International investments in developing countries, 154–55

International Labor Organization (ILO), 196, 200, 218

International markets, access to, 279–80

International Monetary Fund (IMF), 177–84
Asian crisis and, 260
crisis management and, 265

Internationalization
borders and, 9
cultural encounters of globalism, 281–85
East Asia, 102–3
"hypercapitalism" and, 10

Internet, 11–12
access to international markets and, 279–80
women and, 45

Investment
considerations other than wages, 204–5
in developing countries, 154–55, 244–45, 256
in East Asia, 102–3
free movements of capital and, 244–48
risk, 247, 254–56
Tobin tax and, 253–58

Investment boundaries, 243–44

Investors, Asian crisis and herd mentality of, 262

IP. See Intellectual property rights

Iraq, human rights violations, 40

Islam, democracy and, 40

Isolationism, 289

Ivory Coast, development assistance, 183

Japan
employment, 137
government intervention, 100, 102
labor-intensive industries, 172
MITI (department of industry), 174
"open" economy, 103
post-WWII economy, 99
wages, 203–4
wealth, 134

Job creation/dissolution
East Asia, 101
free trade and, 136–44

job market changes, 142–44
technological advances and, 140
wages and, 143–44
Jobs
  lack of challenge and development in, 208
  length of stay in United States, 143
Jospin, Lionel, 17
Jubilee 2000 campaign, 183

Karlsson, Stig, 21–22, 290
Kearny, A. T., 89
Kenya
  equality in, 86
  lack of growth and poverty, 132
  "vampire state," 106
Khatuun, Halima, 279
King, Martin Luther, Jr., 202
Klein, Naomi, 220, 222, 263
Kohl, Helmut, 222
Kraay, Aart, 79, 96, 97
Krugman, Paul, 138, 194
Kuttner, Robert, 15
Kuwait, water supply, 35
Kuznets, Simon, 86

Labor-intensive industries, 172
Labor organizations, transfer of technology to developing countries and, 196
Land ownership
  private, 235–36
  Russia, 94–95
Land socialism, 94–95
Lao Tzu, 70

Latin America
  crisis of 1980s, 252
  dictatorships, 269, 272
  hunger, 31
  lack of growth and poverty, 132
  "open" economy, 103
  in world economy, 289
Legal codes protecting enterprise and competition, East Asia, 100
"Liberal" and "libertarian," term use, 14n
Liberal market economy, 16
  See also Economic liberalization
Liberal society and the right to choose, 18
Liberalization
  freedom of choice and, 278–85
  necessary institutions for, 265
  self-determination and, 286–91
  See also Economic liberalization
Liberalization of thinking/thought, 9, 290
Liberty. See Freedom; Individual liberty
Libya, human rights violations, 40
Life expectancy
  average, 28–29, 75f
  East Asian countries, 100
  South Asian girls', 46
  women in developing countries, 46
Lim, Linda, 219
Liquidity shortage, 262
Literacy/illiteracy, 14, 36, 37f, 53
  illiteracy, 60
Lomborg, Bjørn, 230–35

Mad cow disease crisis, 238
Malaysia
  absolute poverty, 100

Asian crisis and, 260
Berg in, 29
capital regulation, 249–50
government intervention, 100
growth and income differences, 86
labor-intensive industries, 172
"open" economy, 103
Mankind and human relations,
    creativity and man's capacity to
    achieve great things, 17
Manufactured goods, versus raw
    materials exports alone, 169–72
Market economy, versus market
    society, 17
"Market fascism," 268
"Market fundamentalism," 15
Material development/materialism,
    17–18, 27
Mauritius
    free trade, 109–10
    growth and income differences, 86
Meat production and subsidies,
    European Union, 237–38
Mechanization, change brought
    about by, 200
Media, changing people, 22
Medicine, developing countries and,
    186–89
Mercantilism, 120
Merck Corporation, free medicine,
    187
Messerlin, Patrick, 160
Mexico
    air pollution control, 228
    dictatorships, 269
    environmental regulations, 224–25
    equality in, 86

exchange rate crisis, 267
free trade policy and exports,
    171–72
"Tequila crisis," 252
Middle East, 269
    girls attending school, 45
    hunger, 31
    See also specific countries
Milken Institute, Capital Access
    Index, 247–48
Mill, James, 120
Mill, John Stuart, 82
Mismanaged policy, 251
Mixed economy, 17
Mobility
    physical. See Immigration/
    emigration
    social, 82–83
Modernization of thought, 22–24,
    290
Monetary policy, East Asia, 100
Monopolies and trusts, multinational
    corporations, 211–12
Monopoly protection, trade barriers
    and, 123
Monsanto Corporation, "golden rice"
    technology, 187
Morality, multinational corporations,
    222–23
Morocco, equality in, 86
Mortality prevention costs, WHO
    and, 189
"Most favored nation" treatment,
    124–25
Mugabe, Robert, 106, 107
Multilateral trade negotiations,
    123–24

See also Trade agreements; World Trade Organization

Multinational corporations
  bad behavior and morality in, 221–23
  competition and, 213–14
  consumers and, 213
  Daewoo example, 222
  dominance, 216, 217*f*
  economic free zones and, 219–20
  finance of research and long-term projects, 220–21
  in foreign and developing countries, 216–18
  versus government-owned enterprises such as Russia, 212–13
  growth compared to nation states, 214–16
  impartial inspections for worker satisfaction, 218–19
  information technology and, 215
  monopolies and trusts, 211–12
  Nike example, 218–19
  nonemployee wages versus employee wages, 217–18
  oppressive governments and, 222
  positive aura for trademarks, 222
  power, 210–11
  quality and productivity, 213–14
  reinvesting profits in country of operation, 220–21
  sales in relation to GDP, 214–16
  size of firms, 214–16
  technology and environmental regulation compliance, 227–28
  wages, 216–18, 221
  working conditions, 218–19, 220
The Mystery of Capital, 91

NAFTA. *See* North American Free Trade Agreement
Narayanan, K. R., 53
Nation states
  multinational corporations' growth compared to, 214–16
  separatism, 41
National Academy of Sciences, 228
National debts, 271
National financial markets, 242–48
National judicial systems, 287
Natural resources, developing countries, 152–55
Nepal, boycotts, 199
Nigeria, economy, 108
Nike, 218–19
No Logo: Taking Aim at the Brand Bullies, 220, 222
Nordström, Håkan, 132
North Africa, hunger, 31
North American Free Trade Agreement (NAFTA), 171, 204, 224
North Korea
  economy, 72
  exclusion form global environment, 289
  human rights violations, 40
  starvation, 34
  ultra-protectionist policy and controlled economy, 103
Norwegian Institute for Foreign Affairs, global inequality report, 56, 57

OECD. *See* Organization for Economic Cooperation and Development countries
On Asian Time: India, China, Japan 1966–1999, 21, 29
One World, Ready or Not: The Manic Logic of Global Capitalism, 136, 138–39
Openness
  East Asia, 103
  growth and, 129–32
  variables testing for, 131–32
Oppression
  Africa, 105–6, 107
  China, 49
  living in, 291
  multinational corporations' presence and, 222
  overlooking, 202
  of tradition, 284–85
  women, 43–46
Organization, 68
Organization for Economic Cooperation and Development (OECD) countries
  average life expectancy, 28–29
  economic free zones and, 220
  percent of world GDP, 155
Ownership
  private land ownership, 94–95, 235–36
  protection of, 66
  rights of, 91, 100
  See also Intellectual property; Patent rights; Property rights

Pakistan
  growth and income differences, 86
  lack of growth and poverty, 132

Passport requirements, 287, 288
Patent rights, respect for, 196–97
Penetrating new markets, price dumping and, 126
Per capita incomes, 76
Perot, Ross, 204
Personal responsibility, 67
Peru, registering property and businesses, 92, 93
Pharmaceutical companies, 186–89
the Philippines, registering property, 92
Pinochet, Augusto, 168, 287
Pluralism, developments and, 280–82
Political dictatorships, 185, 201, 220, 236, 269, 270, 272, 287
Political institutions, globalized humanity acquiring power at expense of, 10
Political leaders
  development assistance and, 185
  tariff walls and, 174–75
Political power and controls, 9–10, 165–66
Political systems, democratization, 268–76
Politics, 17
  freedoms and voluntary relations in, 17
  impact of African politics on growth and development, 104–11
  impact of East Asian politics on growth and development, 99–103
  playing at business, 16
Pollution
  air, 228, 229, 232

growth and, 229
Poor people, 55–56
  in developing countries, 13–14
  freedom of choice and, 13–14
  property rights, 90–98
Pope John Paul II, 20
Population growth, India, 51, 52
Potable drinking water, 34–35
Poverty, 60
  absolute, 21, 26, 48, 99–100, 108
  East Asian countries, 99
  economic freedom and reduction
    in, 95*f*
  growth benefiting the poor, 79–81
  India, 51, 52
  in last few centuries, 73, 75–76
  long-term growth and, 81
  reduction, 25–30, 132
  remedy for, 83
  "trickle-down" effect and, 80
  United States, 83
Poverty lines, 54–55
Power
  freedom and power over our own
    lives, 11, 290–91
  globalization and local power
    relations with the poor, 90
  globalized humanity acquiring
    power at expense of political
    institutions, 10
  multinational corporations,
    210–11
  political, 9–10, 165–66
  powerlessness/loss of power, 11, 12
  purchasing power, 55–56
Predetermination, 287–88
"Price dumping," 125–26

Prices, 65–66
Production
  environmental problems and,
    236–37
  free trade and, 136–44
  led and driven by trade, 129
  raw materials and, 122, 169–72
  specialization, 115–19, 120
  world output, 129
Productivity
  multinational corporations,
    213–14
  wages and, 194
Profits, 65–66
Property, 67
  as "dead capital," 93
  private land ownership, 235–36
Property rights, 90–98
  See also Rights of ownership
Prosperity
  companies/investors and, 172
  economic freedom and, 73
  environmental protection/
    improvement and, 224–26, 230,
    231*f*
  former colonies, 99
  free trade and, 17, 118*f*
  gender equity and, 44
  growth and spread of, 14, 25, 81,
    134–35
  opportunities for women and, 44
Protectionism
  Africa, 105–6, 107
  backlash, 124
  developing countries' loss sustained
    by, 156–62
  reappearance, 288

trade subject to conditions and,
    192–97
Protectionist countries
    annual growth rates, 129, 130
    financial crises and hyperinflation,
        131, 167
    growth in open poor economies
        versus open affluent ones,
        133–35
    Latin America, 163–68
  . policy results, 129, 130–31
Public spending, 275
    undemocratic societies, 97–98
Purchasing power, 55–56

Qatar, 269
Quader, Noorul, 223
Quantity of trade, 121–22

Rahman, Helen, 46
Raw materials, 233–35
    exports, 163–64, 167
    processing and manufacturing,
        169–72
    production, 122
R&D. *See* Research and development
Reebok, 218
Reforms
    African growth and, 108–9
    demands that parallel debt
        cancellation, 183
    demands that parallel receipt of
        aid, 185
    East Asia, 101
    economic, 15, 179–80
    Latin American crisis and, 252
    welfare policy reform, 149–50

Refugees
    economic, 147–48
    noneconomic, 146–47
Regional trade agreements, 125
Registering property, 92–94
Regression analysis, 131
Regulation, 69–71
    Africa, 155
    agricultural, 95–96
    capital. *See* Capital regulation
    East Asia, 101
    emissions, 226–28
    environmental, 224–28
    Russia, 95
Research and development (R&D)
    drug prices and R&D
        expenditures, 187–88
    multinational finance of research
        and long-term projects, 220–21
Reyes-Heroles, Jesus, 194
Rights of ownership
    East Asia, 100
    economic liberalism and, 91
Risk
    investments and, 254–56
    spreading by diverse investing, 247
Robinson, Joan, 123
Romer, David, 132
Roosevelt, Franklin D., 150
Rothbard, Murray, 126
Russia
    Asian crisis and, 251
    equality in, 86
    exchange rate crisis, 267
    IMF and, 179–80
    modernization of private sector,
        212–13

private land ownership, 94–95
Rwanda, poverty line, 54

Sachs, Jeffrey, 103, 108–9, 129,
    130–31, 133–35, 188
Sala-i-Martin, Xavier, 56
Sand/silicon, 233
Saudi Arabia
    human rights violations, 40
    water supply, 35
    women, 45
Save the Children (Sweden),
    199–200
Saving and investment, 68, 81–82
    innovation and, 76
    See also Investment
Scandinavia, wealth, 135
Schengen Agreement, 145
Schools, quality of, 201
Schumpeter, Joseph, 140
Scully, G. W., 87–88
Self-determination, 286–91
Self-sufficiency policies, 163–65
    post-WWII, 118–19
Sen, Amartya, 27, 34, 70
Separatism in nation states, 41
Service sector, developing countries,
    170
Sex equality. *See* Gender equity
Shang Ying, 44
Short-term capital flows, regulation,
    250–52
Short-term debts, 260–61
Shortages of raw materials, 234–35
Simon, Julian, 149
Singapore, Asian crisis and, 251, 262

*The Skeptical Environmentalist:
    Measuring the Real State of the
    World,* 231–33
Slavery, 23–24
Smith, Adam, 122, 271
Social development, India, 53
Social dumping, 193
Social mobility, 82–83
Socialism, China, 47
Society, freedoms and voluntary
    relations in, 17
South America
    failed government industrial
        initiatives, 174
    meat importation, 238
South Asia
    girls attending school, 45
    girls' life expectancy, 46
    hunger, 31
South Korea
    Asian crisis and, 259–60, 263
    economy, 72
    government intervention, 100, 102
    growth and income differences, 86
    labor-intensive industries, 172
    "open" economy, 103
    post-WWII production and
        prosperity, 119
    standard of living, 99
    wealth, 134
Southeast Asia
    child labor, 200
    dictatorships, 269
    hunger, 31
Soviet Union (former), starvation, 34
Spain, employment, 137
Specialization, 115–19, 120

Speculation, currency, 254–57, 261, 266
Standards of living, 59*f*
  economic freedom and, 74*f*
  HDI and, 56
  income, 77*f*
Starvation, 33–34
  See also Hunger
State-directed capital flows, 247
Steel manufacturing, cleaner technology, 227–28
Stiglitz, Joseph, 15
Stock market fluctuations, 241–42
Subsidies, 157–61, 237–38
  domestic subsidies as de facto trade barriers, 126–27
Sudan, human rights violations, 40
Surplus exchange, 117, 121
  grants and, 159
Sweden
  agricultural efficiency and employment, 138
  child labor, 199–200
  educational voucher system, 201
  employment, 137
  example of "catch-22" in trade conditions, 195
  failure of digital television, 174
  need for immigrants, 148
Symbolic sanctions, dictatorships, 201
Syria, human rights violations, 40

Taiwan
  Asian crisis and, 251, 262
  economy, 72
  government intervention, 100

growth and income differences, 86
labor-intensive industries, 172
"open" economy, 103
standard of living, 99
Tanzania, foreign debt, 182–83
Tariff walls, 174–75
Tariffs and quotas, 114
  antidumping tariffs, 126
  developing countries' tariffs, 173–76
  "infant industry tariffs," 173
  tariff reduction negotiations, 122–25
  tariff reductions, 156–62
  See also Tobin tax, 254
Tax avoidance, 82
Taxation, 82–83, 275
Taxpayers
  debt cancellation and, 182
  subsidies and, 237
Technological advances, 17, 68
  addressing raw material shortages, 234–35
  "creative destruction and," 140
  developing countries and, 278–80
Technology, 23
  cleaner technology, 227–28
  expediting social progress, 45
  growth and, 134–35
  importing new ideas and techniques, 128–29
Terrorist attacks of September 11, 2001, 145–46
Thailand
  Asian crisis and, 259, 260
  equality/inequality, 133
  government intervention, 100

growth and income differences, 86
labor-intensive industries, 172
"open" economy, 103
worker satisfaction, 219
Third World. *See* Developing
   countries
Tobin, James, 253, 266
Tobin tax, 253–58, 266
Trade
   among developing countries, 175
   balance of trade, 121–22
   "catch-22" of trade conditions,
      194–96, 197
   environmental problems and,
      236–37
   increases and rise in per capita
      income, 132
   quantity of, 121–22
   subject to conditions and
      protectionism, 192–97
   See also Free trade; *specific countries*
Trade agreements, 289
   impartial code of rules for
      honoring, 124
   provisions stipulating standards,
      193–96
   regional, 125
   See also World Trade Organization
Trade barriers
   domestic subsidies as de facto
      barriers, 126–27
   Latin America, 163–68
   patent and IP infringement as,
      196–97
   See also Tariffs and quotas;
      Subsidies; Antidumping
      measures

Trade controls, Russia, 95
Trade policy
   East Asia, 103
   separating effects of one policy
      from another, 131
Trade-Related Aspects of Intellectual
   Property Rights (TRIPS)
   agreement, 196, 197
Trade sanctions, dictatorships and
   temporary sanctions, 201
Trademarks, multinationals and
   positive aura for, 222
Tragedies and risks surrounding
   immigration policy, 147
Transportation, environmental
   problems and, 236–37
"Trickle-down" effect of growth, 80
TRIPS. *See* Trade-Related Aspects of
   Intellectual Property Rights
   agreement
Turkmenistan, human rights
   violations, 40

Uganda
   IMF compliance, 181
   liberalization, growth, and
      development, 110
   poverty reduction, 132
UN Food and Agriculture
   Organization, 31
UNCTAD. *See* United Nations
   Trade and Development
   Program
Undemocratic societies, public
   spending, 97–98
Underdevelopment, 60

UNDP. *See* United Nations Development Program

Unemployment
  free trade and, 136–44
  wages and increase in, 194

UNEP. *See* United Nations Environmental Program

Unfair competition, price dumping, 125–26, 160

UNFPA. *See* United Nations Population Fund

Unilateral free trade, 123

United (Dutch charity), immigrant mortality estimates, 147

United Kingdom
  England's wealth, 134
  foreign firm R&D investment in, 221
  Ireland's wealth, 135

United Nations, governing world government, 256

United Nations Development Program (UNDP), 25, 229

United Nations Environmental Program (UNEP), 196

United Nations Population Fund (UNFPA), 148

United Nations Trade and Development Program (UNCTAD), 162, 183

United States
  Africa Growth and Opportunity Act, 161
  antidumping tariffs, 126
  Asian crisis and, 263
  Chinese Exclusion Act of 1882, 146

competition with developing countries, 205

employment, 137

Enhanced Border Security and Visa Entry Reform Act of 2002, 145–46

foreign firm R&D investment in, 221

immigration policy, 145–47

investment considerations other than wages, 204–5

job market, 143–44

poverty line, 54–55

receipt of immigrants, 150

spread of prosperity, 25

stock market, 240–41

subsidies, 161

terrorist attacks of September 11, 2001, 145–46

wages, 143–44

work-related stress and burnout, 206–9

WTO agreements and, 124

"Untouchables," 53

Uruguay Round, 156

U.S. Federal Reserve, 241

Usury, 14

Uzbekistan, poverty line, 54

Vaccinations for children in developing countries, 189

Vargas Llosa, Mario, 283–84

Variables testing for openness, 131–32

Vietnam
  equality/inequality, 133
  labor-intensive industries, 172

liberalization and poverty
reduction, 132
worker satisfaction, 219
Virtual Souk, 279
Vishal, Ram, 286

Wages, 68–69
developing countries, 193–94
East Asia, 101
immigrants and, 149, 150
increase in, 204, 205f
low starting wages, 150
minimum wage compared to
wages paid by multinationals,
219
multinational corporations in
developing countries, 216–18
productivity and, 194, 203–4
U.S., 143–44
Wal-Mart, child labor and, 199
Wall Street Crash of 1929, 288
Warner, Andrew, 103, 108–9, 129,
130–31, 133–35
Wars, diminishing number of, 40–41
Water supply, 232–33
potable, 34-35
shortage of pure water, 60
Wealth and poverty
global inequality and, 54–59
growth and the rich and poor,
79–81
the half truth, 20–24
social mobility and, 82–83
uneven distribution of wealth in
world, 154
See also Poverty
Welfare. See Public spending

Western world
effects of globalization on wages
and productivity, 203–9
protectionism in, 288
See also Industrialized countries
WHO. See World Health
Organization
Wilk, Richard, 228
Women
Africa, 44
in Bangladeshi garment industry,
223
China, 43
democratic process and, 38, 45
economic independence, 78, 223
education, 45–46
freedom of choice and, 13–14
India, 43
Internet and, 45
life expectancy in developing
countries, 46
opportunities and prosperity for,
44
oppression of, 43–46
refugees, 147
Saudi Arabia, 45
Women's rights, 44
Work, 82–83
quantity as a constant, 138–39
stress and burnout from, 206–9
work hours and workday pace,
205–6, 207f
See also Employment; Job creation/
dissolution; Jobs
Worker satisfaction, impartial
inspections of multinationals,
218–19

Working conditions, 193–96
  in multinational firms, 218–19,
    220
World Bank, 177–84
  absolute poverty figures, 26
  on education in India, 45
  on global equality, 57
  on government interventions in
    "miracle" economies, 100
  on growth and inequality, 86–87
  on poverty in China, 48
World Development Report 2000/
  2001, 81
World economies, as business
  corporations, 214–16
World government, administration
  and collection of Tobin tax, 257
World Health Organization (WHO),
  188–89
World hunger, 31–35
World income distribution, 1960,
  1980, and 2000, 58*f*
World population, 26, 290
World Trade Organization (WTO)
  impartial code of rules for
    honoring agreements, 124
  "most favored nation" treatment,
    124–25
  Seattle meeting of 1999, 124

  tariff reduction negotiations,
    122–25
  TRIPS agreement, 196, 197
World War I (WWI), 288
World War II (WWII)
  Japan's economy and, 99
  post-WWII self-sufficiency
    policies, 118–19
Worldwatch Institute, 237
Worldwide depression, 288
WTO. *See* World Trade
    Organization
Wulfstan, Archbishop, 20
WWI. *See* World War I
WWII. *See* World War II

Yang Zhengming, 290
Yao, Shujie, 48
Yugoslavia (former), conflicts, 41

Zaire, "vampire state," 106
Zambia
  IMF compliance, 181
  standard of living, 99
Zhou Litai, 218
Zimbabwe
  as least economically free country,
    107–8
  "vampire state," 106

About the Author

Johan Norberg is a fellow at the Swedish think tank Timbro. His book *In Defense of Global Capitalism* received rave reviews in Europe. He is also the host of a British Channel 4 documentary, "Globalization Is Good." His previous books include *The Resistance Man Vilhelm Moberg*, *The History of Swedish Liberalism*, and *State, Individual, and Market*.

Cato Institute

Founded in 1977, the Cato Institute is a public policy research foundation dedicated to broadening the parameters of policy debate to allow consideration of more options that are consistent with the traditional American principles of limited government, individual liberty, and peace. To that end, the Institute strives to achieve greater involvement of the intelligent, concerned lay public in questions of policy and the proper role of government.

The Institute is named for *Cato's Letters,* libertarian pamphlets that were widely read in the American Colonies in the early 18th century and played a major role in laying the philosophical foundation for the American Revolution.

Despite the achievement of the nation's Founders, today virtually no aspect of life is free from government encroachment. A pervasive intolerance for individual rights is shown by government's arbitrary intrusions into private economic transactions and its disregard for civil liberties.

To counter that trend, the Cato Institute undertakes an extensive publications program that addresses the complete spectrum of policy issues. Books, monographs, and shorter studies are commissioned to examine the federal budget, Social Security, regulation, military spending, international trade, and myriad other issues. Major policy conferences are held throughout the year, from which papers are published thrice yearly in the *Cato Journal.* The Institute also publishes the quarterly magazine *Regulation.*

In order to maintain its independence, the Cato Institute accepts no government funding. Contributions are received from foundations, corporations, and individuals, and other revenue is generated from the sale of publications. The Institute is a nonprofit, tax-exempt, educational foundation under Section 501(c)3 of the Internal Revenue Code.

CATO INSTITUTE
1000 Massachusetts Ave., N.W.
Washington, D.C. 20001
www.cato.org